STEGOSAURUS

THE DINOSAUR WITH THE SMALLEST BRAIN

by

Elizabeth J. Sandell

DINOSAUR DISCOVERY ERA

Bancroft-Sage Publishing

112 Marshall St., Box 1968, Mankato, MN 56001-1968 USA

LIBRARY OF CONGRESS CATALOGING IN PUBLICATION DATA

Sandell, Elizabeth J.
    Stegosaurus: the dinosaur with the smallest brain.

    (Dinosaur discovery era)
    SUMMARY: An introduction to the physical characteristics, habits, and natural environment of the plant-eating dinosaur who measured between twenty and thirty feet but whose brain was about the size of a walnut shell.
    1. Stegosaurus--Juvenile literature. (1. Stegosaurus. 2. Dinosaurs.) I. Oelerich, Marjorie L. II. Schroeder, Howard. III. Vista III Design. IV. Title. V. Series.
QE862.065S35   1988   567.9'7   88-995
ISBN 0-944280-02-1 (lib. bdg.)
ISBN 0-944280-08-0 (pbk. bdg.)

International Standard Book Number:	Library of Congress Catalog Card Number:
Library Binding 0-944280-02-1	88-995
Paperback Binding 0-944280-08-0	

SPECIAL THANKS FOR THEIR HELP AND COOPERATION TO:
Mary R. Carman, Paleontology Collection Manager
Field Museum of Natural History
Chicago, Illinois

STEGOSAURUS

THE DINOSAUR WITH THE SMALLEST BRAIN

AUTHOR
Elizabeth J. Sandell

dedicated to Karen Ruth Leonard

EDITED BY

Marjorie L. Oelerich, Ph.D.
Professor of Early Childhood and Elementary Education
Mankato State University

Howard Schroeder, Ph.D.
Professor of Reading and Language Arts
Dept. of Curriculum and Instruction
Mankato State University
Mankato, MN

ILLUSTRATED BY
Vista III Design

BANCROFT-SAGE PUBLISHING
112 Marshall St., Box 1968, Mankato, MN 56001-1968 U.S.A.

INTRODUCTION: VISITING THE DINOSAUR QUARRY

"A town that named itself after dinosaurs!" Rosa exclaimed. "In Dinosaur, Colorado, they even named the streets after different dinosaurs!"

As Rosa's family drove down the streets, they found *Triceratops* Terrace, *Tyrannosaurus* Triangle, *Allosaurus* Lane, and *Stegosaurus* Street.

"It would be fun to have an address like that!" laughed Rosa's brother, Manuel.

Rosa, Manuel, and their parents were on their way to Jensen, Utah, to see the Dinosaur Quarry at Dinosaur National Monument.

At last they arrived at the Dinosaur Quarry, and Rosa and her family entered the Quarry Building. They met the park ranger, who told them about dinosaurs.

The park ranger said that no person living today ever saw a live dinosaur. We can find dinosaur fossils, though, in exhibits at some museums.

Rosa asked the park ranger, "How did all these dinosaur bones get here?"

The park ranger explained, "Rosa, a long time ago, there was a river here. Lots of dinosaurs lived nearby. As the dinosaurs died, the bones of some of them fell into the sand at the bottom of the river. When the river dried up, the sand slowly turned into rocks. The bones became petrified in the rock layers. This means that sand filled in the bones until they became hard like rocks, too.

"Scientists use the word 'fossils' for these petrified bones," the park ranger continued. "Fossils are the parts which are left of animals and plants that lived many years ago.

"Scientists have found many dinosaur bones in rocks. These scientists are called paleontologists," the park ranger said. "They study fossils to learn what the animals and plants looked like, what the animals ate, and how they lived. They put fossil bones together into skeletons."

As they walked, Rosa saw a wall of rock with many fossils. The wall was 190 feet (58 m) long. While they looked, the park ranger told Rosa and her family all about one special fossil named *Stegosaurus.*

CHAPTER 1: STEGOSAURUS WAS SPECIAL

There are two reasons *Stegosaurus* (steg´ uh sor´ uhs) was special. It had a very small brain. And it had bony plates along its backbone.

STEGOSAURUS HAD A SMALL BRAIN

THE SMALLEST BRAIN

Fossils show *Stegosaurus* had a small brain, about the size of a walnut shell. This brain may have weighed about 2½ ounces (70 gm).

Stegosaurus had a second nerve center in its spinal cord above its hips. This nerve center was twenty times larger than the brain. Some scientists believe that this nerve center gave extra power to the muscles in the hind legs and tail.

BONY PLATES

The *Stegosaurus* skeleton had bony plates along the top of its backbone. These were attached from the neck to the tail. The largest plate, just behind the hip, was about 30 inches (76 cm) high and 31 inches (78 cm) long.

There probably were different shapes of these plates on *Stegosaurus*. Diamond-shaped plates could have been along the back. Rectangular-shaped plates may have been along the neck.

Scientists do not agree about how the bony plates fit along the backbone. Stephen Czerkas, a paleontologist (pa´ le on tol´ uh jist) from Los Angeles, California, studied the skeleton. He believes that the plates were in only one row. Other scientists think that there were two rows of plates.

In Dinosaur Quarry, paleontologists found two baby *Stegosaurus* skeletons without plates. Maybe the very young did not have these plates. It is possible that only grown-ups or only males had them. Perhaps the plates of these young *Stegosaurus* did not turn into fossils. Scientists do not know.

Two rows of plates

Scientists have different ideas about the purpose of these bony plates:

1. To make *Stegosaurus* look bigger than it really was. This would scare its enemies.
2. To keep the body cool. The blood would cool off as it flowed through the plates.
3. To keep the body warm. The plates would warm in the sun, and then the blood would warm as it flowed through the plates.
4. To keep the body cool or warm. Perhaps when the air was hot, the plates helped cool it off. And when the air was cold, the plates helped warm it up.

The name for *Stegosaurus* came from two Greek words. **Stegos** means "covered roof," and **sauros** means "lizard." Scientists once thought that the plates covered *Stegosaurus* like shingles cover a roof.

One row of plates

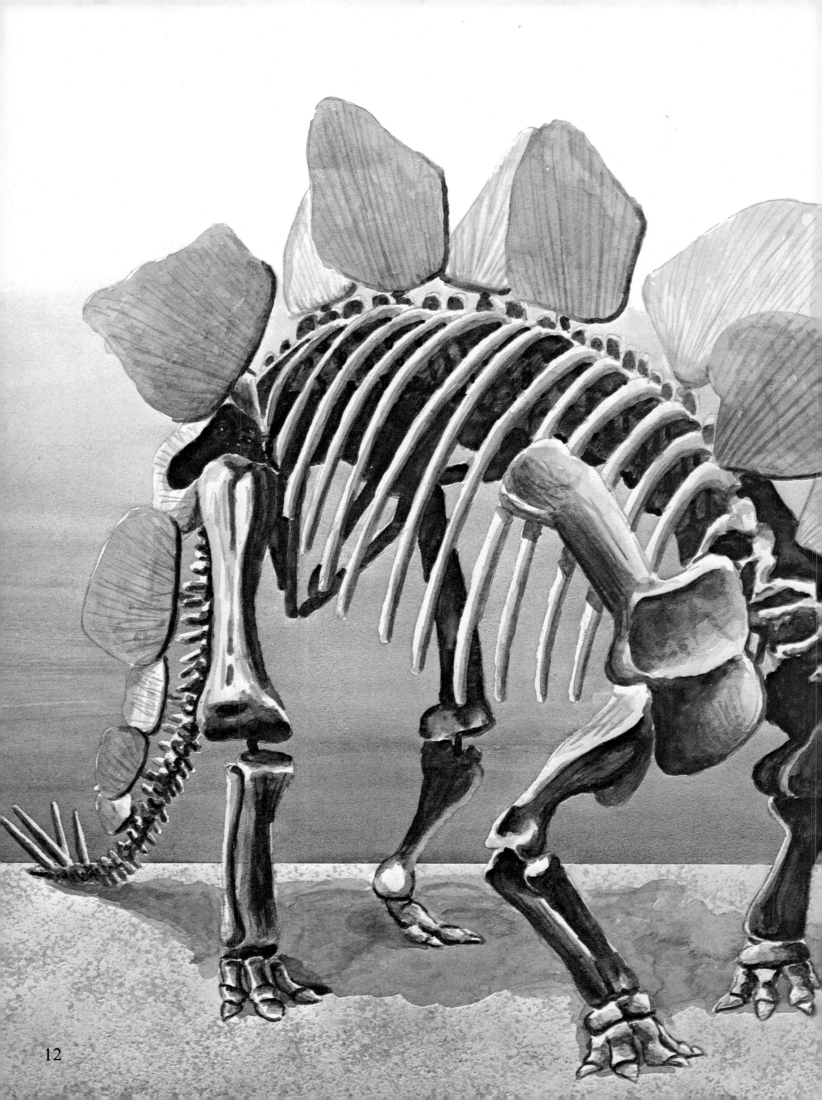

BODY SIZE

Stegosaurus was smaller than some other dinosaurs. It was 20 to 30 feet (6 to 9.2 m) long. This is as long as two school buses. *Stegosaurus* was 11 feet (3.3 m) tall, which is as tall as a one-story house. It weighed 2 to 3 tons (1.8 to 2.7 metric tons).

Stegosaurus walked on all four legs. Scientists believe that its back legs were thick, long, and strong. The back legs were twice as long as the front legs. The hips humped high into the air.

Each back foot had four toes. Each front foot had five toes. Each toe had a hoof-like claw.

CHAPTER 2: STEGOSAURUS' LIFESTYLE

Scientists have found many dinosaur fossils. The name "dinosaur" is from two Greek words. **Deinos** means "terrible," because the animals were very big. **Sauros** means "lizard," because early scientists thought these animals were like lizards.

Paleontologists used to believe dinosaurs were reptiles. There were four ways in which they seemed to be alike.

1. laid eggs
2. breathed air
3. were cold-blooded
4. had scales on their skin

Scientists have looked at many fossils. Now they believe that dinosaurs were very different from reptiles in other ways.

1. Dinosaurs walked on long legs, but reptiles crawl.
2. Dinosaurs took care of their young, but reptiles usually leave their young to grow alone.
3. Dinosaurs might have been warm-blooded, but reptiles are cold-blooded.

DIET OF PLANTS

Stegosaurus ate only plants. With its head low to the ground, it may have chewed ferns and a plant called "horsetails." It could lean its front legs part way up the trees to reach tree ferns. Tender plants were chewed with its small, weak teeth.

SOCIAL LIFE

Fossils of eggs from *Stegosaurus* were found in Portugal (Europe), Canada, and the United States. Groups of eggs were laid in circles in nests near other dinosaur nests.

Many fossil footprints of *Stegosaurus* were found together. This makes paleontologists believe that these animals probably traveled together. Younger animals would walk in the middle for safety.

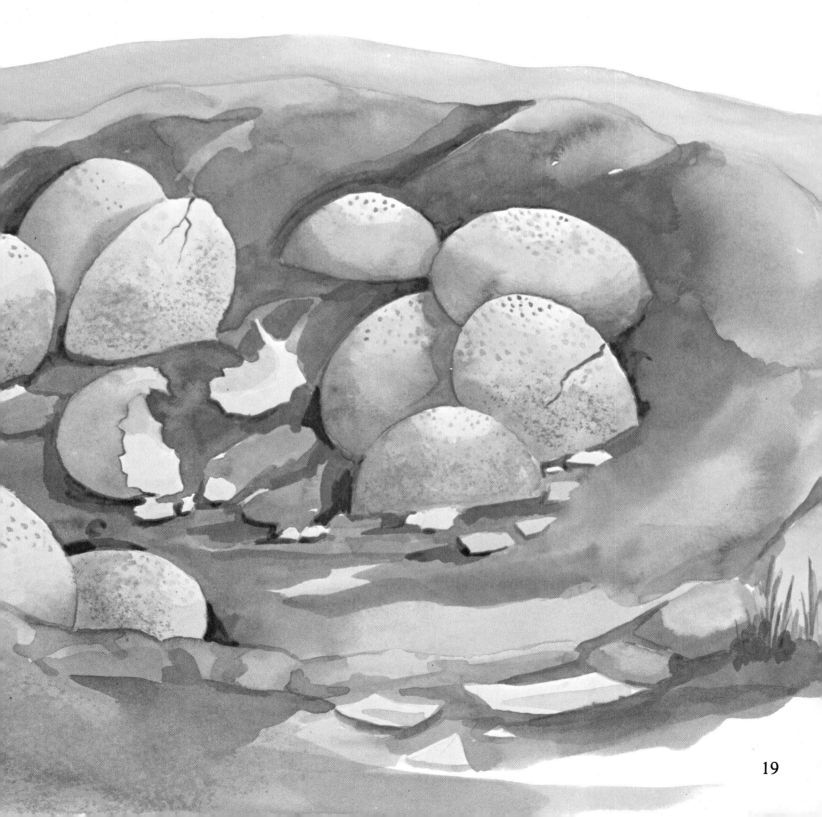

PROTECTION FROM ENEMIES

Stegosaurus had to watch for large, fast-moving, meat-eating dinosaurs. One enemy was a dinosaur called *Allosaurus* (al´ uh sor´ uhs). Because it was so big (about 35 feet or 11 m long), *Allosaurus* had to eat a lot of meat. Footprints show that *Allosaurus* would run on its two hind feet. Each footprint was about 6 feet (1.8 m) apart.

Allosaurus probably would not jump on *Stegosaurus* because of the plates on the back of *Stegosaurus*. With its front legs and hook-like claws, *Allosaurus* would grab at the tail or side of *Stegosaurus*. *Stegosaurus* could lash out with its four tail spikes, each of which was 12 inches (30 cm) long.

CHAPTER 3:
THE AGE OF STEGOSAURUS

Scientists report that some dinosaurs lived to be more than one hundred years old. Some paleontologists believe that *Stegosaurus* may have continued to grow larger all of its life, too.

ROAMING ACROSS THE EARTH

Many scientists believe that, over the years, the land on earth moved slowly apart into continents. Earthquakes and volcanoes caused the land to move around. When *Stegosaurus* lived, the continents were almost touching, so animals could roam over most of the earth.

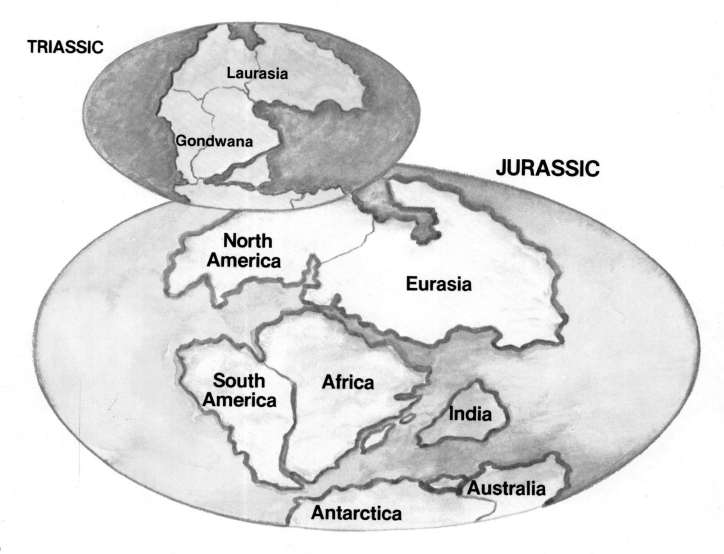

Stegosaurus is the only plated dinosaur ever found in Canada or the United States. The first *Stegosaurus* skeleton discovered in North America was found in Colorado. Many *Stegosaurus* skeletons were found at the Dinosaur Quarry in Utah. Other fossil bones of *Stegosaurus* have been found in Wyoming, and Oklahoma (USA) and Canada.

Stegosaurus fossils have also been found in England; Portugal (Europe); Asia; Africa; and South America.

During these early times, the weather was warm. There were ferns, grasses, and plants. Many kinds of trees grew, such as cycads (like small palm trees), palms, willows, walnut, and oak.

Insects probably bothered the dinosaurs, just like they bother horses and cows today. Scientists have also found fossils of many different kinds of insects.

WHY STEGOSAURUS DIED

All the *Stegosaurus* animals died before all of the dinosaurs disappeared from earth. Perhaps larger meat-eating dinosaurs slowly killed them and then died from hunger.

When *Stegosaurus* died, its body was covered with sand and mud. Some of the bones, the bony plates, and the teeth turned into fossils.

Scientists are not sure how all the dinosaurs died. There are many different ideas. Maybe the weather on earth changed so they could not keep warm. Perhaps water flooded the earth. Perhaps a sickness caused them to die.

27

CONCLUSION: LEARNING MORE ABOUT STEGOSAURUS

"There are many questions yet about the life of *Stegosaurus*," the park ranger told Rosa and her family. "We do not know the sounds it made or what its skin looked like. Most of what we believe are really just ideas. Scientists are still looking at fossils to learn more."

"May we stop at the gift shop?" Rosa asked her father, "I'd like to take a book home to learn more about *Stegosaurus.*"

The park ranger also told them that they could learn more about dinosaurs by visiting certain museums.

"There are friendly people at the museums who want to help you learn about dinosaurs," the park ranger ended.

MUSEUMS

Remains of Stegosaurus fossil bones may be found in the following museums.

American Museum of Natural History, New York, NY.

Carnegie Museum of Natural History, Pittsburgh, PA.

Denver Museum of Natural History, Denver, CO.

Dinosaur National Monument, Jensen, UT.

Exhibit Museum of the University of Michigan, Ann Arbor, MI.

Los Angeles County Museum of Natural History, Los Angeles, CA.

National Museum of Natural History, Smithsonian Institution, Washington, DC.

Nebraska State Museum, University of Nebraska, Lincoln, NE.

Peabody Museum of Natural History, Yale University, New Haven, CT.

Utah Natural History Museum, University of Utah, Salt Lake City, UT.

GLOSSARY

ALLOSAURUS (al´ uh sor´ uhs) means "other lizard" or "different lizard." The Greek word **allos** means "different," and **sauros** means "lizard." The backbone was different from all other dinosaurs.

CYCAD (si´ kad) is a fern-like tree which lived many years ago.

DINOSAUR (di´ nuh sor´) means "terrible lizard." The Greek word **deinos** means "terrible," and the word **sauros** means "lizard."

EXHIBIT (ig zib´ it) refers to objects on display so people can see them.

FOSSILS (fos´ uhlz) are the remains of plants and animals that lived many years ago. The Latin word **fossilis** means "something dug up."

LIZARD (liz´ uhrd) is a kind of reptile. Most lizards are small with slender, scaly bodies; long tails; and four legs.

MUSEUM (myoo że uhm) is a place for keeping and exhibiting works of nature and art, scientific objects, and other items.

PALEONTOLOGIST (pa´ le on tol´ uh jist) is a person who studies fossils to learn about plants and animals from thousands of years ago. The Greek word **palaios** means "ancient," **onta** means "living things," and **logos** means "talking about."

PETRIFIED (pet´ ruh fid) mean parts of plants and animals which have become like stone. This happened when the holes in the material were replaced with mineral grains until the material became as hard as stone.

QUARRY (kwor´ e) is a place from which stone is taken by cutting, digging, or blasting.

REPTILES (rep´ tilz) are cold-blooded, egg-laying animals, such as snakes, alligators, and lizards. The legs grow out of the sides of their body, causing the reptile to crawl rather than walk. The Latin word **reptilis** means "creeping."

SCIENTIST (si´ uhn tist) is a person who studies objects or events.

SKELETON (skel´ uh tuhn) is the framework of bones of a body.

STEGOSAURUS (steg´ uh sor´ uhs) is any of a group of large dinosaurs with rows of bony plates along the back and tail. The name is from two Greek words: **stegos** for "covered roof" and **sauros** for "lizard."

TRICERATOPS (tri ser´ uh tops´) was a large plant-eating dinosaur that had a horn above each eye and one horn above the nose. The name means three-horned faced from the Greek words **tri** for "three" and **keratops** for "horned face."

TYRANNOSAURUS REX (ti ran´ uh sor´ uhs reks) was a huge, meat-eating dinosaur that walked on its hind legs.

TIME LINE

PERIOD

CHARACTERISTIC ANIMAL LIFE

AGE OF THE DINOSAURS

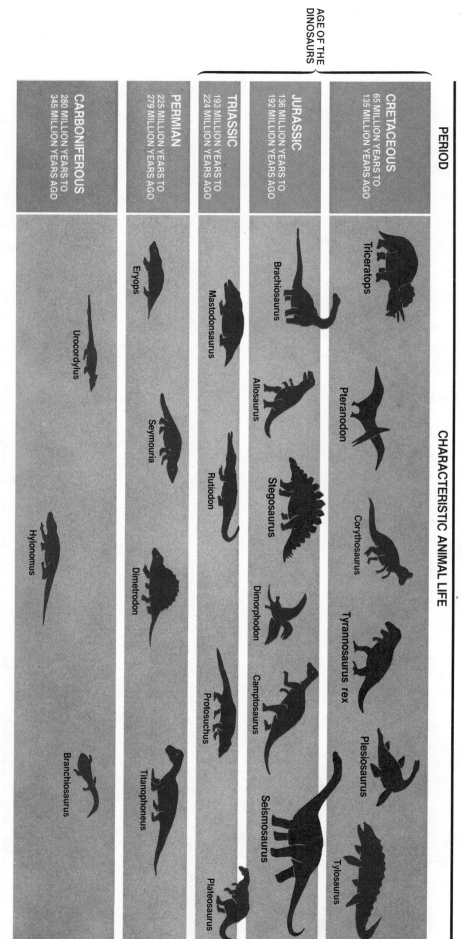

CRETACEOUS
65 MILLION YEARS TO
135 MILLION YEARS AGO

Triceratops • Pteranodon • Corythosaurus • Tyrannosaurus rex • Plesiosaurus • Tylosaurus

JURASSIC
136 MILLION YEARS TO
192 MILLION YEARS AGO

Brachiosaurus • Allosaurus • Stegosaurus • Dimorphodon • Camptosaurus • Seismosaurus

TRIASSIC
193 MILLION YEARS TO
224 MILLION YEARS AGO

Mastodonsaurus • Rutiodon • Protosuchus • Plateosaurus

PERMIAN
225 MILLION YEARS TO
279 MILLION YEARS AGO

Eryops • Seymouria • Dimetrodon • Titanophoneus

CARBONIFEROUS
280 MILLION YEARS TO
345 MILLION YEARS AGO

Urocordylus • Hylonomus • Branchiosaurus

Collaborative Action Research:
A Developmental Approach

Social Research and Educational Studies Series

Series Editor
Robert G. Burgess,
Senior Lecturer in Sociology,
University of Warwick

Social Research and Educational Studies Series: 7

Collaborative Action Research: A Developmental Approach

Sharon Nodie Oja
Lisa Smulyan

The Falmer Press
(A member of the Taylor & Francis Group)
London • New York • Philadelphia

UK	The Falmer Press, Falmer House, Barcombe, Lewes, Sussex, BN8 5DL
USA	The Falmer Press, Taylor & Francis Inc., 242 Cherry Street, Philadelphia, PA 19106–1906

First published 1989

Library of Congress Cataloging-in-Publication Data is available on request

British Library Cataloguing in Publication Data

Oja, Sharon Nodie.
   Collaborative action research: a
   developmental process. — (Social research
   and educational studies series)
   1. Schools. Action research.
   I. Title II. Smulyan, Lisa III. Series
   371.1′02′072

   ISBN 1-85000-520-6
   ISBN 1-85000-521-4 Pbk

Typeset in 11/13 Bembo by
Mathematical Composition Setters Ltd, Salisbury

Printed in Great Britain by Taylor & Francis (Printers) Ltd, Basingstoke, Hampshire

Contents

Series Editor's Preface

The purpose of the Social Research and Educational Studies series is to provide authoritative guides to key issues in educational research. The series includes overviews of fields, guidance on good practice and discussions of the practical implications of social and educational research. In particular, the series deals with a variety of approaches to conducting social and educational research. Contributors to this series review recent work, raise critical concerns that are particular to the field of education, and reflect on the implications of research for educational policy and practice.

Each volume in the series draws on material that will be relevant for an international audience. The contributors to this series all have wide experience of teaching, conducting and using educational research. The volumes are written so that they will appeal to a wide audience of students, teachers and researchers. Altogether, the volumes in the Social Research and Educational Studies series provide a comprehensive guide for anyone concerned with contemporary educational research.

The series will include individually authored books and edited volumes on a range of themes in education including qualitative research, survey research, the interpretation of data, self-evaluation, research and social policy, analyzing data, action research and the politics and ethics of research.

Recent debates in educational research have highlighted the importance of research and development activities in schools and classrooms as well as collaboration between teachers and researchers. It is these two themes that are taken up in this volume that draws on relevant material from different parts of the English speaking world. A distinctive feature of the volume is the extent to which it draws on the authors' own experience of collaborative action research to advance our understanding of the issues involved in such studies.

Robert Burgess
University of Warwick

Preface

Stephen Kemmis (1982) describes four phases in the history of educational research. In the first phase, which he calls interpretive research, educators and philosophers such as Rousseau and Dewey made sense of practice by developing educational theory 'on a grand scale' (p. 7). In the second, or technical, phase, researchers began to use the principles and techniques of science to examine and improve practice. Their approach was optimistic: problems identified in education could be solved through the application of scientific tools and methods. The third, or pessimistic, phase which followed was a reaction to the separation of theory from practice which resulted from the technical approach. Research came to be seen as irrelevant to practice, the domain of technicians or bureaucrats who had little understanding of life in schools. Consequently, educational research has moved in a fourth, self-reflective, phase which recognizes practitioners' rights and skills as professionals and encourages their involvement in the examination of practice and the clarification of theory. Collaborative action research, which engages teachers in all aspects of the research process as they study their classrooms or schools, provides a methodology for this current phase of educational research.

As action research has reemerged as a viable method for educational research in the United States, United Kingdom and Australia, researchers have begun to study the process itself, to use some of the skills and techniques of self-reflection to examine what happens as teachers and university researchers come together to identify and work on problems of practice. Such examination allows us to plan and implement action research projects which meet the combined goals of improved practice, greater theoretical understanding, and professional development. This book uses the Action Research on Change in Schools (ARCS) project as a case study for analyzing key elements of effective collaborative action research. It focuses in particular on the collaborative processes which interact with, and influence, the research process and outcomes of an action research team, drawing on theory in the fields of group dynamics and adult development to explain how individuals and groups develop through their involvement in action research. Collaborative action research provides practitioners with the supports and challenges needed for personal and professional growth; it is in turn influenced by the interpersonal needs and skills of the participants and the context within which the project occurs. Group leaders who are aware of individuals' differing perspectives can help a group achieve its goals and support individual growth in the process.

This book is intended for both university researchers and practitioners who engage in action research. We expect that it will be comprehensible and interesting to readers with a wide range of backgrounds: people interested in the field who have little background in educational research, group process, or adult development; graduate students in education; and practitioners and professionals in public school and university settings. Although it is not a 'how to' guide, it offers several new lenses for analyzing what contributes to and impedes an action research project's ability to reach its goals. In Chapter 1 we provide an historical overview of action research in education, noting that action research past and present tends to involve collaboration, a focus on problems identified by practitioners, and an emphasis on professional development. This chapter also introduces recent action research projects in the United States, United Kingdom and Australia which are used as examples throughout the book. Chapters 2 through 5 focus primarily on the ARCS project as an example of school-based collaborative action research. Chapter 2 describes the purposes and objectives of the ARCS study, noting the features which differentiate it from other recent collaborative action research projects. It then examines the project participants' academic and personal backgrounds and uses phase theories of adult development to analyze their career and age-related reasons for joining the team. Finally, the chapter includes descriptions of the school context in which the project occurred and the research project on teacher morale undertaken by the action research team. In Chapter 3 we analyze the ARCS team's research and group processes, identifying five phases through which interpersonal issues and research tasks shifted over the two years of the project. Research directions and demands influenced the ways in which the group members interacted, and the group's work on interpersonal concerns affected the research project and process. This chapter also explains how teachers began to redefine research, see themselves as researchers, and clarify their goals as a result of their participation in the project.

Chapter 4 uses a cognitive-developmental framework to examine teachers' thinking and behavior as members of the collaborative action research team. Case studies of the five teacher participants, each at a certain stage of development, illustrate qualitative differences in teachers' perceptions of five issues: power, decision making and change; group organization and process; authority and leadership; the school principal; and the goals and outcomes of the collaborative action research project. Theories of adult development provide new insight into teachers' experiences and suggest how to support and challenge individual teachers to grow and learn through the process of action research.

Individual roles taken by team members in an action research project are not static; roles change over the course of a project, reflecting shifting research tasks and patterns of group interaction as well as teachers' changing perceptions of themselves as researchers. Chapter 5 analyzes the roles taken by ARCS team members as they address individual and group demands. It also examines team leadership and the role of the 'outsider,' or university researcher, as a developmental leader in action research. In Chapter 6 we broaden the perspective, presenting several of the key issues or dilemmas characteristic of collaborative action research: establishing a productive relationship between school context and the research project; balancing project control and leadership; and choosing and achieving project goals. Within this chapter, we analyze responses to these issues reflected in recent action research projects and suggest approaches which contribute to successful collaborative action research in schools.

We would like to thank a number of people and organizations who supported our work in this project. First and foremost, we wish to recognize the teachers who contributed their time and efforts to the collaborative action research project undertaken in their school. The opportunity to work with them allowed us to investigate the issues discussed in this book.

In connection with the original ARCS project (1981–83) which involved two universities and two middle school/junior high school sites, we wish to express again our deepest thanks to Gerald J. Pine, Oakland University, for the chance to work with him as co-principal investigator; to Joseph Vaughan and Jay Stratoudakis at the National Institute of Education, who were enthusiastic about our work and helpful regarding NIE procedures; and to the project's advisory board, Leslie Huling, University of Texas at Austin, Norman Sprinthall, North Carolina University, and Beatrice Ward, Consultant for Interactive Research and Development, for their expertise and suggestions over the course of the project. Sincere thanks again to Bob Jebb for organizing and editing the final report format and to Priscilla Woodman for typing the project reports during 1982 and 1983.

This book grew out of our desire to focus in-depth on the investigation of group process and adult development in collaborative action research. In the years since the project we have reanalyzed our data, reviewed recent research, and studied other collaborative action research projects to help us further understand the issues. In writing this book we wish to thank Rita Weathersby, University of New Hampshire, for her useful suggestions concerning the treatment of adult development and presentation of the case studies in Chapter 4; Maryellen Ham for her assistance in conceptualizing figures used in Chapter 5; Judith Randall for her helpful comments after reading the manuscript in its entirety; and Robert Burgess, the Series Editor at Falmer Press, for his critical reading of the manuscript. In using our personal computers for all of the writing we have found heretofore unknown capabilities in ourselves and a variety of software programs which, at the end, allowed Lisa to integrate all our work into the final printout at Swarthmore College. We thank the University of New Hampshire's Education Department and the Program in Education at Swarthmore College for numerous forms of support. Finally, we are especially grateful to Jon McMillan and Michael Markowicz for their patience, encouragement and help throughout the writing process.

The authors undertook to write this book in the spirit of collaboration which characterized the larger project. We provided each other with much of the encouragement and guidance needed to carry out the study and complete the manuscript, and we each appreciated the personal and professional support that we experienced in the process. Collaboration is not always an easy process, but our experience suggests it can be both rewarding and productive.

Sharon Nodie Oja
University of New Hampshire

Lisa Smulyan
Swarthmore College

1
Collaborative Action Research

Introduction

During the past forty years, collaborative action research has been adopted, rejected, modified and revived as a way of meeting the investigative needs of the educational community. Action research, a term first used in the 1940s by Kurt Lewin, implies the application of tools and methods of social science to immediate, practical problems, with the goals of contributing to theory and knowledge in the field of education and improving practice in schools (Kemmis, 1980). Collaborative action research suggests that each group represented in the process shares in the planning, implementation, and analysis of the research and that each contributes different expertise and a unique perspective. Today's collaborators often include school district personnel, university faculty or educational research and development center staff and national education agencies which provide financial support and guidance.

Action research projects have three general aims: staff development, improved school practice and the modification and elaboration of theories of teaching and learning. Staff development through action research may take a number of forms, including increased teacher understanding of the classroom and school (Carr and Kemmis, 1986; Grundy and Kemmis, 1982; Nixon, 1981); increased self-esteem resulting from active involvement in research, professional conferences, and perhaps publication (Elliott, 1985; McCutcheon, 1981; Sheard, 1981) and greater feelings of competence in solving problems and making decisions related to teaching and learning. Improved practice results from practitioner participation in the investigation of actions and issues of immediate importance. Contributions to educational theory include the discovery and elaboration of theoretical frameworks underlying teacher practice (Carr and Kemmis, 1986) and the development of theory grounded in the realities of the school and generalizable to other educational contexts. Although not every project aims at or meets all of these goals, most include elements of all three.

This chapter presents an historical overview of the use of action research in education and examines the basic assumptions, expectations, and conditions which continue to characterize collaborative action research today. In so doing, it suggests a basis for examining both the processes and outcomes of specific projects and a guide for developing effective action research studies.

Collaborative Action Research: History

In the early 1940s Kurt Lewin used the term action research to describe research which united the experimental approach of social science with programs of social action to address major social issues (Ebbutt, 1985; Kemmis, 1980). Lewin, an American social psychologist, believed that social problems should serve as the impulse for social inquiry. From the research which followed, theory would emerge, and necessary social change would be achieved.

Lewin suggested that action research could take two forms: (i) comparative research on the conditions and effects of various forms of social action; and (ii) research that responded to a particular social conflict and led directly to social action. In either case, 'Research that produces nothing but books will not suffice' (Lewin, 1948, p. 203). Kemmis (1980) summarized Lewin's goals for action research as follows:

> Knowledge (theory) about social action could develop from observation of the effects of action in context: simultaneously, social needs and aspirations might be met because action programs were aimed at addressing them directly (as action not as principles which might later be applied in action). (p. 15)

Kemmis (*ibid*) suggests that Lewin's adoption of methods of action research stemmed in part from a growing awareness after World War II of significant social problems, including prejudice, authoritarianism, and industrialization. Much of Lewin's early work focused on helping minorities address psychological and social problems caused by prejudice. External consultants worked with community groups to develop and implement change experiments that would help individuals and the community understand and address their biases.

Lewin challenged the traditional role of social scientists, who he felt needed to address these problems directly: 'Socially, it does not suffice that university organizations produce scientific insights' (Lewin, 1948, p. 206). In order to understand and change social practice, social scientists had to include practitioners from the social world under investigation in all phases of their research. Practitioners had to understand that only through the use of the social sciences could they 'hope to gain the power necessary to do a good job' (*ibid*, p. 213). By working together, social scientists and practitioners could discover new theory and take action which addressed important social concerns.

Chein, Cook and Harding (1948) described action research in its early stages, noting the unification of theory and practice through the interaction of practitioner and social scientist:

> (Action research) is a field which developed to satisfy the needs of the sociopolitical individual who recognizes that, in science, he can find the most reliable guide to effective action, and the needs of the scientist who wants his labors to be of maximal social utility as well as of theoretical significance. (p. 44)

The action researcher studied problems which grew out of the community, rather than his or her own knowledge, and worked to make discoveries which could be applied in the community setting.

Practitioners had to be involved in action research not only to use the tools of social science in addressing their concerns, but also because their participation would make them more aware of the need for the action program chosen, and more personally invested in the process of change (*ibid*). Lewin advocated the incorporation of group work into the research process because of the power of group interaction in producing commitment and change in attitude and behavior (Kemmis, 1980; Lewin, 1952). Chein, Cook and Harding (1948) suggested that when practitioners were involved in all phases of the research, the degree of precision of the research findings was less important than the appropriate direction of the resulting action or change. Lewin (1948), however, insisted that action research involving practitioners was as scientifically valid as any other:

> This by no means implies that the research needed is in any respect less scientific or 'lower' than what would be required for pure science in the field of social events. I am inclined to hold the opposite to be true. (p. 203)

Stephen Corey (1952 and 1953) was among the first to use action research in the field of education. He argued that the scientific method had never become an important part of educational practice and that most educational researchers arrived at generalizations with no intention of doing anything with the results of their research. Through action research, however, changes in educational practice would be more likely to occur because teachers, supervisors, and administrators would be involved in inquiry and the application of findings. Teachers themselves supported Corey's assumptions:

> We are convinced that the disposition to study, as objectively as possible, the consequences of our own teaching is more likely to change and improve our practices than is reading about what someone else has discovered regarding the consequences of his teaching. The latter may be helpful. The former is almost certain to be. (Corey, 1953, p. 70)

Corey had more limited claims than Lewin for the results of action research. He believed that the value of action research lay in the extent to which it led to improved practice; the generalizations which emerged from action research applied to the present situation rather than a broad, representative population. Corey may have recognized what other action researchers would later experience: the difficulty in producing both traditionally defined educational theory and improved practice through action research. This conflict has led current action researchers (Adelman, 1985; Carr and Kemmis, 1986) to redefine educational research and theory as that which is grounded in and guides teacher practice. Because education is action-oriented and practical in nature, educational research must address practical problems, rather than theoretical (or context-free) problems (Carr and Kemmis, 1986). In many action research projects, especially in the United Kingdom and Australia, 'the emphasis has come to be on the overriding need for practical, specific solutions in education rather than the search for elusive truths' (Nisbet and Broadfoot, 1980, p. 27).

Corey, like Lewin, emphasized the need for researchers and teachers to work together on common concerns. Cooperation among teachers and between teachers and researchers increased the likelihood that participants would be committed to changing their behavior if the study indicated change was necessary. It provided a support group within which members could risk change and experimentation, and prevented those involved from being manipulated or coerced. Instead of being subjects of an experiment, teachers became the experimenters. Cooperation also provided a greater range and variety of perceptions and competencies from which the group could draw, and increased the probability that the study would be within the realm of possibility (Corey, 1953).

Corey felt that only minimal differences existed between scientific research and the commonsense problem-solving methods used by practitioners, although he argued that action research required more careful and systematic inquiry and interpretation than the common-sense method. In the action research process he outlined, teachers defined a problem, hypothesized or predicted consequences of a certain action, designed and implemented a test, obtained evidence, and generalized from the results. Practitioners used this experimental or hypothesis-testing model of research to provide them with a basis for future decisions and actions.

Between 1953 and 1957, interest in action research in education declined. University scholars attacked action research as method-ologically poor and unscientific, and researchers withdrew to the universities to produce studies more acceptable to their colleagues. Practitioners, too, questioned whether or not action research lived up to its promises of helping them improve school practice and began to use other action-oriented methods of inquiry, such as evaluation (Kemmis, 1980).

In 1957 Hodgkinson wrote a critique of action research in edu-cation in which he presented the basic arguments against its use. Practitioners, he said, lacked familiarity with basic techniques of research, and 'research is no place for an amateur' (Hodgkinson, 1957, p. 142). Teachers did not have time to do research, and the time they did put into research detracted from their teaching. The use of substitutes for teachers engaged in action research also diminished the quality of students' education, and placed an extra financial burden on the school. Hodgkinson argued that no-one had ever examined what happened to teachers after they put the results of their research into practice. He suggested that teachers might actually become more resistant to change because they could defend their present practice by saying that it had been researched and proven good, a defense based on the false assumption that the class or classes researched represented all future classes.

According to Hodgkinson, action research detracted from edu-cation in ways other than its negative effects on pedagogy. Within a school, action research required a group leader who was sensitive to individual and group needs. 'If people of this sort are not available, group cooperation and consensus may be difficult or impossible to obtain. This could lead to failure concerning the action research, distrust of the teacher for colleagues, and a general lowering of school morale' (p. 143). Action research also emphasized the separate local school and threatened a consistent national program of education.

Finally, Hodgkinson argued that action research was not really research, because it did not meet the criteria of valid scientific methodology. Action research did not go beyond the solution of practical problems and often did not involve controlled experimentation because of teachers' lack of training in research. Action researchers did not look for broad generalizations in the field of education, nor did they relate their findings to a larger body of theory or knowledge. Hodgkinson's conclusions directly contradicted Lewin's belief that action research was valid scientific inquiry:

> Perhaps it would be better to define action research as quantified common sense rather than as a form of scientific, empirical research. (*ibid*, p. 146)

Sanford (1970) points out that the shift away from action research and back toward a distinct split between science and practice was advocated in the 1960s by the social science establishment in addresses at annual meetings and public panels and in reports from commissions. Social problems were distinguished from sociological problems, and only the latter were considered to be appropriate for academic research. As a result, policy and practice-related research fell into disfavor (Finch, 1985). Most educational research in the 1960s and early 1970s was done within a particular social science discipline, such as sociology or psychology. Educational issues were discussed in relation to key topics in that discipline and in a language which was unknown and inaccessible to most practitioners (Threadgold, 1985).

Federal funding agencies in the United States institutionalized the separation of scientific inquiry and educational practice during this time period (Sanford, 1970). Between 1954 and 1972, the federal government's goal in educational research and development was to promote 'improvement oriented change' (Guba and Clark, 1980, p. 9). Federal education agencies used a social science model, in which university scholars applied for federal funding, did their research, and presented the funding agency with a report of their findings. The federal government made no provisions for linking the research to development or dissemination processes so that it could be used to create change in schools. Only after the passage of the 1972 Education Amendments Act which established the National Institute of Education did the federal government begin to fund educational research and development centers which coordinated efforts for research, development, diffusion, and adoption (*ibid*). This movement was paralleled in the United Kingdom by the establishment in 1964 of the Schools Council, which also provided official support for educational research and development. In the 1970s, however, both the National Institute of Education and the Schools Council faced problems of translating research into practice, disseminating ideas to a broad range of practitioners, and providing teacher training which would allow for effective implementation of new programs (Lawton, 1980). These concerns may have contributed to the shift in the 1980s to more locally controlled, school-based action research.

Because of the critiques of action research as unscientific and unproductive and the emphasis in the social sciences and federal funding agencies on the separation of research and practice, action research in the 1960s and the early 1970s became inquiry done by practitioners with the help of a consultant (Ward and Tikunoff, 1982). During these years, action research was used to provide in-service teacher training and to improve practice rather than to produce generalizable results or theory.

> Action research emphasizes the involvement of teachers in problems in their own classrooms and has as its primary goal the in-service training and development of the teacher rather than the acquisition of general knowledge in the field of education. (Borg, 1965, p. 313).

The consultants or scientists involved in action research projects served as 'democratic leaders' who would 'stimulate and develop the talents of the group and train and supervise the participants' as they planned, conducted, and evaluated their research (Good, 1963, p. 234).

An example of this focus in action research in the United States is Schaefer's (1967) proposal that teachers use action research to make their school a center of inquiry rather than a distribution center for information. Through their investigations, teachers could find better ways of teaching a diverse student population the skills and knowledge they needed in society while simultaneously contributing to their own intellectual health, growth and professionalism. Schaefer did advocate school-university collaboration in action research, but the goal of inquiry remained the professional development of teachers and the production of situation specific, immediately useful knowledge. In the

7

United Kingdom, a similar pattern emerged from Lawrence Stenhouse's Schools Council Humanities Curriculum Project (HCP) in 1967. While the HCP produced curriculum materials, Stenhouse also focused on helping teachers examine the effects of new strategies for teaching controversial issues in the classroom. His goal, like Schaefer's, was to help teachers become self-reflective researchers, practitioners who could examine their own practice critically and systematically (Stenhouse, 1975). The understanding which resulted from investigating and reflecting on their own practice helped teachers make decisions in their classrooms and allowed them to clarify, modify, and elaborate the theories which informed their teaching (Nixon, 1981). Those who worked with Stenhouse later applied his ideas to several other teacher-based action research projects, such as the Ford Teaching Project (Elliott, 1977) and created organizations to support teacher researchers such as the Classroom Action Research Network, established in 1976 and coordinated from the Cambridge Institute.

In the mid-1970s, new and expanded views of action research in education began to appear, first in the United Kingdom as the result of continued interest in action research in other fields, and later in the United States (Kemmis, 1980; Ward and Tikunoff, 1982). The resurgence of action research as a cooperative venture which simultaneously contributed to knowledge in the field and improved practice reflected growing researcher dissatisfaction with traditional research methodology and design and teacher dissatisfaction with available in-service programs designed to help them develop and improve their practice.

In the 1970s, researchers began to question the applicability of quantitative, experimental methodologies to educational settings and problems. Traditional research methods adapted from the natural sciences tended to restrict the researcher's focus to short run events, isolated variables, and a limited range of meanings, creating an oversimplified picture of a complex classroom reality (Hall, 1975; Mishler, 1979; Nixon, 1981). The experimental method also required that conditions be held constant throughout the experiment and yielded data about the effectiveness of a project only after it had been completed. Both of these requirements conflicted with a teacher's need to modify and improve a 'treatment' throughout the process and therefore limited the usefulness of the research as a decision making tool for practitioners (McCutcheon, 1981; Pine, 1981). Clifford (1973), Mishler (1979), Mosher (1974) and others saw action research as a method which would help researchers more successfully examine the contexts and context-dependent actions and meanings in which learning occurred while helping teachers address their more immediate teaching concerns. Researchers began to articulate the value of more qualitative research methods which allow them to develop 'theoretically grounded critical accounts of "what happens"' which lead to an understanding of both practice and generalizable 'underlying social processes' (Finch, 1985, p. 114).

Another reason for the shift back to action research was researcher and teacher dissatisfaction with the linear model of research and development in which researchers validate new knowledge, develop it into a practical format, and disseminate it to practitioners for adoption (Krathwohl, 1974). This process created a gap between the researcher and user, and it usually resulted in little or no implementation of research findings at the classroom level. Research infrequently reached practitioners, and when it did it was often reported in language which had no meaning for them. Teachers often felt that much of the research available to them lacked practicality and was inconsistent with classroom reality (Cassidy, 1986; Cummings, 1985; Fisher and Berliner, 1979; Huling, 1981).

The linear process of educational research and development also imposed implementation models and procedures on practitioners who had no ownership of or commitment to research in which they had had no part (Clifford, 1973; Hall, 1975; Huling, 1981). Elliott (1977) explains that teachers must become conscious participants in the development of theories which arise from their practical concerns in order to make fundamental changes in their practice. Only through participation in planning and implementing new practices and observing and analyzing their effects will teachers accept and use research findings (Anning, 1986; Elliott, 1977). In the 1970s, action research was seen as an alternative to the traditional, linear approach of scientific research, because it included practitioner involvement in research which would be of immediate use in the school setting.

Practitioner participation in action research also addressed growing concerns during the 1970s that traditional staff development programs did not meet teacher needs. Action research would provide teachers with the opportunity to gain knowledge and skill in research methods and applications and to become more aware of options and possibilities for change. Teachers participating in action research would also become more critical and reflective about their own practice (Oja and Ham, 1984; Pollard, 1988; Street, 1986). Elliott (1977) quotes one teacher involved in an action research program who said, 'Indeed the value of this research to us may be in the analysis the teachers make of their methods and their whole approach to teaching' (p. 13). Teachers' heightened perceptions and understanding gives them greater control over their own behavior and makes them independent of others for professional growth (Elliott, 1977; Griffiths, 1985; Mosher, 1974; Pine, 1981). Lieberman and Miller (1984) see staff development through action research as a model for professional growth and an ongoing process of problem solving and program building within a school.

Action research, initiated in the 1940s by Kurt Lewin, and adapted by educators soon after, has reemerged in the 1970s and 1980s as a viable method for conducting educational research which contributes to knowledge in the field, change in school policy, and improved practice. While earlier studies of action research tended to report project outcomes, recent studies have begun to examine the processes or methods involved in action research with the assumption that an understanding of the elements underlying successful action research will lead to more effective research processes and designs. John Elliott (1985) describes such analysis as 'second order educational research' which focuses not on the issues teachers are studying but 'on the actions of those responsible for facilitating teacher deliberation' (*ibid*, p. 239). In the United States, these studies include Tikunoff, Ward and Griffin's (1979) Interactive Research and Development on Teaching study, which found that interactive research and development can produce rigorous research and stimulate staff development under certain conditions; Little's (1981) study which examined staff development in a school district; Hord's (1981) study which focused on the collaboration between a research and development center and a school district whose goal was to raise student performance on achievement tests; and Evans, Stubbs, Duckworth and Davis' (1981) Teacher Initiated Research, a project which aimed to give teachers the opportunity to improve their practice while producing practice-based research.

Another recent study is Huling's (1981) Interactive Research and Development project in which she used the Concerns-Based Adoption Model (Hall and Loucks-Horsley, 1978) to determine the effects of participation in a collaborative action research project on teachers' concern for and use of research findings and practices. She found that teachers who participated in the project demonstrated significantly greater changes in concern about the use of research findings in their practice, higher levels of research and development skills, and more positive attitudes about using research findings in their teaching than teachers who did not participate.

In the United Kingdom teachers in John Elliott's Teacher-Pupil Interaction and the Quality of Learning project (TIQL) (Elliott, 1985; Ebbutt, 1985) at the Cambridge Institute of Education focused on the gap between teaching for understanding and teaching for assessment. In their analysis of this project, Elliott (1985) and Ebbutt (1985) examine the dilemmas which arise in the collaboration between outside researchers with a research agenda and teachers who want to examine and reflect on their own practice. Their results (referred to again in Chapter 6) suggest that project success depends on a constant monitoring of the needs of practitioners and of the demands of educational research. Insistence on addressing both leads to improved practice, professional development, and further understanding of educational theory.

Whyte (1986) and Kelly (1985) address some of the same concerns in their examinations of their project, Girls Into Science and Technology (GIST). Their analyses of the processes and outcomes of this project suggest some of the difficulties in collaborating on an issue (sex bias in science and technology education) which must first be introduced to teachers as a concern and then acted upon. Other studies examining the process of action research include works by Elliott (1981) and Kemmis and McTaggart (1982) each of whom has developed a sequence of spiral steps designed to guide others through the process of action research. Volumes by Nixon (1981), Burgess (1984, 1985a, 1985b and 1985c) and Hustler, Cassidy and Cuff (1986) include essays written by teachers and researchers engaged in a range of action research projects in schools.

These studies suggest researchers' concern for the acceptance of action research as a valid, rigorous and productive form of educational research in the 1980s. To avoid the criticisms of the past and to meet the combined goals of improved practice, expanded theory, and staff development, educational researchers involved in collaborative action research must examine the processes in which they are engaged and use their findings to improve both the process and products of action research in the schools.

Characteristics of Collaborative Action Research

Ward and Tikunoff (1982) point out that the underlying premises and requirements of current action research projects closely resemble those applied in action research conducted thirty and forty years ago. Despite the fact that the specific forms and definitions of action research differ from project to project, each 'grounded by the participants and institutions they represent' (*ibid*), certain common characteristics emerge. Four basic elements of action research are its collaborative nature, its focus on practical problems, its emphasis on professional development, and its need for a project structure which provides participants with time and support for open communication. Each of these elements is described below.

Collaboration

The key characteristic of action research past and present is collaboration, which allows for mutual understanding and consensus, democratic decision making, and common action (Carr and Kemmis, 1986; Street, 1986).

> Action research aims to contribute *both* to the practical concerns of people in an immediate problematic situation and to the goals of social science by joint collaboration within a mutually acceptable ethical framework. (Rapoport, 1970, p. 499)

Hord (1981) distinguishes between cooperation and collaboration, suggesting that in the former, participants reach some agreements but proceed individually toward self-defined goals, while in the latter, participants work together on all phases of a project which provides mutual benefits. Grundy and Kemmis (1982), Little (1981), and Oja and Pine (1981) also emphasize that in collaboration, teachers and researchers set common goals and mutually plan the research design, collect and analyze data, and report results. They claim that the involvement of both groups in every stage of research, development and application allows for the connection of theory and practice throughout a project and provides both teachers and researchers with the 'opportunity for reflection and for unexpected insight into situational realities' (Little, 1981, p. 4). According to Tikunoff, Ward and Griffin (1979):

> Collaboration is viewed as teachers, researchers and trainer developers working with parity and assuming equal responsibility to identify, inquire into, and resolve the problems and concerns of classroom teachers. Such collaboration recognizes and utilizes the unique insights and skills provided by each participant while, at the same time, demanding that no set of responsibilities is assigned a superior status. (p. 10)

Wallat *et al.* (1981) point out that 'parity and equal responsibility' in collaboration 'do not mean that each member has an equal role in decision making or input during all phases of the study. Role shifts occur depending on the needs of the situation. Continuity is provided by the researchers through the communication and collaboration network they establish with those involved in the study' (p. 94). In collaborative action research, researchers and practitioners contribute their knowledge and skills to a jointly defined research project and process.

Collaboration can take a number of forms, depending primarily on the degree to which practitioners are included in the project. For example, in Whyte (1986) and Kelly's (1985) GIST project, the research team introduced teachers to the concern about sex bias in science and technology through a series of workshops. Teachers were involved in some of the programs and changes which followed, but researchers initiated most of the action. In the first stage of Susan Florio's (1983) collaborative writing project, teachers were involved in data collection and dissemination of results. In the Action Research on Change in Schools project (Oja and Pine, 1983) described in Chapter 2, teachers identified a research question, designed a study, collected and analyzed data, and disseminated their findings. At different stages in the process, teachers with skills in research design, statistical analysis, and other needed skills assumed leadership roles in the group.

Collaboration also assumes that researchers and practitioners will communicate frequently and openly throughout the process to avoid possible conflicting perceptions and assumptions which result from their different positions in the field (Cummings and Hustler, 1986; Threadgold, 1985). Grundy and Kemmis (1982) call for a democratic process of 'symmetrical communication' (p. 87) which allows all members to participate on equal terms. For teachers, this may require a willingness to discuss their own problems and limitations, to share in the activities and ideas of others, and to be open to learning new skills and behaviors of use in the research process (McLaughlin and Marsh, 1978; Pine, 1981). Researchers must convince university peers and funding agencies that working in schools is viable research (Fisher and Berliner, 1979; Rapoport, 1970) and must themselves accept that 'getting their hands dirty' in classroom complexities is an appropriate and rewarding research process (Pine, 1981, p. 13). In order to make collaboration succeed, researchers must learn to work with teachers as peers and be sure that their work supports rather than interferes with teachers' on going school responsibilities. Bown (1977) suggests that 'collaboration is an endless series of daily acts which respect equal partnership in joint undertakings rather than a flag to be saluted annually with glib rhetoric' (p. 7).

Focus on Practice

Most collaborative action research focuses on immediate problems defined by the participating practitioners (Cummings and Hustler, 1986; Ebbutt, 1985; Elliott, 1977; Rapoport, 1970; Wallat *et al.*, 1981). If university researchers are involved, they may provide an overall issue or framework or plan additional research in conjunction with the teachers' project, although the imposition of such a framework may limit practitioners' freedom to work on issues of importance to them (Elliott, 1985). Different projects again vary in their approach to this characteristic. Teacher-as-researcher projects (Cummings, 1985; Evans *et al.*, 1981; Nixon, 1981) focus primarily on teacher-initiated issues. Teachers may come together to share insights and develop generalizable ideas (Ebbutt, 1985; Hustler *et al.*, 1986) or they may use their findings primarily in their own classrooms. In other projects, such as Teacher-pupil Interaction and the Quality of Learning (TIQL) (Elliott, 1985) a general topic or issue is introduced to teachers who may then choose a related classroom problem to pursue. Because action research aims to change and improve the situation in which it is carried out, the research ultimately focuses on the classroom or school and the actions of practitioners in that situation.

Professional Development

Kurt Lewin advocated action research into social problems in part because he believed that social change depended on the commitment and understanding of those involved in the change process (Lewin, 1948). Action research in education has often been seen as a way of involving teachers in changes which improve teaching practice. The assumption, based on Lewin's work, is that if teachers work together on a common problem clarifying and negotiating ideas and concerns, they will be more likely to change their attitudes and behaviors if research indicates such change is necessary (Anning, 1986; Cassidy, 1986; Hall, 1975; Hodgkinson, 1957). Elliott (1977) and Little (1981) both suggest that collaboration provides teachers with the time and support necessary to make fundamental changes in their practice which endure beyond the research process. Teachers themselves explain that participation in action research groups gives them the support and impetus to change both their classroom practice and their approach to professional problems (Enright, 1981; Evans *et al.*, 1981; Smulyan, 1984).

Another expected outcome of action research in education, beyond change in practice, is teachers' professional growth. Collaboration provides teachers with many different perspectives. Through action research, teachers gain new knowledge which helps them solve immediate problems, broaden their general knowledge base as professionals, and learn research skills which can be applied to future interests and concerns (Mosher, 1974; Street, 1986). Teachers tend to emphasize that their new knowledge of the process of action research (knowing how to analyze a problem, work with others to solve it, and evaluate their results) is as useful to them as the specific product produced by their initial efforts in action research. Teachers who participate in action research projects become more flexible in their thinking, more receptive to new ideas, and more able to solve problems as they arise (Groarke *et al.*, 1986; Pine, 1981).

Noffke and Zeichner (1987) analyze several major action research projects carried out in the United States, United Kingdom and Australia to document the effects of action research on teachers' thinking. They find evidence for a number of developments: changes in teachers' definitions of professional skills and roles; increases in teachers' feelings of self-worth and confidence; increases in teachers' awareness of classroom issues; changes in teachers' disposition toward reflection; increases in teachers' awareness of and/or changes in specific educational beliefs; development of greater congruence between teachers' practical theories and practices; and a broadening of teachers' views on teaching, schooling, and society (pp. 4–5). The authors note that changes in teacher thinking may take different forms in studies conducted in the United States and United Kingdom or Australia. For example, in the United States, changes in professional skills resulting from participation in action research often include the development of skills necessary for traditional social science research, while in the United Kingdom, new professional skills and knowledge tend to include a greater self awareness in the classroom and understanding of the institutional, social and political constraints on one's work. Noffke and Zeichner suggest that these differences reflect differences in each country's perceptions of the profession of teaching and the concept of what constitutes professionalism in education.

Hall (1975) points out that action research also benefits the community in which it occurs, in this case the school or district, as well as the individual teachers who participate. Hall and others claim that through the process of collaboration, teachers tend to arrive at research questions which address school or district concerns rather than the problems of an individual teacher in the group. Their research results can then be used in the school or system as well as in participating teachers' classrooms (Borg, 1965; Griffiths, 1985; Nixon, 1981). Teachers who have participated in collaborative action research projects say that the process created new patterns of collegiality, communication, and sharing in their schools which carried over into and improved other activities and projects (Little, 1981). Some studies indicate, however, that the impact of collaborative action research on the school or system depends to a large extent on the involvement and support of administrators who can provide a project with legitimacy and continuity (Cohen and Finch, 1987; Elliott, 1985).

Project Structure: Conditions Necessary for Collaborative Action Research

Successful collaborative action research depends on a project structure which allows the prior three characteristics (collaboration, focus on practice, and professional development) to emerge. A project structure conducive to effective action research consists of at least four elements: (i) frequent and open communication among participants; (ii) democratic project leadership; (iii) spiraling cycles of planning, acting, observing, and reflecting; and (iv) positive relationships with the school context within which the project occurs.

Communication

Hord (1981), McLaughlin and Marsh (1978), and Wallat *et al.* (1981) all stress the importance of negotiating and articulating clear and specific goals from the outset of the project. Clear goals provide all participants with a sense of the project's value and what they will gain from it and establish a shared frame of reference from which hypotheses and future plans can be generated. Although defining mutual goals may consume a large part of the group's initial meeting time, this process provides the research group with a shared sense of commitment, mutual understanding and a framework for future tasks.

Shared goals imply patterns of communication which facilitate interaction. Communication between university researchers and teachers can often break down due to differences in language, perceptions, and expectations which result from their different positions in the field (Cummings and Hustler, 1986; Holley, 1977; Threadgold, 1985).

> Given this natural breach of language, and more importantly the thinking it represents, a collaborative research effort must take special pains to ensure that the different members of the collaborative team use the same language and understand each others' concerns. (Mergendoller, 1981, p. 6).

Frequent interaction among participants in the research project, through team meetings and more informal discussions, is a requirement of action research which helps to overcome communication difficulties and contributes to mutual understanding of goals, techniques, and perspectives (Corey, 1953; Elliott, 1985; Hord, 1981).

Leadership

Many of those studying action research also call for strong leadership in a collaborative action research project, by someone who can set a positive example as a collaborator (Ebbutt, 1985; Grundy and Kemmis, 1982; Hord, 1981; Nixon, 1981). This often means that the leader must disperse his or her power, sharing control and allowing others to delegate and assume responsibility. Recent studies of action research projects show a growing awareness of the need for a democratic process that considers each participant's needs, perspectives, and skills. Successful action research projects may struggle with and find ways to balance the concepts of collaboration or democracy and leadership which allow the project to move forward. (Chapter 5 discusses in more detail the role of the outside researcher as leader in collaborative action research.)

Spiraling Cycles

Lewin (1948) explains that action research proceeds through spiraling cycles of planning, execution, and reconnaissance (or fact-finding) in order to evaluate and perhaps modify the plan. Elliott (1981) and Kemmis and McTaggart (1982) adapt Lewin's description, each providing a model of the process of action research which emphasizes recurring cycles of planning, acting, observing, reflecting, and revising (see Figures 1 and 2). They, too, use a spiral pattern to indicate that initial

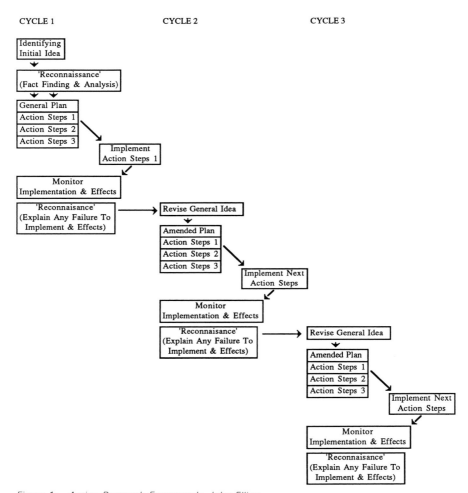

Figure 1: Action Research Framework: John Elliott

Source: Ebbutt, D. (1985) 'Educational action research: Some general concerns and specific quibbles,' in Burgess, R., (Ed) *Issues in Educational Research: Qualitative Methods*, Lewes, Falmer Press, p. 165, figure 2.

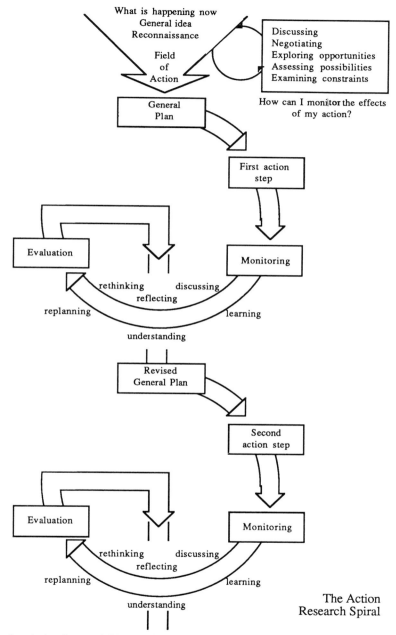

What is happening now
General idea
Reconnaissance

Field
of
Action

Discussing
Negotiating
Exploring opportunities
Assessing possibilities
Examining constraints

How can I monitor the effects
of my action?

General
Plan

First action
step

Evaluation

Monitoring

rethinking   discussing
reflecting
replanning   learning
understanding

Revised
General Plan

Second
action step

Evaluation

Monitoring

rethinking   discussing
reflecting
replanning   learning
understanding

The Action
Research Spiral

Figure 2:   Action Research Planner: Stephen Kemmis

Source: Ebbutt, D. (1985) 'Educational action research: Some general concerns and specific quibbles,' in Burgess, R., (Ed) *Issues in Educational Research: Qualitative Methods*, Lewes, Falmer Press, p. 163, figure 1.

ideas shift over time and that recurring reflection leads to modification of plans throughout the process. Grundy and Kemmis (1982) explain that spiraling cycles are necessary 'to bring action research under the control of understanding, in order to develop and inform practical judgment, and in order to develop an effective critique of the situation' (p. 85). Ebbutt (1985) sees the process of action research as a 'series of successive cycles, each incorporating the possibility for feedback of information within and between cycles' (p. 164) (see Figure 3). The emphasis remains the same, however; an action research project must provide participants with the opportunity to work through several cycles in order to be effective. This recursive rather than linear research process allows practitioners to use their own reflections, understandings, and developing theories to inform both practice and research (Oja and Pine, 1988). Action research projects must therefore be structured to allow this cyclical process to occur.

School Context

Certain elements of the school environment contribute to the effectiveness of action research projects. Projects are most successful when the school climate encourages communication and experimentation and when the administration supports the project (with technical support and/or assurances of further implementation or continuation). Studies by Elliott (1977), Whyte (1986) and Cohn and Finch (1987) all indicate that the school context affects teachers' willingness and ability to participate in the process of action research. Corey (1952) and Pine (1981) suggest that teachers need an atmosphere in which they are free to identify problems for inquiry, experiment with solutions, and express and share ideas with colleagues and administrators. Some of this freedom comes from an administration which recognizes collegial rather than hierarchical authority and allows teachers to make decisions which influence their practice and inquiry (Schaefer, 1967; Stenhouse, 1975). Ideally, the administration not only provides teachers with the freedom to experiment, but gives them the recognition needed to legitimize their project and ensure its continuation in the future (Cohn and Finch, 1987; McLaughlin and Marsh, 1978).

Administrative support may take the form of resources such as time and the technical and material assistance necessary to the research project's success. Many who advocate collaborative action research claim that time restraints often limit the research. In 1967, Schaefer said that teachers needed reduced teaching loads in order to step back from

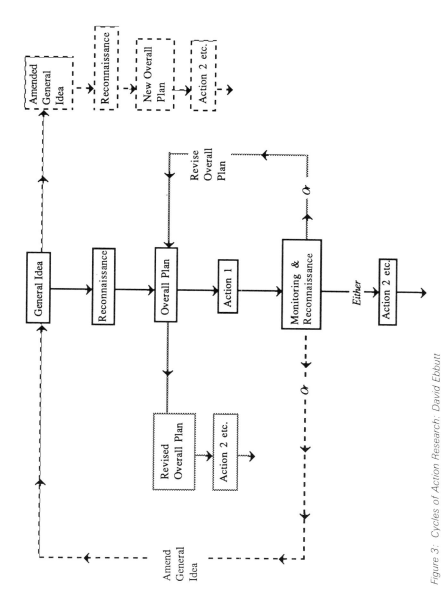

Figure 3: Cycles of Action Research: David Ebbutt

Source: Ebbutt, D. (1985) 'Educational action research: Some general concerns and specific quibbles,' in Burgess, R., (Ed) *Issues in Educational Research: Qualitative Methods,* Lewes, Falmer Press, p. 166, figure 3.

and reflect on teaching and learning. More recently, as economic and demographic pressures decrease the amount of in-school free time available to teachers, those writing about action research suggest only that 'participants must be willing to devote the necessary time to joint endeavors' (Hord, 1981, p. 9). Although the question of how to provide it remains unanswered, agreement exists that time is a valuable resource and a necessary condition for successful collaborative action research.

Action research also requires technical assistance and material support, which may include xeroxing, locating literature, and designing data collection tools. Teachers may need training in research techniques or new classroom practices and the input of observers or consultants in their classrooms as they conduct their inquiry. At times these resources can be provided by the university participants in the project; in other cases the school or system may agree to support the project in these ways.

Action research can exist without administrative or school support; teachers may work individually or in small groups to carry out projects in their classrooms (James and Ebbutt, 1981) or outsiders may provide the initiative, materials, and professional support needed to implement a project (Cohn and Finch, 1987; Whyte, 1986). Most projects which engage in these more independent forms of action research later reflect that greater school/administration involvement might have helped expand the impact, the longevity, and the legitimacy of the project. As Carr and Kemmis (1986) note when describing a project in which they had worked:

> The situation did not change as radically as the teachers involved had hoped, but they learned something about the change process itself: that they needed to involve others in the learning process they had gone through, and to involve them early. (p. 170)

Forms of Action Research

As we have previously suggested, action research can take a variety of forms. The characteristics of any particular project will depend on the particular goals emphasized, the degree of collaboration between practitioners and outside researchers, the processes used in carrying out the research, the relationship of the project to the school, and the project outcomes. Grundy and Kemmis (1982) and Noffke and Zeichner (1987) suggest that differences in action research reflect different countries' educational and research perspectives and priorities. They claim that British and Australian action research share a collaborative style but British action research is 'less strategically oriented and probably less politically aware. It emphasizes interpretive inquiry where Australian action research is more critical. ... And American action research tends to be more technical where Australian action research is more teacher-oriented and teacher controlled' (Grundy and Kemmis, 1982, p. 83).

Alison Kelly (1986) outlines three strands of action research in the United Kingdom: the teacher-as-researcher model exemplified by Stenhouse's work, the experimental social administration model which originated in Lewin's work, and the simultaneous-integrated model which draws on both of the others. Each of these is briefly described below along with a fourth form, collaborative action research, prevalent in the United States. Although projects from any country may fit neatly into one category or another, it is expected that many will have characteristics of more than one.

Teacher-As-Researcher

This form of action research aims to improve educational practice by engaging teachers in the processes of planning, acting and reflecting. Teachers provide the problems to be solved; if outside researchers are involved, their role is to help teachers as they examine their own practice. Eventually, the need for an outside facilitator is alleviated as practitioners take on responsibility for the process (Carr and Kemmis, 1986). While some of those engaged in teacher-as-researcher projects place less importance on the generalizability of outcomes and the contribution to educational knowledge and theory, others emphasize the importance of having teachers move to the step of sharing, generalizing, and writing about their insights (Elliott, 1985; Sheard, 1981). This form of action research, while most prevalent in the United Kingdom and Australia, appears in the United States as well (Cohn and Finch, 1987; Evans *et al.*, 1981).

Experimental Social Administration

Kelly (1986) describes this model of action research as aiming to affect policy and practice rather than engaging teachers in reflection on their own practice. In this model, researchers 'take a research-based hypothesis, test it in an experimental action project, and evaluate its effect' (p. 130). Practitioners have little input into the process and researchers remain outsiders to the situation in which the action occurs. This model does not clearly meet the expectations of collaboration, professional development, and a focus on practical problems which characterize most action research projects as we have defined them.

Simultaneous-Integrated Action Research

Kelly (1986) draws on the work of Hult and Lemming (1980) in defining this model of action research which contributes to both practical problem solving and scientific knowledge. Like the experimental social model, it is concerned with contributions to theory, but it allows practitioners to participate and involves a less rigid experimental design. Like the teacher-as-researcher model, it engages teachers in action and reflection on an immediate, practical situation, but the problem under investigation may be initiated by outside researchers; teachers may be collaborators but not necessarily innovators in the project. Kelly describes the GIST project as fitting this model; teachers were collaborators in the research project which was initiated and evaluated by outside researchers. Such a model is necessary, Kelly explains, when teachers are unaware of the problem and possible solutions.

Collaborative Action Research

A fourth model of action research has grown out of the projects funded in the United States by the National Institute of Education. This model brings together teachers, staff developers, and/or university faculty with the goals of improving practice, contributing to educational theory, and providing staff development. This form of action research tends to be carried out in teams which may or may not be school based. Each team negotiates a group project which addresses its members' concerns and then uses a recursive process of action research in carrying out its project in classrooms, schools, or school districts. In most of these projects, teams publish or present the results of their studies, and the projects themselves are documented and analyzed by researchers who look for insights into the processes of effective action research.

Examples of this form of action research include the Interactive Research and Development on Teaching Study (Tikunoff, Ward and Griffen, 1979), the Interactive Research and Development on Schooling Study (Griffin, Lieberman and Jacullo-Noto, 1983), and Interactive Research and Development studies by Huling (1981).

Conclusion

An examination of the history of action research in education helps explain the range of projects presently underway and the difficulties some of them face. Each project must establish a successful process of collaboration that meets the personal and professional needs of participants. Each must negotiate an appropriate place for itself within its school or system. Each must define its goals — how will it contribute to practice, theory, professional growth — and design a project to meet those goals. Many of those engaged in action research describe its inherent 'messiness,' the result of people from different areas of education working together to examine, change, and reflect on a setting that is itself volatile and alive.

The chapters which follow describe and analyze an action research project modeled on those described under the heading of collaborative action research, above. The Action Research on Change in Schools (ARCS) project (Oja and Pine, 1983) reflects the historical trends from which it grew and includes, in some form, all of the characteristics of action research described earlier in this chapter. In Chapter 6, we will return to some of these characteristics, using the ARCS project to reexamine the dilemmas, conflicts, and issues involved in meeting the expectations and demands of collaborative action research.

2
The ARCS Project

Introduction

The Action Research on Change in Schools project proposed to examine the relationships among teachers' developmental stages, action research in schools, and individual teacher change. By studying the process in which teachers engage while carrying out an action research project in their school, the principal investigators, Sharon N. Oja, University of New Hampshire, and Gerald J. Pine, Oakland University, investigated the following questions:

(i) To what extent do teachers' stages of development (ego, moral and conceptual) influence and affect the changes they undertake?

(ii) How do the contextual variables of the school, i.e. role definition, rewards, expectations, norms, social climate, structure, etc. affect individual teacher change?

(iii) What is the role and impact of action research on the promotion of individual change? (Oja and Pine, 1981, p. 1)

The study was, itself, action research, in that it aimed to improve educational practice and contribute to theories of teacher change and growth. The investigators assumed that their study would provide insight into the design and implementation of staff development programs that encourage teacher growth and improved instruction. The approach was one of 'ongoing tentativeness' (*ibid*, p. 39) which allows for continuous revision of questions, hypotheses, and generalizations as data is collected and analyzed. 'Tentative generalizations will lead to probes about individual change which will lead to new data which are then accumulated with existing data so that tentative generalizations may be revised, which will then lead to revisions of the problem(s) and probes which lead to new data, and so forth' (*ibid*, p. 41). The study did not intend to prove a particular set of hypotheses but rather to generate hypotheses and ideas based on teachers' perceptions, experiences, and deliberate study of the issues they chose to investigate.

The three general questions on which the study was based each led to a series of further themes to be investigated as the two-year study progressed. The first question asked: 'To what extent do teachers' stages of cognitive-development (ego, moral, conceptual) influence and affect the process and outcome of a collaborative action research project?' Issues of importance which emerged were: the individual's inter-personal reasoning in the collaborative group organization and process, the individual's perception of authority and leadership of the university researcher, and the individual's initial goals and expected outcomes of the project.

The second question asked: 'How do the contextual variables of the school affect individual teacher perceptions of, and participation in, a collaborative research project?' Issues of importance were: teachers' receptivity to new ideas, prevailing patterns that created possibilities or set limits in a collaborative research project, and the teachers' perception of the principal and their attitudes toward power, decision-making, and change.

A third set of questions asked: 'How does collaborative action research affect teacher/school development?' and 'To what extent does collaborative action research provide support and challenge for teacher/school development?' Issues which emerged in relation to this purpose were: the importance of the principal's relation to the collaborative research team in effecting school change, the teachers' changing perceptions of themselves as researchers, the teachers' research skill development, and the teachers' unique perspectives, abilities and roles on the team.

The study was implemented in two junior high schools, one in New Hampshire and one in Michigan. The schools were matched for size, grade levels, racial distributions, number of students qualifying for federal aid, and history of school change. In September 1981 all teachers in both schools received a letter introducing and briefly describing the project. At an introductory meeting for interested teachers at their respective sites, eight to ten teachers indicated an interest in the project. All were interviewed and asked to complete a number of questionnaires, including the Loevinger Sentence Completion Test (1970), Rest's Defining Issues Test (1974) and Hunt's Assessment of Conceptual Level (1973). The questionnaire responses were used to choose five teacher participants from each site who represented a range of subject areas, interests and stages of development.

In October 1981, each group of teachers began meeting with one of the principal investigators, who took the role of university researcher on the team, and a research assistant, who would document team meetings and provide research assistance to the team. Each team met weekly from October 1981 until May 1982, and again from September 1982 through May 1983. The team's goal was to conduct a research project in an area chosen by the teachers and to report its results to its funding agency, the National Institute of Education, and wherever else it felt such a presentation would be appropriate. The New Hampshire and Michigan teams worked independently of one another, with the exception of a joint weekend meeting in May 1982 where team members shared and compared progress and problems and their tentative research proposals which they would be sending to NIE in June. This book focuses on the research team located in New Hampshire as a case study of collaborative action research.

ARCS as Collaborative Action Research

The ARCS project fits into the model of collaborative action research described at the end of Chapter 1. In this model:

(i)   Teachers, staff developers, and/or university faculty join together with the goals of improving practice, contributing to educational theory, and providing staff development.

(ii)   Action research is carried out in teams which may or may not be school based.

(iii) Each team negotiates a group project which addresses its members' concerns and then uses a recursive or cyclical process of action research in carrying out its project.

(iv)   In most projects, teams publish or present the results of their studies.

(v)   The projects themselves are documented and analyzed by researchers who look for insights into the processes of effective action research.

The ARCS project reflects this model and, in addition, had certain planning and design features which made it unique. In particular, the characteristics of teachers according to their cognitive-developmental stage scores were used to examine individual teacher participation and perception of issues related to the collaborative research process. The analysis of the individual teachers and their stages of cognitive development provided a new way of examining how a collaborative action research project supports or influences teachers' personal and professional development and their ability to propose or initiate change in school practice. In addition, examination of the ARCS project using theoretical perspectives from group process research offered new insights into the phases of a collaborative action research team and the roles taken by group members.

In the sections which follow we describe the ARCS project in more detail, explaining how it fits each aspect of the model of collaborative action research described above and how it is unique.

Description of Participants

A characteristic of collaborative action research is that participants include teachers, staff developers and university faculty. The ARCS project was no exception. One unique feature was that the university education department faculty member involved in this project was experienced in staff development practices and fulfilled the role of both staff developer and experienced researcher on the team. In addition, the university faculty member was a principal investigator of the project. This provided a different perspective on the collaborative research process. Also new was the use of participant observation by a graduate research assistant experienced in qualitative methods of research to document team meetings. This documentation provided the basis for analysis of the collaborative team process and individual teacher differences.

Participants for the collaborative action research teams were selected to represent a variety of adult stages of cognitive-development. This, too, was an unusual feature of the ARCS project. Chapter 4 describes adult development theory, how teachers were selected from the larger group of interested school staff members, and how five teachers at different stages of development varied in their behavior patterns in the group research process and task. Here we describe the participants as a group in terms of their age, teaching experience, and previous research experience.

Of the five teachers, four were male and one female. They ranged in age from 33 to 41 and in teaching experience from nine to nineteen years. They had taught at the junior high for varying amounts of time, three to seventeen years (see Table 1). These teachers had a total of twenty-seven years teaching experience outside of the junior high, and

Table 1: Team Members' Professional Background

Name	Subject Area	Education	Professional experience	Previous research and training
Brooks Johnson	Reading	B.A, Nasson College Springvale, Maine M.A, University of New Hampshire	One year working with mentally retarded Two years instructional assistant Six years New Hampshire Junior High School*	Title I, educational background in experimental design and methods, grant writing
Ted Williams	Social Studies	B.S, University of Maine M.A, University of Maine	Ten years in Maine elementary schools Two years elementary school principal Three years New Hampshire Junior High School	Developed reading and sports programs
George Rosewater	Math	B.S, University of Maine M.A, University of South Maine	Four years Maine secondary schools Seven years New Hampshire Junior High School	Mathematics Accountability Testing Committee Independent research on teacher learning style
Jack D. Part	Math/House coordinator	B.A, University of New Hampshire M.A, University of Maine	Seventeen years New Hampshire Junior High School	Project funded to investigate school problems Teacher Corps project
John Alden	Science	B.A, University of New Hampshire	Eight years junior high schools in New Hampshire Eleven years in New Hampshire Junior High School	Development of own courses Teacher Corps project TRACT program

* New Hampshire Junior High School was the site of this collaborative action research project.
Pseudonyms are used to identify participants

a total of forty-four years at the junior high. One had twelve years experience in administration and another had two years in addition to their teaching responsibilities; they had both been house coordinators in the school-within-a-school program. One teacher had been an elementary teacher for ten years and an elementary principal for two years before coming to the junior high just three years before the project began. A teacher who took a job at the senior high school during the second year of the collaborative action research project had taught four years at the secondary level before joining the junior high staff seven years before. Only one teacher had gained his entire seventeen years of teaching experience at this junior high (he had also twelve years part-time administration experience during this tenure), and he became a principal at a nearby elementary school during the second year of the project. Four of the five teachers taught one subject to one grade: one teacher taught social studies, one taught science, and two taught math. These four teachers taught at the eighth grade level. The fifth teacher taught seventh and eighth grade reading.

In terms of previous research and training, all had developed curriculum, and four had been involved in a previously funded Teacher Corps Project from 1977–79. The Teacher Corps project provided the opportunity for teachers to explore innovative teaching techniques, focus on ways to individualize instruction, and address developmental needs of junior high students. University and outside consultants worked regularly with the teachers in university masters level courses and workshops taught on site in the school and offered during the summers. One teacher had been involved in Title I (now called Chapter One) which is a federally funded reading program designed for those students who fall within the 20–35 per cent range on standardized reading tests. The Title 1 teacher worked closely with other academic classroom teachers to reinforce the students' reading skills, course assignments, and homework required. This ARCS teacher also had extensive educational background in experimental design and methodology and the writing of research proposals. The ARCS teacher who taught mathematics had been involved in the Mathematics Accountability Testing Committee and had done independent research on teacher learning style. Four of the teachers had master's degrees.

The teachers' views of educational research varied. The two teachers most experienced with research design and methods indicated that although research was meant to improve education, most educational research topics were too narrow; they questioned what research could be replicated and urged that teachers needed more time to do their

Table 2: Critical Issues by Life Phase

	Thirties Transition	Settling Down	Becoming One's Own Person		Midlife (40s) Transition
	Brooks (33)	George (34)	Jack (38)	Ted (39)	John (41)
1 Separating myself from my family and/or my parents' expectations					
2 Seeing myself as an adult becoming part of the adult world					
3 Starting a career and/or exploring family or community roles	4*	5			
4 Parenting ... raising my children as I'd like to (or deciding to be a parent)	4	5		5	4
5 Developing my sense of myself as an adult				4	
6 Making deeper investments in my choices for life and work, setting long range goals and meeting them	4*		4	4	
7 Becoming recognized for my contribution and achievement in roles I value	5*	5		4	
8 Becoming my own person with identity and direction, not dependent on boss, spouse, colleagues, critics, or mentors					

9	Changing my activities and ambitions to reflect more realistically who I am and what I want from my life and work	5			
10	Sharing my knowledge and skills, contributing to the next generation, being helpful to younger friends and associates	5	5		5*
11	Sharing everyday human joys with others; maintaining warm relationships with friends, family, spouse, and colleagues	5*	4	5	4
12	Accomplishing a few important things in the finite period I have left	4*	4	5	
13	Accepting what has transpired in my life as "mine," valuing myself and my choices	5			

Key: 5 = very important — a key issue now
4 = becoming increasingly important

* respondent added written comments

33

own research. Of the remaining three team members, each with little experience in educational research, two gave no initial impressions, while one said that educational research needed to identify a problem, not deal in generalities, and was a waste of time if it did not result in effective change.

Life/Age Cycles

Why do teachers choose to participate in a project on collaborative action research? In order to find out more about teachers' reasons for participating, we used surveys and interviews prior to the project to ask teachers about their current lives, feelings of transition or stability, key issues they were dealing with personally or professionally, and their previous success levels in staff development activities in the school. The key issues identified in Table 2 (Critical Issues by Life Phase) and Table 3 (Life Age/Cycles) are related to adults' life cycles and the patterns of stability or transition that most adults follow at different ages in their lives. The average age of the teachers at the junior high school at the time of the collaborative action research project was 40. The descriptions of five teachers on the junior high team give a flavor for the diversity of life ages, career cycles, and personal concerns for five teachers who are fairly close in age (33–41). One would expect that any collaborative group of teachers would have a varied age range and experience range, and that life age/cycle and career cycle characteristics would affect their reasons for participation.

The teachers are introduced here by name (self-chosen pseudonyms), age, and years of experience; often, this is the most that outsiders ever find out about the teachers who participate. Then we describe more, using the teachers' own voices about their different reasons for participating which related to their career cycles and life age/cycles and influenced their goals and expectations. In the teachers' reasons for participating one can hear varied goals related to improved practice, staff development, and contributions to educational theory.

Brooks

Brooks (age 33) was a reading teacher with nine years of experience, six at the junior high school, who clearly described her use of ARCS as an

Table 3: *Life/Age Cycles*

Theorist	15	20	25	30	35	40	45	50	55	60	65	70	75
Levinson (1978)	leaving the family			settling down			restabilization						
		getting into the adult world				becoming one's own person							
				transitional period									
			mentor plays a significant role										
						mid-life transition							
Gould (1978)	leaving parents	leaving parents		becoming adult	question-ing life's	continuing questioning		occupational die is cast		mellowing, spouse increasingly important			
	breaking out	staying out		marriage work	meaning	values: realization that time is finite; often responsible		interest in friends, reliance on spouse		review of contributions			
			reliance on peers				for parents as well as children						
Sheehy (1976)	pulling up roots	provisional adulthood		age 30 transition	rooting	mid-life transition		restabilization					
Age	15	20	25	30	35	40	45	50	55	60	65	70	75

Source: Oja, S. N. (1980) 'Adult development is implicit in staff development', *Journal of Staff Development* 1, 2, p. 12.

aid in coping with the changes she saw in the school and with the personal issues she was confronting in her life and teaching. She was concerned with handling problems in the school and thinking about leaving teaching.

> I, personally, am trying to discover the effects that these changes have on me ... (talking about finding another job) ... I just don't seem to be able to cope with all these changes. (interview 9/81)

In the late 20s or early 30s the 'age 30 transition' confronts the new adult. The individual asks, 'What is life all about?' In confronting this question, the adult reexamines the initial life structure and the commitments made in the twenties. This may result in restabilization or change in a career or in personal relationships. The adult may go back to school, get divorced, get married (or remarried), change jobs, or change occupations. Of particular interest is the question of what options exist in the teaching profession for those teachers who wish to make a change. As Brooks continued, she also described her skills and interests as they related to action research:

> I said I better really deal with this issue now. So I came back to school resolved that I better deal with what I've got here, before I even try to look for anything else if I want to go on. Another thing, I just thought it would look great on a resume. I just mentally like to keep active, I guess. I want to understand why I'm unhappy about the system and the institution of teaching. I felt that keeping a journal would help. I needed some motivating reason to get me to write. As an undergraduate in college I had visions of becoming a researcher in psychology. I really like researching. It's like solving a puzzle. (interview 9/81)

Like other adults at the age 30 transition, Brooks indicated she had come through a huge transition and was on the verge of making a lot of changes in her life and/or work. She clearly recognized that finding another job and leaving teaching was not the only answer.

> Finding another job at this time would only be fueling my idealism. I really like my colleagues (very few that I don't like), and I enjoy the junior high age group, and I am a talented teacher. So why do I want to leave teaching? I find most of my problems are with administrators and administrative methods.

I feel so helpless and frustrated that their power is affecting my personal life. (interview 9/81)

Brooks' state of transition is apparent by her mention of being hard at work on five key issues (from Table 2) with four additional issues becoming increasingly important to her. Two of the issues were sharing everyday human joys with others (she said, 'Every day I work at this — I'm aware of its importance') and changing her activities and ambitions to reflect more realistically who she was and what she wanted from her life and work. Brooks also keyed in on the issue of being recognized for her contribution and achievement in roles she valued and added, 'This is the crux of the problem at school.' Brooks became involved in ARCS for conscious reasons of personal and professional growth amidst this transition time of the 30s.

Brooks' additional key life issues at the time were valuing herself and her choices and contributing to the next generation. She was the only one of the ARCS teachers who valued personal development goals slightly over work and career goals at this time in her life. Having been very satisfied with, and rated herself as very successful in, previous staff development programs, she noted that since the Teacher Corps project had begun at the school five years ago, the junior high 'has gone through one change right after another. I, personally, am trying to discover the effects that these changes have on me.'

George

George (age 34) had dealt with the issues of the age 30 crisis and was settling down in his early thirties, reaffirming commitments and choosing his career as the most highly valued investment of time and energy. His children were in school; his wife had returned to work. Settling long-term goals both for work-related and family-related activities becomes important to adults in this phase. George, a mathematics teacher of eleven years, six of these at the junior high, was originally somewhat hesitant to commit himself to the two-year action research project because he was preparing to 'advance to a role of more responsibility' most likely outside the teaching field.

> Very recently I have questioned my motivation in meeting weekly and discussing educational topics; I'm a little burned out from that as a result of my pursuing the Masters degree in Education I did recently. I'm considering moving out of

education. I wouldn't want to sit on a committee, sit on this team rather, and be only halfway involved and have one part of me saying what am I doing here. (interview 9/81)

In making a conscious decision to participate he indicated a clear sense of commitment. He said, 'ARCS will ideally motivate thought and greater precision in my conceptualization of issues relevant in an advanced position.' George also indicated an awareness of his own skills as he added, 'I derive pleasure from such activities (research); I am skillful ... I can make significant contributions.' Although only moderately satisfied with previous staff development activities, he definitely enjoyed participating in research activities in the school during the previously federally-funded project. George indicated that prior staff development activities were somewhat helpful to him in negotiating changes in his life or work in terms of 'motivation to learn and filling voids in knowledge background.'

George felt he was on the verge of making a lot of changes. (And, in fact, at the end of the first year of the project, he did transfer from the junior high to the senior high mathematics department and into computer education.) There was a sense that George had wrestled with, and made decisions on, a number of life dilemmas and was on his way in the life period titled 'settling down after the thirties transition'. George's three key issues were parenting, starting a career and/or exploring family and community roles, and being recognized for his contribution and achievement in roles he valued. Similar to many men in this age cycle, George indicated work and career goals as significantly more important than personal goals; he said, 'My personal life right now is substantially involved in planning and preparing for professional growth and change.'

Jack

In the late thirties and early forties the adult is concerned with becoming his/her own person. In most professions promotions are crucial markers of success at this time. While work relationships are important, the adult seeks to break away from advisors and mentors in order to become more independent in work. At this life age/cycle as well as at each of the previous and subsequent cycles, the adult is trying to create a better fit between the life structure already defined and the reality of life's current challenges. Of particular importance in public education are the concepts of promotions and mentoring.

Jack (38 years old) seemed to be tackling issues in this stable life period of Becoming One's Own Man. He had seventeen years of teaching experience (all at the junior high) including twelve years as a part-time school administrator in addition to teaching duties. Jack indicated that he had just come through a period of 'transition' in his life and work and was now in a period he titled 'happy'. Jack's key issue in life was sharing knowledge and skills, contributing to the next generation, and being helpful to younger friends and colleagues. Work and personal goals were equally important. Another indication of Jack's stability was the feeling of being more independent in his work, not relying on the old advisors but becoming open and aware of other opinions in the school.

Jack's reason for participating in the collaborative action research project was that, 'It sounds like an interesting challenge. I could do it now because my outside school commitments are fewer.' He was also interested in getting ideas from others and saw that as a benefit of his participation.

> I'm in hopes the purpose of the project is to look at some of the problems that maybe are unique to this school but also affect junior high education across the country. Well, just participating and sitting and talking with other people, getting other ideas, there have to be benefits you know, to yourself. Even if they are accidental there have to be benefits. It's easy for me to sit there as one of the administrators in the school and also as a teacher and not see some of the other problems that have gone on in the school. I think it's great to get a cross section, and of the six people interested right now, we have a cross section somewhat of teachers in the school. (interview 9/81)

Although only moderately satisfied and rating himself as moderately successful in prior staff development activities, he stated, 'I have not taken too many past (staff development) activities too seriously. I have taken them to satisfy recertification requirements. It is now time to do something constructive.' Jack titled his next life period as 'growth' and saw three life issues as becoming increasingly important: accomplishing a few important things in the finite period left, making deeper investments in choices, and sharing everyday human joys with others. A definite sense of career expansion was visible in Jack's choice to focus on more meaningful activities in the school now that other major life decisions were made.

Ted

Ted (age 39) was also in the phase of Becoming One's Own Person. Ted, like Jack, indicated, 'I have the time and desire to participate in a research project.' He had ten years of teaching experience at the elementary level, two years as an elementary principal, and he had been teaching social studies at the junior high for three years. When the ARCS Project began, Ted felt he was consolidating a major period of work and professional change. Work and personal goals were equally important. Four key issues were: parenting his two elementary aged children, sharing everyday human joys with others, sharing knowledge and contributing to the next generation, and accomplishing a few important things in the period of life left. These issues were similar to Jack's key issues and are reflected in Ted's description of his expectations for ARCS in terms of improving understanding and practice.

> I think the purpose is that we're going to focus on something that all of us have a deep caring for or we're going to analyze a problem and maybe reach some kind of conclusion about it ... something that will make you understand it better and make you a better teacher, maybe a better person and will meet at least some of the needs of the people. (interview 9/81)

Ted wanted a 'clearer focus and understanding of issues' such as 'classroom management, personal growth (kids and teachers), importance of subject matter (what we teach), lack of time and effort spent in developing character in pupils.' Ted spoke of goals for the project mainly in terms of hope for school improvement. An indication that Ted may have been approaching a time of transition, the forties transition, was that a number of additional issues were becoming increasingly important to him: developing my sense of myself as an adult, making deeper investments in my choices for life and work, setting long range goals and meeting them, and becoming recognized for my contributions and achievement in roles I value. The breadth of key issues in Ted's life was much more extensive than teachers who seemed to be in more stable life age/cycles; this is an indication that for Ted transition was near.

The mid-life transition of the forties occurs as one realizes that life ambitions might not develop. The disparity between the benefits of living within one's stable life structure and the recognition of what else one wants in life urges a person to try to create a better fit between one's life structure and self. The mid-life transition is a time of redefining one's work in conjunction with a deeper understanding of self.

John

After the forties transition, one again experiences a period of restabilization to enjoy one's choices and life style. John (age 41) reflected the characteristics of a stabilization period. He had the time and energy to become involved in new pursuits, and at the same time he enjoyed being an informal advisor and mentor to less experienced teachers.

John had been teaching science at the junior high school for eleven years and had nineteen total years of teaching experience. He was Chairman of the staff development program for the school and had been part of the team that designed the current district-wide staff development plan, having to appear personally before five town school boards to negotiate approval. Because of the experience, he said, 'I can deal with administration and school boards better than ever before.' He felt he was in a relative period of stability; evidently this was important to his reasons for becoming involved in the ARCS program. He had come through a transition initiated by a divorce and had total responsibility for raising his junior high aged son. In the current period of stability, John could combine study of action research with his family responsibilities and enjoy both.

> I enjoy teaching junior high students. I have taught in public and private, small and large schools (and have seen many changes good and bad), and have many ideas of how to improve. In the past my personal life has been hectic so extra time could not be used. Now I have the time. (interview 9/81)

John's main issue in life was mentoring. Very important to him was the one key issue of sharing his knowledge and skills, contributing to the newer generation of teachers, and being helpful to younger colleagues. On a regular weekly basis during the project, John shared his project journal comments with the Principal and at least 25 per cent of the school staff. Important in his career he said was 'what is good for students'. He saw the ARCS group as a potential sounding board for his ideas.

> Benefits? For me, yes, because in dealing with people you're working with, if you're talking with them on a basis in which

you are constantly sharing ideas, it can't help but help either you or them; even if you may not agree with the idea, if they have a sounding board, if it helps them, it helps you. (interview 9/81)

Another aspect of the stabilization after either the thirties or forties transition is a response which indicates pursuing long-term goals and accelerating progress or satisfying intellectual curiosity and exploring personal interests. John illustrates this latter facet of stabilization when he said that he's not done much with educational research and 'that's part of the reason why I'm getting involved now, to find out more about it'.

As can be seen in the above descriptions, teachers' reasons for participating in collaborative action research varied. Their goals included improved practice, personal and professional development, and the possibility of contributing to educational theory. Their reasons for participating often correlated with their particular career cycles and life/age cycles. For examples of all the questionnaires used to determine teachers' life age/cycles and career cycles, see Oja (1983). For a further description of the research and literature on career and life/age cycles, see Oja (1985 and 1988b).

School Context

Collaborative action research occurs in school-based teams because groups allow teachers to support each other, take risks, explore new ideas, learn from each other, and because groups encourage teachers to work on classroom or school-based issues of concern to practitioners. The school setting and history will influence the team's process and outcomes.

ARCS Team

The ARCS project drew on the experience of three prior collaborative research projects funded by the National Institute of Education: the Interactive Research and Development on Teaching Study (IR&DT) (Tikunoff, Ward and Griffin, 1981), the Interactive Research and Development on Schooling Study (IR&DS) (Griffin, Lieberman and Jacullo-Noto, 1983), and the IR&D projects by Huling (1981). The research teams in these prior projects were not all school-based. The IR&DT study involved two collaborative research teams; one team consisted of teachers, researcher and trainer/developer all from the same school district but different schools, and a second team consisted of a university researcher, three teachers from different schools in the same school district, and two trainers/developers. The IR&D strategy was next used by Huling (*ibid*) to establish collaborative study between researchers from the Texas Technology University faculty, staff developers from the Teacher Corps staff, and thirteen teachers from local school districts. Six collaborative research teams were formed based on individuals' research interests and team member preferences, but not all involving teachers from the same school. Next, the IR&DS study extended the collaborative research focus to three varying teams (i) teacher specialists working out of a teacher's center, (ii) high school teachers from two cooperative school districts; and (iii) elementary school teachers from the same district and different schools.

In the ARCS Project all five teachers on each team were from the same school. This made it possible to examine their different perceptions of the same school; these perceptions affected their goal setting and problem solving in the group. Recognizing the teachers' reasons for participating is only part of the investigation of the group process and school context in a collaborative action research project. In the ARCS project, because the collaborative action research team was school-based, it is important to understand the context and school climate in which such a project takes place.

Description of the School Setting

The junior high school site was located in a city which was a microcosm of America's largest cities. As one junior high school teacher put it, 'We have all the ingredients of a large urban environment within a small community.' The city had a stable middle class, an affluent population, and an economically disadvantaged population. Of the 680 students in the junior high school, about 15 per cent qualified as educationally disadvantaged according to Title I Reading Scores. Approximately 7 per cent of the junior high students were Black, Indian, Hispanic or Asian.

In 1970 the school consisted of two buildings designed to hold 550 students yet it housed as many as 1000 students. From 1970 to 1982 the school experienced a number of organizational, physical and demographic changes of a substantial nature. These changes included double-tracked ability grouping in mathematics and English, flexible multilevel parallel tracking, a new science program, the initiation of a faculty senate, the dissolution of a faculty senate, classroom accommodations for parochial students, split sessions, homogeneous grouping, heterogeneous grouping, department head organization, house coordinators and five different principals. Continuous changes in leadership and organizational structure with little teacher involvement in decision-making had a negative effect on teacher morale over the years. In 1982, midway through the second year of the collaborative action research project, the new Principal, in his second year in office, replaced the house coordinators responsible for each school-within-a-school by department chairs. The move toward a more traditional junior high organizational structure had begun.

Class size at the junior high school averaged twenty-two to twenty-five students when the ARCS Project began. Sixty-one staff members worked with approximately 660 students. The schedule was a traditional junior high format of 45-minute class periods. Students were basically heterogeneously grouped with some advanced mathematics and English classes. At the beginning of the collaborative action research project, the school had three house coordinators, one for each of the schools-within-a-school. The following year, the second year of the project, the new Principal had replaced the house coordinators with department chairs. The team's research focus was a reaction to the number of principals and organizational changes it had experienced. The new Principal was perceived as receptive and the team hoped, with his apparent sensitivity to teachers' needs, 'that morale would improve and things would be on the upswing'.

Teachers' Perceptions of School History and Climate

For teachers in the ARCS Project the efforts to initiate change were influenced by their school context. The teachers' perceptions of their school organization and environment are in part a function of their school histories and organizational structures. Influential school context issues include: decision-making processes, staff interaction and cooperation, administrative support, communication between teachers and administrators, and teacher and administrator influences on curriculum and departmental issues. Although there are many formal and informal ways to assess these school context matters, the ARCS project chose the Organizational Environment Assessment Instrument (Pine, 1979), an inventory similar in its design to the Organizational Climate Description Questionnaire (OCDQ) developed by Halpin and Croft (1963). In addition to this questionnaire, data on the school context was generated through audio tape recordings of the team meetings, interviews with teachers and principals, and analyses of teacher journals kept over the life of the project. A full report on school context variables of both ARCS teams can be found in Pine (1983).

Teachers in the action research team responded to the organizational environment questionnaire at the beginning of each of the two years of the project. At the beginning of the first year, the team members responded to the questionnaire in August, before any official notice was given that the current Principal of six years would leave the school in September. The following results of the first year data are presented to illustrate the similarity or diversity of team members' impressions. Of five teachers in the collaborative action research team, all agreed that the behavior of the administration was somewhat supportive. Three perceived that the school administration had little confidence and trust in teachers while two felt that the administration had substantial confidence and trust in teachers. All five agreed that teachers in the school had little confidence and trust in administrators. Four teachers on the team felt that there were sometimes hostile and unmotivating attitudes among the staff toward the school and its goals. Three team members felt that teachers in the school had very little influence in shaping the goals and activities of their teacher teams and department; one indicated moderate influence. Four of the team members felt that teachers were seldom involved in decisions related to their work. While three members agreed that the administration could substantially influence the goals and activities of teams and departments, two members anticipated only moderate or very little influence possible.

Teachers' responses at the beginning of the second year showed definite changes in their perceptions. These changes probably resulted from the administrative change experienced in the junior high school during the first year of the project, which was also the first year of the new Principal's administration. Team members' responses showed a general shift toward a perception that administration had more confidence in teachers, was more generally supportive of teachers, and knew and understood the problems teachers faced. These changes may have reflected teacher optimism and belief in the teacher-orientation of their new Principal, who had himself taught at the junior high school. The collaborative action research team members also saw staff attitudes toward the school and school goals as more favorable and motivating than they had in the beginning of the first year. They also had a greater sense that teachers could influence the goals and activities of departments and teacher teams in the school. Again, these shifts may have been influenced by teachers' perceptions of the Principal as more open to teacher opinions.

There was also a shift in team members' perceptions of the level at which decisions were made. At the beginning of the first year of the project, they indicated that they saw decision-making as a top-down, administrative process. At the beginning of the second year, teachers tended to see decision-making as a process which could occur at, or among, a number of different levels. This shift corresponds to teachers' individual perceptions that participation in the action research process gave them a better understanding of the workings of the school (see Chapter 3).

Action Research Project

In collaborative action research each team negotiates a group project which addresses its members' concerns and then uses a recursive process of action research in carrying out its work. In the ARCS Project research problems were mutually defined by teachers and researchers; the university faculty and classroom teachers collaborated in seeking solutions to the practitioner-defined problems. Teachers and researchers spent a long time at the beginning of the project negotiating mutually acceptable goals for the research purpose, design, and ongoing framework. This joint goal setting allowed all participants to feel ownership in the research and kept the project and participants going over the two-year period, even when the work became confusing or frustrating during successive recycling of the action research process.

The team depended upon a process of recursion in carrying out their research. This flexible approach involved redefining research questions and analyzing data and research problems taking into consideration developing themes and new directions during the life of the research and group process. An example of recursion in research problem identification is illustrated in Figure 4. The recursion process as experienced in the ARCS project was similar to aspects of Kemmis'

PHASE OF RESEARCH PROCESS   **RESEARCH PROBLEM**

Year 1

Phase 1: Negotiating Research and Group Boundaries
October–December 1981
Problem identification related to discussion of school contexts

Defined as
● low levels of communication and collegiality among teachers and between teachers and administrators
● low teacher morale
● problems in scheduling that affected teachers and students

Phase 2: Pursuing Tangents
January–March 1982
Survey of staff to help in problem identification

Redefined as
● creating an ideal schedule or specific schedule changes or a philosophy statement about good scheduling practice
● examining scheduling issues: "schools within a school" class length student ability grouping
● investigating a variety of scheduling issues and suggesting alternative schedules to the principal

Phase 3: Reaching Consensus
March–May 1982
Research design and development

Redefined as
● how scheduling changes adopted by the school administration for implementation in the Fall of Year 2 affected teacher morale

Year 2

Phase 4: Reinterpreting the Task
September–December 1982
Data collection and deciding how to analyze data

Redefined as
● how scheduling *and* other organizational changes in the school affected teacher morale

Phase 5: Evaluating the Project and Process
January–June 1983
Data analysis and presentation of results at national conference and local school boards and final report with recommendations to staff and principal

Redefined as
● effect of organizational changes on staff morale/job satisfaction
● effect of organizational changes on staff's perception of teaming, grouping of students, communication with colleagues and administration, time management, and teaching assignment
● relationship of goal clarity and involvement in decision making to staff morale/job satisfaction

Figure 4:   Example of Recursion in Research Problem Identification

planning model (1982), Elliott's framework spirals (1981), and Ebbutt's cycles of action research (1985).

As will be discussed in Chapters 3 and 4, group process theory and adult cognitive-developmental stage theory provide two new lenses with which to examine group and individual patterns of how new data, fed into the action research project at successive points, affected the research process and project. This analysis furthers understanding of why some action research ends up as simply fact finding rather than 'analysis as well as fact finding' (Ebbutt, 1985, p. 162) which is necessary for change.

Research Project Carried Out by ARCS Team

An integral element of collaborative action research in general, and in this project in particular, was the direct involvement of teachers in the research process. By identifying and discussing problems in education and their own school, the teachers were given the opportunity not only to examine change in the school setting but also to develop ways in which they might bring about change. The teachers participated in developing research designs, collecting and analyzing data to respond to research questions, and presenting their findings and conclusions. The university researchers on the team were also given the unique opportunity to participate with teachers in an ongoing research process, to reflect on how they worked as individuals and as a group in recognizing and effecting change, and, of primary importance, to observe how the teachers' stages of cognitive development impacted on the group process and in change in schools.

The action research team was organized in September 1981 and began meeting in October. Over a period of two years, the team identified and developed research questions that addressed their concerns. During the first school calendar year, the team investigated their concerns about the organizational practices of teacher teaming and student ability grouping. They identified their research questions and designed research strategies and frameworks. The second year was devoted to collecting and analyzing their data, developing findings and conclusions, and compiling a final report, *Action Research on Change in Schools: The Relationship Between Teacher Morale/Job Satisfaction and Organizational Changes in a Junior High School* (Blomquist *et al.*, 1983).

In their proposal in the first year of the project, teachers described an evaluation study of organizational decisions around scheduling in their own and several other junior high schools. Within this framework, the team decided to undertake a descriptive case study of its own school context, the school philosophy, and the match between the philosophy (goals, objectives, and junior high priorities) and the organizational practices related to teacher teaming and student ability grouping. The team planned to analyze the strengths and weaknesses of current practices in light of teacher morale, job satisfaction, and student learning. Site visits to other schools and a review of relevant literature would provide data on alternative organizational and scheduling procedures. The study would culminate in a recommendation to the school Principal of organizational and scheduling modifications which were consistent with the team's operational definition of the junior high and substantiated by the team's surveys, literature review, and field observations.

During the second year, the team narrowed its focus. Preliminary investigation into the issue of scheduling the first year, coupled with organizational changes made by the new Principal, led the team to redefine and specify its concerns. The team chose to investigate the relationship between teacher job satisfaction/morale and a number of organizational changes and practices which were occurring at the junior high. Research questions were developed to study new organizational changes at the school affecting the staff's perceptions of: morale/job satisfaction, teaming, communication with colleagues, communication with administration, teaching assignment, time management and planning, clarity of goals, and teacher involvement in decision making. Morale/job satisfaction was measured using the Maslach Burnout Inventory (Maslach and Jackson, 1980) revised for the teaching profession by Schwab (1983). This survey is commonly referred to as the Human Services Survey and is used to determine staff perceptions of the teaching/learning environment. The team created its own second instrument labelled the School Survey to probe teachers' perceptions of the organizational and scheduling issues listed above.

Conclusions of the study indicated that the staff at the school felt teaming was beneficial to teachers, but that they did not have time to communicate with other staff members to share ideas and materials, and they did not have enough time to manage and plan assignments. In addition, staff felt that they had little involvement in decision making. When the total staff was divided into high, moderate, and low groups based on their morale/job satisfaction scores, staff in high and low groups differed in three areas of response: (i) communication with colleagues; (ii) communication with administration (i.e., clarity of goals and involvement in decision making); and (iii) time management.

Dissemination of Results

In the ARCS Project, teachers and researchers co-authored their research reports. Written reports, available for some form of public

Date	Presentation	Audience
May 1982	Syracuse workshop Two ARCS teams met to present research proposals and share ideas	Michigan team
November 1982	Presentation to National Staff Development Conference. Report on ARCS project and process of collaborative action research	Staff developers and teachers from United States and Canada, principal and superintendent from Michigan school site
February 1983	Presentation to District Staff Development Committee. Report on ARCS project and process of collaborative action research	One teacher representative from each elementary, junior, and senior high; school principal; assistant superintendent
April 1983	AERA symposium. Report on ARCS project and process of collaborative action research	Researchers, teacher educators and representatives of federal agencies from United States and Canada
April 1983	Presentation to University of New Hampshire graduate course on Stress in Educational Organizations. Report on ARCS project and process of collaborative action research	Inservice teachers and part-time University of New Hampshire Masters and CAGS students in Education
May 1983	Presentation to University of New Hampshire faculty colloquium. Report on ARCS project and process of collaborative action research	Education Department faculty
June 1983	Lesley College Middle School Conference. Report on ARCS project and process of collaborative action research	Middle School teachers and administrators
June 1983	One team member appointed to National Middle Schools Task Force	
April 1984	Northeastern Educational Research Association Meeting (NEERO). Present results of Teacher Morale study	Teacher Educators and Researchers from Universities in the Northeast United States
April 1984	One team member attended AERA and National Middle School Task Force	

Year after ARCS project ↑ | ↓

Figure 5: Presentation of Collaborative Action Research Project and Process by School and University Participants

critique, are crucial in helping teachers reflect on the research in which they have engaged (Ebbutt, 1985); in the ARCS project the teachers and university researchers found that writing together reinforced collaboration and helped them clarify findings. In addition, the ARCS collaborative action research team engaged in numerous presentations describing the research project and its process. These presentations are listed chronologically in Figure 5 with a description of the audience for each presentation. The presentations proved crucial to the participants' feelings of success in the project (see Chapter 3).

Meta-Research Project

In collaborative action research, the projects themselves are documented and analyzed by researchers who look for insights into the processes of effective action research. The development of the ARCS study was unique in that a study of how teachers' cognitive-developmental stages (ego, moral, conceptual, and interpersonal) affected change processes in action research was carried out simultaneously and in conjunction with the teachers' design and study of a research question focusing on change in their school setting. Although previous studies had effectively utilized collaborative action research in which both teachers and university researchers join in defining research questions and conducting research, this study expanded the experience to make fuller use of both teacher and university involvement. In addition to the recursion process and single school context mentioned in preceding sections, the following planning and design features illustrate the differences from past studies:

Participant-observer documentation
A participant-observer documented team meetings. This documentation (plus audio-tape transcripts) provided the basis for analysis of the collaborative team process and individual teacher differences. Although this intense documentation process is not always feasible, it is very useful in examining the processes of collaborative action research teams (Kelly, 1985; Smulyan, 1984).

Investigator involvement
Principal investigators were team members and served as the researchers on the team. This provided a unique perspective on the collaborative research process.

Teachers' perceptions

Teachers' voices became an integral part of the project. Teachers' perceptions as illustrated in logs, interviews, and team meeting documentation provided researchers with data needed for triangulation, challenging and supporting hypotheses developed through participant observation.

Two key aspects of the role of the investigator on the team differentiate this study from previous collaborative action research projects. First, the investigator was a university professor rather than someone from the school or school district with research skills. Another person (i.e., district personnel with research skills) assuming the researcher role may be perceived differently from the university professor filling such a role. When discussing teachers' thinking and attitudes toward the researcher, this study refers to the university professor as the researcher (in the role of team member). This role is analyzed because of the important school-university connections that collaborative action research can develop.

Second, the university researcher was the principal investigator for the NIE project. The role of the principal investigator as an active team member has unique benefits. One obvious advantage is his or her greater flexibility in organizing problem solving sessions. The principal investigator also served in the role of researcher and technical assistant. Thus the collaborative action research process was observed firsthand by the principal investigator who knew both traditional (experimental and quasi-experimental) research as well as action research and more situation specific approaches to inquiry. Because of its localistic nature, action research presents some very complex questions of whether it can contribute to (generalizable) educational theory. In discussing differences between teacher-researcher action research and experimental research, Kelly (1985) cites the work of Cummings (1985) and Sharples (1983) to illustrate the perspective that questions of academic respectability and generalizability are irrelevant to the teacher involved in action research. 'Sharples argues that an enhanced understanding of the particularity of a teacher's situation is more important then generalizability, and that replicability and transferability are less important than authenticity and accountability' (Kelly, 1985, p. 131). Others, ourselves included, think that the issues of generalizability and replicability can and should be addressed in collaborative action research without negating the importance of particularity, authenticity, and accountability. Familiarity with traditional methodology as well as action research approaches allows university researchers to help the team address issues of generalizability and make decisions in the research process.

Conclusion

This chapter has described one Action Research on Change in Schools team in terms of its participants, the school setting in which it took place, and the action research project undertaken by the team. Teachers' life age/cycles and career cycles have helped to clarify reasons for these teachers' participation in the collaborative action research project. In the chapters which follow, as we describe our findings in the meta research study, we explain how these teachers participated in the group process and the research process. Group dynamics theory provides an initial framework for examining the group process of collaborative action research (Chapter 3), and adult development theory provides a framework for analyzing individuals' attitudes and behavior related to the group, decision making, change, and authority in the team and the school, all of which affect the group's effectiveness in defining and reaching its goals (Chapter 4). Together, theories of group dynamics and adult development enhance the framework for analyzing leadership behavior and group interaction in the process of collaborative action research (Chapter 5).

3
The Group Process of Collaborative Action Research

Introduction

When asked what stood out for him as he looked back over the two years of the project, one ARCS participant said:

> Working with the people mostly, and getting to know the people that have been on the team. Working with them is the most important factor. (interview, 6/83)

Another team member gave a similar response:

> Working as a group, really working closely with a group that meets consistently on a basis that has a common understanding, common goal. ... The key was that it was a collaborative research group and I think the workings of the group was really what was the focal point. (interview, 6/83)

What did it mean to these people to 'work as a group'? What constituted the group process they experienced? How did this process affect their research project and outcomes?

Previous studies of action research explain that collaboration is an essential element of action research. All participants in an action research group are expected to share in setting research goals, designing the research project, collecting and analyzing data, and reporting results, always contributing their unique skills and insights to the group. Collaboration provides a supportive setting which allows participants to experiment with change and draw on the ideas, perspectives, and skills of colleagues from school and university (Corey, 1953; Tikunoff, Ward and Griffin, 1979). This kind of support and experimentation may also contribute to individuals' developmental growth, as we explain in Chapter 4.

Although those reporting on previous action research projects have recognized the importance of collaboration and discussed some of the problems involved in implementing it (Ferver, 1980; Hord, 1981; Pine, 1981), few have discussed the *process* of collaboration or how that process affects the resulting research project and staff development. The purpose of this chapter is to describe and analyze the collaborative process of an action research team and the relationship of that process to a group's research project and outcomes. Traditional group dynamics theory provides a lens for examining the process; the ARCS team experience provides examples to illustrate general trends.

Group Dynamics Theory

Collaboration on an action research team is a dynamic process. As a team moves forward on its project, research tasks change, demanding different forms of interaction, different roles, and different patterns of behavior. As team members work through interpersonal issues, their understanding and perceptions of the project change, they interact differently, and they approach their research in new ways. How a group interacts over time thus influences the development of their research project, the project's outcomes, and the quality of the experience for group members.

Studies of group interaction in small problem-solving groups provide one framework for analyzing the process of collaborative action research teams. Research in group dynamics suggests that members of a group work through sequential or cyclical phases of group development and establish and maintain group norms, decision-making processes, patterns of communication, roles, and interpersonal structures. The group's negotiation of these aspects of its interaction affects its goals and results.

Research in group dynamics developed out of Kurt Lewin's use of action research to address social problems. Lewin believed that group decisions to act produced commitment and changes in attitudes and behavior not attainable through lecturing or individual treatment (Lewin, 1952). To bring about enduring, effective social change, Lewin found it necessary to consider the process of group interaction and its effects on individual and group decisions and actions. At the Research Center for Group Dynamics established at the Massachusetts Institute of Technology in 1945, Lewin used experimental methods to investigate group processes in a variety of settings. His work fulfilled his own requirements for action research: it generated new theory and knowledge in the field of group dynamics while addressing practical social concerns of practitioners (Kemmis, 1980).

Since Lewin's original research, the field of group dynamics has branched in several directions, each of which emphasizes a different approach to and use of research in group processes (Bolman, 1982). Despite the variations in approach and purpose which characterize these different types of research in group dynamics, common characteristics of group interaction emerge which provide insight into the process of collaborative action research. In particular, many theories describe the process of group development over time, noting that problem-solving groups tend to move through a series of phases, each with certain characteristics.

Bales and Strodtbeck (1951) explain that a phase hypothesis of group development rests on the 'assumption that there are internal tendencies of interaction considered as a system distributed between persons and through time' (p. 493) in all groups. A number of external conditions affect a group's development through its phases, including the duration of group life, its setting and purpose (for example, laboratory group, therapy group, production group), the individual personalities of group members, and the nature of the task (*ibid*; Obert, 1983; Schutz, 1958; Tuckman, 1965; Tuckman and Jensen, 1977). When these external variables are controlled for or in some way taken into consideration, 'internal conditions create qualitatively different subperiods within a total continuous period of interaction' (Bales and Strodtbeck, 1951, p. 485). Each phase of group development consists of interpersonal and task–related issues which the group must address as it proceeds.

Tuckman and Jensen (1977) see the group simultaneously developing a structure of interpersonal relations and patterns of task activity. In the first stage, 'forming', group members orient themselves to each other and the task, testing to identify the limits of interpersonal and task behaviors. Stage two, 'storming', is characterized by conflict, polarization, and resistance. The initial dependence on a leader may be challenged as members resist group influence and task requirements. In the third stage, 'norming', the group overcomes resistance, resolves interpersonal conflict, and establishes cohesiveness, standards of behavior and new roles. In the fourth stage, 'performing', the interpersonal structure becomes a tool of the task activities as the group channels its energy into task performance, and in the fifth and final stage, 'adjourning', the group deals with issues of separation.

Bennis and Shepard (1956) agree that group development involves overcoming obstacles to communication and developing methods for achieving and testing consensus. Drawing on Bion's (1959) work on basic assumptions which motivate group members, Bennis and Shepard describe two phases of group development: dependence, in which group members work through issues related to the leader's authority, and interdependence, in which they confront interpersonal concerns for intimacy and identity. In the first phase, attempts to cope with dependence may take the form of flight or avoidance as members discuss problems external to the group. Resolution of this phase involves a revolt against the leader, similar to Tuckman's storming phase. In the phase of interdependence, group members struggle with conflicts between identity, self-esteem, and intimacy, often forming sub-groups in the process. A group reaches maturity when it can resolve its own internal conflicts and take intelligent action based on consensual validation of the group experience.

While Tuckman sees task and interpersonal issues developing together, and Bennis and Shepard concentrate on the development of interpersonal concerns, Schein (1969) describes the group moving from interpersonal to task-oriented issues. In phase one, individual group members must choose a role acceptable to themselves and to the group, find answers to questions of control, power, and influence, expose and share personal needs and goals which must be integrated into group goals, and find comfortable levels of acceptance and intimacy. Schein suggests that individuals may cope with these concerns differently. Some may take a tough, aggressive stance which tests and challenges others as emotional issues are addressed. Others may seek support or withdraw a part or all of themselves from the group process. As group members resolve these issues, they become less preoccupied with their own feelings and more able to listen to one another and address task problems.

In phase two, group members focus on task and maintenance functions. The former include actions which move the group forward on its agreed upon task, such as initiating, opinion and information seeking and giving, clarifying, elaborating, summarizing, and consensus taking. Maintenance functions, such as gatekeeping, encouraging, harmonizing, and compromising, help the group maintain its positive interpersonal relationships as it proceeds on its task. Schein's phase two parallels Tuckman's performing stage, during which interpersonal and task behaviors complement and reinforce one another.

Schutz (1958) suggests a cyclical, rather than sequential, pattern of group interaction. He compares the group process to changing a tire. In the latter, you go around and tighten the bolts one at a time, in the same sequence, repeatedly. In the former,

> ... need areas are worked on until they are handled satisfactorily enough to continue with the work at hand. Later on they are returned to and worked over to a more satisfactory degree. If one bolt was not tightened well on the first sequence, on the next cycle it must receive more attention, and so on. (p. 172)

Schutz begins the group cycle with an inclusion phase, in which the individual deals with problems of commitment to the group and interpersonal boundaries. Like Schein (1969), Schutz describes behaviors in this initial phase as individual-centered, such as over talking, withdrawing, and reciting biographies and previous experiences. In this phase, the group may focus on 'goblet issues' which are of minor importance to the group but which provide lenses through which individuals can examine and get to know other members of the group.

Once the group has resolved issues of inclusion, it moves into a control phase, in which problems of sharing responsibility and distributing power and control arise. Behaviors which mark this stage include competition and a struggle for leadership, discussion of group orientation to the task, structuring of rules of procedure and methods of decision-making, and a sharing of responsibility for the group's work.

Like Bales (1951), Schutz believes that a task-oriented phase which may create some conflict is followed by a phase focusing on socioemotional issues. His third phase, an affection phase, serves to reintegrate emotional needs into the task and structure decisions of the control phase. Also like Bales, Schutz sees that behavior in this kind of phase can take positive forms such as expressing positive feelings or pairing to enhance performance, or negative forms, such as expressing hostility or jealousy. In this phase, each member tries to obtain a comfortable amount of affective interchange with other group members. Resolution of these concerns leads the group back to issues of inclusion, and the cycle repeats.

Srivastva, Obert and Neilsen (1977) recognize the complexity of group development by suggesting that a group grows along six dimensions: members' relations to one another; members' relations to authority; the group's relation to its organizational environment; the group's task orientation; the group's orientation to learning; and the group's mode of reacting to its larger environment. In each of these dimensions, the group moves through five stages, shifting from individualistic and dependent modes of interacting, through stages of competition and conflict, to a stage of cooperative independence which allows for task concentration and performance (Obert, 1983). This perspective on group development reflects both the interpersonal and task demands a group experiences as well as the group's changing interaction with the environment within which it works.

Phases in the Group Process: Collaborative Action Research

Research in group dynamics suggests that a group progresses through a cycle of phases which reflect both personal and task needs. It is not enough, therefore, to examine an action research team's research process and outcomes, as previous studies of action research have done (Elliott, 1981; Kemmis, 1981; Tikunoff, Ward and Griffin, 1979). Many of these studies suggest that an action research team works sequentially or cyclically through a number of research steps, such as identifying an issue to be studied, identifying research strategies and data needed, collecting and analyzing data, and reporting conclusions (Delamont, 1984; Hammersley, 1984; Porter, 1985). While a collaborative action research group will work on each of these steps at some point (or at several different points) over time, other group process issues interact with and influence the group's approach to the research project.

Recent studies of collaborative action research illustrate that research teams experience phases in the group process (Smulyan, 1984 and 1988; Trubowitz, 1986), often moving from an interpersonal orientation to a more task-oriented focus over time. Although boundaries between phases may not always be sharply defined, each phase is characterized by distinct research tasks and interpersonal concerns. The cycles of action research, described by Lewin (1948), Elliott (1981) and Kemmis and McTaggart (1982), occur within and across the phases described; the phase description adds the interpersonal dimension which influences the cycles of planning, acting, and reflecting.

The ARCS team experienced five phases in its process of interaction, phases which seem to parallel those described by theorists who examine problem solving groups (see Table 4). What follows is a summary of phases experienced by the ARCS team, each phase generalized to be applicable to other settings. Awareness of these phases

Table 4: Phases of the Group Process

Phase	Research Process Issues	Use of Team Time	Group Interaction Issues
Phase 1: Negotiating Research and Group Boundaries October–December 1981	– Problem identification	– Discussing school context	– Establishing trust – Sharing opinions and ideas: building a common base – Setting boundaries – Establishing norms
Phase 2: Pursuing Tangents January–March 1982	– Data collection (Staff Opinion Survey) – Unclear goals: avoidance of research issues	– Discussing school context and data collection tools	– Feelings of being "on hold" – Challenging group leader – Unfocused discussions
Phase 3: Reaching Consensus March–May 1982 (Summer Break)	– Research design and research question	– Discussing research project	– Feelings of frustration, time pressure – Concern with group consensus – Group writing for reasons of "fairness"
Phase 4: Reinterpreting the Task September–December 1982	– Data collection (MBI, School Survey, interviews) – How to analyze data	– Discussing research project	– Feeling that interpersonal issues resolved in year 1 – Questions of individual commitment to group project – Resetting boundaries
Phase 5: Evaluating the Project and Process January–May 1983	– Data analysis – Presentation of results	– Working on data analysis, final report	– Feelings of working hard and accomplishing much – Emphasis on group rather than individual work – Positive group feelings – Attempts to remove boundaries with school

will help those who participate in action research be more sensitive to the possible issues that arise in the collaborative process and more successful in addressing them.

Phase 1: Negotiating Research and Group Boundaries

Phase 1 in a collaborative action research team parallels Tuckman and Jensen's (1977) 'forming' stage, during which the group begins to establish trust, boundaries, norms, and an initial feeling of group solidarity. Because action research teams often bring together school and university people who may not share common experiences, expectations, or language for talking about educational issues, this phase of development may initially be characterized by miscommunication and frustration and by lengthy discussions of issues only tangentially related to the research project (Adelman, 1985; Hammersley, 1984; Threadgold, 1985). Conversations around these external 'goblet issues' (Obert, 1983; Schutz, 1958) provide an opportunity for group members to observe, listen to, and get to know other members of the group. Not all conflicts will be solved, but participants begin to create patterns of interaction which will allow them to join together on a common task.

The ARCS team spent its first two months simultaneously team building and discussing possible researchable problems they might address. At the first weekly meeting, the university researcher reintroduced action research and the steps the team might take in carrying out a research project. Team members each identified and then discussed several problems they believed education was facing.

In the second and fourth meetings, the team discussed questions provided by the university researcher. The first set of questions asked teachers how change occurred in their school. The second set of questions asked about individual teacher and student change in the school. Team members used these questions as the basis for conversations about the role of the principal in their school, the role of the central administration and school board, and the changes in their school over the past fifteen years. They also raised particular issues of concern, such as low levels of communication and collegiality among teachers and between teachers and administrators, poor teacher morale, and problems in scheduling that affected teachers and students.

During these first two months, the team also discussed some of the parameters or goals of their research project. Two teachers suggested that the team do a group project on a school issue rather than individual, classroom-based projects, and the team agreed. Team members asked whether or not their project should create a change of some kind in the school, and they questioned whether or not teacher-initiated change was possible given traditional change and decision-making patterns in the school and system. Team members had different ideas about the outcome of the project at this point: Were they involved in this project for personal satisfaction or to create a change in their school? Would the results be used or filed away somewhere? These questions frequently reemerged for team members as they faced decisions about what data to collect, how to design the project, and how to analyze collected data.

During the fifth team meeting in November of the first year, one team member suggested that by investigating scheduling the group could address several of the concerns they had identified in previous discussions, including the issue of low teacher morale. During the next two meetings, the group agreed that they would study scheduling.

Jack: I guess I'm suggesting that what John said earlier about scheduling seems to me to be (i) something that affects everybody in the whole school; and (ii) something that is more tangible that you can do some research on. It isn't in the abstract — it's there ... you can go, you can look, you can gather data. It would be very beneficial for everyone in the school, and I think that some of the things that I have listened to here and some of the things that Brooks has mentioned can be part of that scheduling problem. (transcript, 2 December 1981)

In December of year one, the group focused on the question, 'How can we make scheduling changes to benefit our school?' and identified issues which they might investigate in order to answer that question, such as ability grouping, the house or team system within which the school functioned, class length, and rotating schedules. They decided on several forms of data collection including a survey of their staff to determine their opinions on these issues, site visits to other schools, and an ERIC search to find out what other research had been done on these scheduling practices.

During this initial phase, team members used discussions of school context (which consumed half to three-quarters of the team meeting time) to establish trust and share ideas. Topics of discussion included the new principal appointed in November; problems with particular students or types of students; teacher-student-parent relationships, and the roles of house coordinators and department chairpeople. These discussions served as the basis from which the team generated its research problem, but they also provided team members with the opportunity to find out about each other, find their own place in the group, and see how the group might work together (Bennis and Shepard, 1956; Obert, 1983; Schein, 1969; Schutz, 1958). Team members had never worked together before and saw themselves using meetings during this initial phase as a way of learning the opinions, thoughts, and insights of their colleagues.

> I see the greatest benefit of the first five meetings of getting to know each other, getting to know each other's feelings, a little bit of how each person operates, and just being comfortable with each other. I see that as being the most important thing in the first five meetings. (interview, 12/81)

> I guess it's very important for each group member to have a fairly good idea of what all the others are thinking, and we've accomplished that. We just (each) communicated to the others (our) feelings and thoughts on our school. (interview, 12/81)

Sharing their thoughts and feelings allowed the team to develop an initial sense of group solidarity. This issue arose again as the team faced more complex and demanding research tasks in later phases. At this point, group togetherness was experienced as sharing a common set of ideas:

> I think it made us a team, you know, you feel more comfortable with the people now ... you feel like we've all arrived at the same place. (transcript, 10 February 1982)
> If you've never really worked together closely I think there's a certain group process ... that must take place in order for a group ... to have some identity as a group. (transcript, 10 February 1982)

During phase 1, team members worked through and appeared to resolve issues of trust and confidentiality which might have prevented group cohesion. During interviews and team meetings, several group members raised concerns about the confidentiality of group discussions. Could they trust their colleagues not to repeat or use their openly shared ideas about the school? Brooks described her concern:

> Well, you see, most of us haven't worked that closely with each other and any group has to spend a month or two months

really building trust and building who's who and do I trust this person, do I say what's really on my mind, can I be frank with people, will someone come around the corner at me at some other point and hit me with something I've shared that's kind of personal? Or, you know, how far does one go? (interview, 12/81)

Although team members explicitly raised this question they never directly or openly answered it. Instead, they increasingly exhibited their trust of one another by sharing opinions, supporting and challenging each others' statements and ideas, and referring to the group as a whole to which they belonged. For example, during a team meeting in November, George said that he had some ideas about a possible project, but felt that if he brought an article in, people would think he was too pushy. Brooks replied, 'Teaching is sharing'. Later in the same meeting, Brooks asked George to bring in the work he had done on teacher evaluation. He said he had been 'kind of shy until now' but would be happy to bring it to the next meeting. This kind of interchange typifies interaction which contributed to team members' growing feelings that they could trust one another and work together.

Another way in which the team developed feelings of cohesion during this early phase was to establish group boundaries. This issue took other forms later in the project, but at this point it focused on the question of whether or not to include the Principal in the group's research process. Some team members suggested that the Principal's input would be valuable if he was interested in sharing his ideas, although they agreed that the team alone would make a final decision about what project to do. Other team members argued that the Principal should have been included from the first meeting if he was to be involved, because they had just spent the first five meetings 'finding out where everyone in the group was coming from'. The team chose not to include the Principal, in part because the new Principal did not begin work until late in November of the first year of the project, but primarily because team members perceived of his presence as an infringement on their control of their research project and process. They did agree to keep him informed; John became the informal liaison to the Principal, sharing the initial questionnaire with him in advance to solicit his input and bringing it to him after implementation and analysis to share results.

During this initial phase, team members also established some patterns of interaction which became norms, or accepted operating procedures. One such norm was the use of a question to begin a task or raise a new idea. The university researcher took a non-directive or facilitative role after the first two or three meetings, choosing to let teachers direct the flow of talk and make their own decisions. When she did enter the discussion to direct the task, she tended to use a question rather than a statement: 'What should we plan to do next week?' or 'Do we want to do the school context readout?' Other team members adopted this method of initiating new ideas or tasks and carried it through the two years of the project. Each team member tended to use this form of directing the discussion most when he or she took on a leadership role in the group over a several meeting period (see Chapter 5).

Another team norm set during these first few months was the use of a weekly agenda. The university researcher introduced this pattern, too, asking team members each week what they wanted to do the following week. At each meeting she would list those items on the agenda (a large pad) and ask the team for others. When the university researcher was not at a meeting, other team members made the agenda, an action which signalled the official start of the meeting. Both the university researcher and other team members used the agenda during team meetings as a way of refocusing a discussion or moving the team on to another item or task.

Another norm established during phase 1 was that explicitly set group rules governing team members' behavior tended to be ignored. Over the course of these first three months, the group explicitly established three rules:

(i)   If a team member could not attend a meeting, he or she would inform Jack, who would call the university researcher.
(ii)   Anyone who missed a meeting was responsible for finding out what they had missed.
(iii) School context discussions would be limited to approximately one half hour so that they would not prevent the team from focusing on research tasks and issues.

After the meeting at which the team agreed to each of these rules, the rule was infrequently adhered to and rarely, if ever, mentioned again. Team members usually (but not always) told someone on the team if they could not attend a meeting, but they did not usually inform Jack, and he never called the university researcher. When team members missed a meeting, they often came to the next without having talked to another team member about what had transpired. And although the amount of meeting time devoted to school context discussions decreased over the two years of the project, the shift was not due to enforcement of the half-hour limit but resulted from the team's need to use meeting time for research-related issues. Team members apparently established these rules to help them adapt to and become a part of the group during its initial phase. Because they developed feelings of group cohesion and an ability to work together in more indirect ways, the rules were not needed. After phase 1 the team did not explicitly set rules to govern team members' actions or interactions, having established many of the interpersonal norms needed for group work (Schein, 1969; Zander, 1982).

A final norm was established at the end of this phase as the team moved into its first research tasks. Team members had decided to survey the staff on their opinions about scheduling issues and had talked briefly about what would be included in the survey. One team member offered to bring a draft of the survey to the next meeting for the team to work on. In an interview, he explained that he offered to write the draft 'because I thought that we had, during that discussion, ... brainstormed all the items of information we'd like to cover in the interview, and I didn't feel like going through it all over again'. When he brought the draft in, he told the team he had written it so they would have a draft to work with, but he had 'no personal stake in it so you can comment freely'. Team members initially accepted the draft as written and then gradually began questioning and revising. George's actions here set a precedent for team members volunteering to begin a task on their own and bring it back to the team for revision. As others began to bring work in for group appraisal, they echoed George's disavowal of personal feelings involved in the task. Other team members first accepted their colleague's work, providing a cushion of support before going on to analyze and rework the drafted piece. When the team was not involved in group data analysis and writing, this pattern of individual task assumption and team reaction dominated their work on the research project.

Although individual teachers reacted differently to each phase, in part because of differences in developmental stage, some patterns emerge in their perceptions of the experience. In retrospect, team members saw phase 1 as a necessary time of group building. They also described it as confusing and frustrating, a time in which the research task was undefined and the research project non-existent.

Jack: I know we have to brainstorm to start with and spend a considerable amount of time — I guess if we just sat and talked for six, seven, eight weeks the purpose it serves is getting to know and trust each other as fellow workers ... I don't think we really, any one of us, really knows where we're going or have identified the problem yet to the point of carrying it further. (interview, 12/81)

Despite their feelings that they spent more time on interpersonal than task issues, team members also believed that phase 1 provided a necessary foundation for proceeding on the research project. First, it gave team members a feeling of ownership and control:

George: I think the basic element in this collaborative action research is that it should accomplish whatever the participants want it to accomplish. Now it took us a while before people in the group had a sense for that but now we do, so it's like now we're free to move on. (interview, 12/81)

Second, it began to provide a sense of what, as a group, the team might be able to do:

John: I think we have got to come to some conclusions about a project or a theme to research ... and begin to focus in on the tools that we're gonna take to either try to solve these problems or come up with ideas about solving the problems so that we can hand them over to someone who can do something about it. (interview, 12/81)

Team members suggested that phase 1 as they experienced it, benefited both the group process and the research project:

Brooks: I think that every group ... goes through that sort of finding a niche, building who's who in the group and what function and whether it's stated or implied, and I think that's gone on. And I think now the group sort of feels that they come in, and they have a task to do, and we may not know where we're ending up but now we know we're in the process. (interview, 12/81)

The process of collaboration requires the time for a research team to define a researchable problem, establish effective patterns of communication, and develop a sense of itself as a working group. Although this team would continue to negotiate group interaction and research project issues throughout the project, it now did so with a basic belief that problems could be resolved, the group would be maintained, and the project would move ahead.

Phase 2: Pursuing Tangents

Several theories of group dynamics suggest that in its second phase, a group experiences conflict around issues of leadership and power (Bennis and Shepard, 1956; Schutz, 1958; Srivastva, Obert and Neilsen, 1977; Tuckman and Jensen, 1977). In a collaborative action research group, this problem may be exacerbated by perceived differences in status and power between school and university participants. University faculty or researchers often initiate collaborative projects and are, at least initially, the group facilitators or leaders. School practitioners may, in this phase, need to establish ownership and true collaboration in the project by experimenting with the limits of their colleagues' power and asserting their own voices in the group process. Elliott (1985) points out that this process may swing the project away from its initiator's goals, as teachers begin to identify their own concerns. But it appears to be a necessary step in the collaborative process.

Another key element in phase 2, not reflected in theories of group dynamics, is that school practitioners may discover that they know little about conducting educational research (Jacullo-Noto, 1984; Lieberman, 1986; Smulyan, 1984). Consequently, they may back away from their enthusiasm for a chosen topic and hesitate in making decisions which would move the project forward. This lack of research knowledge and self-confidence in themselves as researchers may contribute to the dynamics that encourage the group to challenge its leaders. Successful group leaders can help the group through this experience by providing research support and by using a non-directive approach that allows team members to assume control when they are ready to do so (Carr and Kemmis, 1986; Grundy and Kemmis, 1982).

The ARCS experience reflects these patterns. Between January and March of year one, the team collected and analyzed data, discussed their research design and research questions, and planned future data collection procedures. During December and January, the team designed and administered their Staff Opinion Survey to all school staff in order to identify specific researchable issues within the broader topic of scheduling. They then collated and analyzed the data and presented the results to the teachers and administration. Survey results indicated that of the nine scheduling issues listed, the staff's top three concerns were effective 'schools-within-a-school', class length, and student ability grouping. Although the Staff Opinion Survey had provided the team with the information they had wanted, analysis of the survey led them to consider their overall research design, or in their words, 'Where do we go next?' Their process here illustrates the stage of reflection found in the cycles of action research described by Carr and Kemmis (1985); having planned and acted, team members stepped back to examine their actions and modify their plans.

Many of those engaged in action research describe this experience of shifting the focus of their research, their project design and the processes of data collection after their initial phase of work (Ball, 1984; Hammersley, 1984; Fuller, 1984). One researcher explained this process:

> Clearly, in the early weeks or months in the field that which is to be 'important' is the object of the discovery process not its organizing principle. One result of such an orientation to the field, indeed it is an expectation of ethnographic study, is that the process of fieldwork is marked by changes in direction, focus, and scope of the research objectives. These changes, some short-lived and unprofitable, some profound, are accompanied by the problem of false trials, dead-ends and the collection of much useless or irrelevant data. (Ball, 1984, p. 74)

The shifts that occur in research direction and process result from participants' increased understanding of issues under investigation, changing patterns of group interaction, and pragmatic or context-related situations which arise.

At the beginning of the second phase in their project, the ARCS team had planned to describe a schedule or beneficial schedule changes, implement the changes, and evaluate them. After having administered and analyzed the Staff Opinion Survey, however, the team began to question how they might use the information from the Survey to carry out a research project and what the parameters and goals of that project would be: Did they really have the power to influence or change the schedule? Should they develop an ideal schedule, or specific schedule changes for their school, or a philosophy or statement about good scheduling practices? They also discussed their concern that research results might contradict preferences indicated by teachers in the survey. How then could they implement the changes their research indicated would be beneficial? In answer to these questions, the group decided to investigate a variety of scheduling issues and suggest several alternative schedules to the Principal, although individual team members disagreed on the potential impact of their work on the school.

As teachers worked on clarifying their research question they also continued to generate and develop data collection procedures. One teacher began to compile a history of changes in the school during the past ten years. The team discussed possible tests to use in examining student achievement under different scheduling practices, wrote a form letter and sent it out to approximately twenty-five agencies and organizations requesting information about other schools they might visit, and began to write survey questions to use when they visited other schools. This focus on specific data collection procedures led the team to question the nature of the data they wanted to collect. For example, they discussed desirable characteristics of schools they would choose to visit and what information they wanted to collect during those visits. These considerations and the need to begin to make methodological decisions led the team back to another reexamination of their research question and design.

At this point, the ARCS team seemed uncertain about their next step; they questioned their control over scheduling issues and their ability to influence administrative decisions in this area. This second, reflective phase of their group process was characterized by hesitancy and a tendency toward non-research related and free flowing discussion. One team member wrote in his log, 'Now that the survey is done, what do we do next? I feel we are beginning to wander, or maybe it's the mid-winter slump.' During meetings, team members avoided focusing on the research project, usually choosing to spend time on agenda items (such as events in the school context or when to meet) which were only indirectly task-related. The university researcher's attempts to tie school context discussions back to the research task were acknowledged but infrequently built upon by other team members. One team member said during this time: 'It looks like the further we go the less anxious we are to take on the real issues'.

During this phase, some team members also challenged the university researcher's role as team convener. The specific conflict arose over when to meet; several teachers wanted to replace one week's team meeting with an open meeting with the school staff during an in-service day. The goal of this meeting would be to discuss any questions raised by the collated survey results which had been distributed to the staff that week. The university researcher suggested the team meet twice that week to preserve the team meeting time. The university researcher said she would not decide for the group, despite one team member's attempts to persuade her to agree with him and change the team meeting time. The conflict was resolved when team members decided to meet during their regularly scheduled time and not have a meeting with the school staff. However, one or two team members continued to challenge the university researcher's ideas and suggestions in this phase. This pattern of behavior parallels what Tuckman and Jensen (1977) refers to as 'storming' and what Bennis and Shepard (1956) see as a move away from dependence in the second stage of group development. Once the group has formed and established some ties, they tend to challenge the group leader in order to define and limit that person's power. Although this pattern occurred primarily with one person on the team and diminished as the team became more research oriented in phase 3, it seemed to represent a testing of the university researcher's role in the group and may have reflected the group's uncertainty about the research process in which they were engaged.

Phase 3: Reaching Consensus

Resolution — at least tentative — of patterns of group interaction and leadership conflicts in phase 2 lead in phase 3 to a period characterized by productive work on the research task (Obert, 1983; Schein 1969; Schutz, 1958; Tuckman and Jensen, 1977). Although this phase is not necessarily conflict free, the primary focus shifts from interpersonal to task issues as the group moves toward its goals. The shift from phase 2 to 3 may be influenced by time pressures to perform, group members assuming new leadership roles (see Chapter 5), and/or growing feelings of comfort and trust among group members. Even if some tensions remain around issues of parity, successful action research teams move at this point to more task-related concerns (Lieberman, 1986).

On the ARCS team the shift to phase 3 occurred in April of the first year, when team members asked the university researcher and research assistant to bring models of possible research designs to a meeting for the team to examine. The group discussed the models, questions, and designs in terms of their own preferences and what they thought was feasible within the time constraints of school scheduling practices and the two-year research project. They also considered the nature of data they would need to collect to investigate each question and possible data collection procedures useful in carrying out each design.

By the beginning of May of the first year, the team had decided to study how teacher morale was effected by scheduling changes adopted by the school administration for implementation in the fall of year two. After examining several questionnaires and discussing the project with a University of New Hampshire professor working on issues of teacher burnout, one team member suggested that the team use the Maslach Burnout Inventory (MBI) as a measure of teacher morale. The team planned to administer the MBI to teachers at their school in June 1982, and again in December 1982 in order to assess the effects of scheduling changes. Attached to the MBI would be a team-designed School Survey to solicit staff opinions about scheduling practices. The team planned to do follow-up interviews with a sample of teachers in the fall of 1982 to probe questions addressed in the MBI and the School Survey and an interview with the Principal of the school in May or June 1982, to determine his scheduling goals and definitions of scheduling terms. They also agreed that they would survey or interview teachers in other schools, although they did not decide what information these site visits would provide or how they would be used. The team saw this design as a form of evaluation research in which they would evaluate changes made in scheduling practices in terms of level of teacher morale and job satisfaction. Their goal in carrying out this design was to make recommendations to the Principal about effective, satisfactory scheduling practices at their school. The team spent its last meeting of the school year planning the administration of the MBI and School Survey. Team members administered the instrument to school staff during the last week of May.

The team spent most of its meeting time during this phase discussing concerns directly related to the research project: research question, design and methodology. Team members indicated that the shift toward more task-oriented interaction in this phase may have come from a number of sources: team member frustration with a lack of task or focus; a readiness to take on more abstract research issues; and approaching deadlines — a presentation to another action research team in late May and a research proposal due at the National Institute of Education in June.

> I think everyone felt kind of muddled and unsure, and then I think what happened was that we had discussed scheduling and we started doing the ERIC searches and reading literature then as things became more narrow I felt, okay, let's get it under way, let's nail something down. (interview, 5/82)

During this phase, teachers continued to learn about and become familiar with research process and terminology. One teacher, who had earlier noted that because he did not have the language to talk about the survey results he was 'making it up', now said that he had become familiar with the language and format of research papers and could not only read them but also critique them. The teachers on the team began to see themselves as researchers who could both solve school problems and contribute to knowledge in the field of education.

Concentrating on the research project and deciding on future directions seemed to draw the group closer together. Team members used weekly meetings to work on materials provided by the university researcher, research assistant, and one another rather than to discuss more open-ended concerns about their school. They left meetings with the feeling that they had worked hard. The group demonstrated its feelings of joint ownership and shared responsibility in this phase when it decided that all team members should help write the research proposal required by the National Institute of Education. They felt as though they had united around a common goal and finally begun to work on their research project.

Phase 4: Reinterpreting the Task

Schein (1969) and Schutz (1958) suggest that task-oriented phases may be followed by interpersonally-oriented phases. This reorientation allows the group to address interpersonal issues which have arisen or been neglected as the group focused on task completion. Action research groups experience this shift in orientation at this point in the process for several reasons. First, action research depends on the process of recursion rather than on a strictly sequential or experimental research model (Elliott, 1981; Kemmis, 1981; Oja and Pine, 1988). During the research process, continual analysis of research design, procedures, and data may lead action researchers to reconsider, redesign, and refocus their work to better meet research goals and school context needs (Ball, 1984; Fuller, 1984). Thus, a task-oriented phase in an action research group may be followed by an interpersonal phase which allows the team to step back, evaluate its process, and move ahead in the desired direction. An interpersonal phase also allows task-related conflict to surface and be addressed.

Second, school-based collaborative action research projects are subject to breaks in the process due to school vacations and to personnel changes as teachers change jobs. These external changes require the group to reexamine its structure, processes, and goals before moving ahead on task issues. An interpersonal stage at this point in the process differs from the initial phases in that the team does not need to establish basic norms and boundaries or deal with fundamental issues of trust. As one ARCS team member said, because the group now shares ' a whole body of common knowledge ... you can just — off the top of your head say something and a team member will connect with it, whereas before it didn't always work that way'. The interpersonal concerns in this stage are more task-related, focusing on conflict over research process, individual team members' commitment to the group task, and an evaluation of where the team has been and where it is going.

The ARCS team spent from September to December of year two collecting data and beginning to analyze results. During the first several meetings of year two they clarified and refocused their research question and design and decided what data they needed to complete their research. Team members concluded that they were examining how scheduling and other organizational changes in the school affected teacher morale. Two team members generated a list of these changes to use as a reference in discussing their research results (see Table 5). As a result of this clarification, the team decided that they would not need to collect data from other schools but would concentrate instead on interviewing selected teachers from their own school, readministering the MBI and twenty-two item School Survey, and reading materials gathered through an ERIC search on teacher morale and teacher burnout.

During this three-month period devoted primarily to data collection, the team began to consider techniques for analyzing collected data. Except for a brief analysis of their initial Staff Opinion Survey in January of year one, the team had done little or no data analysis up to

Table 5: Organizational Changes in the Junior High, September 1982

1 Homogeneous grouping expanded to include three seventh grade advanced English and three seventh grade pre-algebra classes.
2 House coordinators replaced by department heads.
3 All classes 45 minutes long.
4 Salary raises, pay period choice of 26 or 21 days.
5 All faculty members have duties (homeroom, bus duty, cafeteria).
6 IEPs completed by teachers for whole year rather than each marking period.
7 Two behavioral management homerooms established.
8 Specials (art, music, shop, home economics) rotate on four-day schedule.
9 Students have elective choices within some specials.
10 No in-school suspension.
11 Bells and tardy bells for changing classes added.
12 Students not allowed to go to lockers between periods.
13 Computer scheduling of classes.
14 New Principal opens school (came in mid-year last year).

this point. From September to November of year two, most of their discussions focused on how to collate and analyze data, for example, deciding how to score surveys and identifying computer programs which might be useful in analyzing patterns or trends. Actual data analysis did not begin until December of year two.

Refocusing the question and considering methods of data analysis led the team to discuss how their results might be presented, to whom and to what end. They debated again the possibility of presenting recommendations to the school Principal and the likelihood of a change resulting from their proposals. During one team meeting, George described the project in its relation to school change:

> In terms of the visitations, last year we were looking for a good schedule for our kids, but we've come to realize that we have no effect on changes. We saw some changes occurring that we had no control over, and we were not in a position to dictate changes. What we are doing is good, showing the effects of the changes on teacher attitude. (documentation, 13 October 1982)

The team also began to look at their project in the larger context of research on schooling, discussing who might read the report and why, and how others might be able to do comparative or follow-up studies using this project as a starting point. Issues of dissemination frequently arise at the point in a project when teachers begin to recognize the value of the process they are experiencing and the results they are generating (Florio, 1983; James and Ebbutt, 1981; Sheard, 1981). Although the ARCS team dealt more fully with this concern in the fifth and final phase, it began to see here the need to expand its vision and perhaps its impact beyond the team and even the school.

During phase 4, two team members questioned their commitment to the group, in part because of the team's increased emphasis on the research project. Both of these team members challenged the value of the project, noting that the group now aimed to describe teacher morale in the school rather than to make any concrete changes or improvements in school practice or policy. Although both doubting team members stayed with the group, only one became more committed to the project and involved in carrying out research tasks. Other team members supported him through his period of questioning by asking him about his new job at the high school, welcoming him if he arrived late, and raising the possibility of his carrying out an adjunct project in an area of special interest to him.

The other hesitant team member used his disenchantment as an excuse for saying he did not know what was going on and as a way of avoiding concrete research tasks. Frustration with this team member surfaced several times during the fall of the second year, often in the form of sharp retorts for his apparent misunderstanding of what was happening in the project. In late October, the tensions led to a confrontation (an unusual occurrence) between this team member and another who had provided much of the team's leadership in phase 3. Ted, the uninvolved team member, had missed an extra meeting scheduled to work on scoring surveys; he was told that others were frustrated because the team had a lot to do, time was running out, and he was not helping and did not even seem to know what was going on. Ted blamed the missed meeting on miscommunication and dismissed the other problems. Although Ted's behavior changed very little, the open conflict seemed to ease previous tensions and 'cleared the air' for the team. As one team member said, 'Now I can see him in a different perspective. Like sometimes his questions seem off the wall, but they sort of end up clarifying what we are doing' (interview, 12/82). The behavior of this recalcitrant team member gradually led other team members to discount his willingness or ability to contribute, however, and they increasingly ignored him as they continued the project. It is not unusual for a group to reject a member who will not conform to group goals and behaviors (Miller, Jackson and Mueller, 1987). To some extent, however, the group's desire to maintain a positive group experience kept it from seriously considering the discordant but valid issues about the goals and outcomes of the project (for example, its immediate usefulness to the school) raised by these two team members. The team's emphasis on the value of the group process, which emerges even more strongly in phase 5, allowed it to set aside questions about the ultimate value of the research project to school practice.

The team also readdressed boundary issues in the fourth phase. At the beginning of phase 4, one team member left the team when he accepted a principalship in another town. The team decided not to replace him for both group interaction and task reasons: they did not want to take the time to rebuild trust and understanding with a new group member, nor did they want to spend time filling someone in on the project when there was so much to be done. The team also chose, for similar reasons, not to seek the help of another university faculty member who had done related work in teacher morale and burnout. One team member explained that he did not want to spend 'a lot of time explaining to some outsider what we wanted done' or do the team's project in order to add to someone else's research. Thus, in phase 4, the team moved forward on its research task while redefining and solidifying its boundaries and membership. It resolved the interpersonal concerns and conflicts of this phase in ways which allowed it to devote its energy to the research project alone in phase 5 but which also influenced the form that final project would take.

Phase 5: Evaluating the Project and Process

During the 'performing' (Tuckman and Jensen, 1977) stage in a problem-solving group, the group focuses its energies on task completion, using all of the interpersonal ties and task skills its members have developed to facilitate its performance (Srivastva, Obert and Neilson, 1977). In a collaborative action research group, this task–oriented phase produces a renewed sense of group cohesion based on common knowledge and experience and often a feeling of success, both personal and professional (Jacullo-Noto, 1984). Different action research groups will experience this phase differently. For some, it may not be a final stage, but a performance-oriented task phase signalling completion of one part of an ongoing series of collaborative projects. This may be followed by a period of regression and/or renewal which allows the group to reform and refocus (Schutz, 1958; Trubowitz, 1986). Other groups will disband having completed this project, possibly experiencing a short, interpersonally oriented follow-up phase of leave-taking or adjournment (Tuckman and Jensen, 1977).

In the ARCS group, team members used meetings in phase 4 to talk *about* the research project; data collection occurred outside of team meetings. In phase 5, team members used group time to *work on* specific tasks, such as collating data, analyzing computer printouts, and writing their final report. One team member developed computer programs which allowed the team to analyze data collected from the MBI and School Surveys administered in year one and year two. The computer program classified each school staff member as high, moderate and low on each of the six sub–scales on the MBI. The university researcher ran t–tests and found no significant shift in scores on any MBI subscale from May to December. In their final report, the team gave two explanations for the minimal change in teacher morale from year one to year two: first, teachers expressed mixed reactions to the organizational changes made in the junior high school, and second, teachers had not been involved in making these changes.

The team grouped the twenty-two questions from the School

Survey into categories including teacher teams, ability grouping, communication with administration, communication with colleagues, and time management/planning. They found some shift in teacher responses on these questions from May to December 1982, and found that teachers in different subject areas responded differently to certain items. The team also analyzed how school staff members ranked high, moderate, and low on each sub-scale of the MBI and how they had responded to each item on the post test of the School Survey. While results differed from question to question, the team found that in general, staff members who felt more stressed tended to feel less satisfied with existing opportunities for communication with colleagues and administrators and with time available for planning.

In March and April of year two, the team drafted its final report and presented its research process and findings at the annual meeting of the American Educational Research Association (AERA) and at a University of New Hampshire class and faculty colloquium. Team members chose to write their final report as a group; much of the writing was done at four all-day meetings held during school vacation or on Saturdays or Sundays in March and April. The team divided the report into seven sections: the research problem, research question, related literature, methodology, findings, conclusions and implications for further research.

As team members discussed the sections on research problem and question, they reviewed their research process, trying to piece together a description of what they had done. They explained that they had begun with the issue of scheduling in an attempt to address staff concerns as identified in their initial Staff Opinion Survey. In retrospect they noted that they had shifted to the issue of teacher morale for several reasons:

— scheduling proved to be too large and unwieldy as a research problem;
— the issue of teacher morale was connected to many of the same concerns as scheduling (teaming, ability grouping, opportunity for staff communication);
— they had found an instrument which measured teacher morale; and
— one team member showed strong interest in the issue of teacher morale, and, in her words, 'railroaded it through.' (documentation, 13 March 1983)

As a result of their discussions and writing, the team decided it had actually investigated three questions:

(i)   Do organizational changes effected between 1981/82 and 1982/83 at the junior high school affect school staff morale/job satisfaction?

(ii) Do organizational changes at the junior high school affect school staff's perceptions of teaming, grouping of students, communication with colleagues and administration, time management, and teaching assignment?

(iii) Is goal clarity and involvement in policy decision making related to staff morale/job satisfaction? (Blomquist *et al.*, 1983)

In answering these questions in their final report, the team drew on previous work done on teacher morale and compared their findings to those of other researchers who had used the Maslach Burnout Inventory to measure teacher burnout (Schwab, 1983). Although their results were site specific, the team suggested that their findings provided further insight into causes of low teacher morale. Specifically, they noted that teachers' lack of participation in decision-making processes in the school, lack of clarity on school goals and objectives, and lack of time to communicate with colleagues contributed to lower levels of morale. They suggested that further studies in the relationship between these school context issues and teacher morale would reveal ways of improving teacher morale and assessing the effects of different levels of morale on student achievement. Complete results of the team's research can be found in their final report to the National Institute of Education (Blomquist *et al.*, 1983).

Team meetings during phase 5 had the same feeling of intensity as those in phase 3. Meetings tended to last an hour longer than at any other time during the project, and all team members contributed to data analysis and report writing. Team members frequently commented on how much there was to do, but also noted how much they had accomplished. In phase 2, the group had argued about holding an extra meeting; in this phase, team members initiated and held several all day meetings to work on the project, meeting twice during school vacation and three times on weekends. No one questioned the extra time; group involvement and commitment reached its highest point during this time.

Team members' intense, shared work on the project and their group presentations at conferences led to strong feelings of group cohesion. In team meetings the group resisted any suggestions to divide up the work of data analysis or report writing. In phase 3, the rationale for group writing had been fairness. During phase 5, team members

79

wanted to write together because they felt the group provided necessary intellectual and emotional support during the difficult processes of data analysis and writing.

Group data analysis and writing led to a unique pattern of interaction for the team during this phase. Team members composed aloud, building and rebuilding sentences as everyone added to and amended the words and statements of others. This kind of interaction arose from the nature of the task and promoted feelings of group solidarity; team members encouraged one another, applauded good or appropriate words and phrases, and laughed together at awkward or over-used terms.

The team's close group work during this phase led them to emphasize team members' commitment and their mutual sense of respect when they described the team to others. They emerged from this phase — and the two year project — with strong feelings that the group process was the most valuable part of the experience for them. One teacher explained: 'Way back, we said it would be nice if it counted (made a difference in the school), but it doesn't matter. It's going through the process from here to there that matters.'

The team also reexamined its boundaries during this final phase. Not only did they present their research at several local and national meetings, they also had to decide who in their own school and system would be invited to share in what had become an insular group process and project. Carr and Kemmis (1986) note that this gradual expansion of boundaries is a natural part of the action research process: 'As an action research project develops, it is expected that a widening circle of those affected by the practice will become involved in the research process' (p. 165). The team decided to invite the Principal to a team meeting and present their results to the staff at a special meeting called for this purpose. These actions reversed their previous decisions to depend primarily on their internal resources and reflected an attempt to integrate the research project back into ongoing school practice. Few teachers attended the meeting called by the team to explain their results, however, and although the Principal attended their meeting and heard their results, he ended the year saying only that he would consider their ideas. The team therefore emerged from phase 5 with positive feelings about the group process and their own professional development but mixed feelings about the success of the research project.

And so maybe as a style of doing a research project, I think we did a good job. As far as our research is concerned, I feel very uncomfortable about it because I don't think we did prove much ... We did do the research, we do have all of the information, just nothing really basically came of it. (interview, 6/83)

Outcomes of the Collaborative Process: Personal and Professional Growth

Previous work in collaborative action research has proposed that teacher participation leads to teachers' professional growth (Griffiths, 1985; Mosher, 1974; Noffke and Zeichner, 1987; Pine, 1981); greater school staff collegiality and experimentation (Little, 1981); and improved practice among participants (Hall, 1975; Elliott, 1977). On the ARCS team, despite teachers' perceptions that their work might have little effect on the school, team members believed that the two-year experience had been worthwhile. The value lay in individuals' increased feelings of confidence, expertise, and understanding of both research and the school context. It also grew out of teachers' belief that their work provided a model for other school practitioners who wanted to try action research. As several team members pointed out in their final interviews, the project was successful because they had shown that teachers could indeed be researchers.

The development of teachers' belief in the value of their work is reflected in several themes. First, teachers' understanding of action research changed over time. Changing definitions of action research grew out of team members' experience in the project and allowed teachers to explain and legitimate the process they had experienced. Second, teachers' perceptions of themselves as researchers evolved over time, shifting in at least one case from a teacher feeling he knew nothing about research to describing himself as an expert in this particular area. Finally, as a result of clarifying what was meant by action research and developing a sense of themselves as researchers, team members began to identify ways in which the action research process could be of further use to them in their classrooms, school, or professional careers. Each of these patterns is discussed below.

Changing Definitions of Research

Many teachers approach action research with caution; prior experience with research has usually been unproductive and meaningless, something passed down from those who have little feel for the exigencies of classroom or school life (Day, 1985; Hammersley, 1984). The ARCS teachers, too, had limited experience with or belief in the usefulness of research. In initial interviews, three of the five team members explained that they had done little or no research outside of developing courses and curriculum. Those who expressed opinions about research said that although it should affect teaching and learning in some way, it usually does not. Jack, for example, said that the purpose of doing research in many cases was 'to write somebody's doctor's thesis'. He also noted that research

> can be beneficial, but I think you really have to identify a specific problem, zero in on it ... and come up with some conclusions. But if the conclusions you come up with aren't going to have any effective change on your staff or on education then it's a waste of time. (interview, 9/81)

At a meeting in late March, the university researcher reminded the team that they had to submit a research proposal to the National Institute of Education by the end of year one. This sparked a discussion about what the team had done and planned to do and how their actions related to their understanding of action research. At this point in the project, teachers asked questions about action research in order to determine how their experience compared to traditional research patterns or models. This discussion and the need to clarify their research question and design led, the following week, to teachers asking the university researcher and research assistant to bring sample research designs to the next team meeting for consideration. As suggested, their request indicated the first shift away from teachers' perception of research as data collection. They began instead to envisage a more abstract and comprehensive research project. By the end of the first year, teachers had begun to describe action research as a process which allowed for constant change and adaptation, a description noted by many involved in qualitative research for the first time (see chapters in Burgess, 1984; Hustler, Cassidy and Cuff, 1986). This definition of action research prevailed among team members throughout year two, although it was expanded to include several other dimensions. John suggested, for example, that given the nature of action research, conclusions may not emerge:

> I see regular research as sitting down and coming up with almost the end. This is what they want as an end and then they do the research to get there. ... Action research is research that

is ongoing, and as the answers to your questions come up or a shift in what you want to research comes up, you just keep right on going researching, whichever direction. ... I honestly feel you may not come to any conclusions about things if you are doing action research. (interview, 12/82)

Teachers also noted that action research tends to be site-specific.

Ted: I just think action research is a term applied to people closest to the problem doing it, teachers. (interview, 12/82)

George: It is a process which might not stand close academic scrutiny, but is highly likely to solve site located problems — whatever problems that the group involved decides to address. (interview, 12/82)

Team members themselves did not make a direct connection between the flexible, cyclical quality of action research and its use in solving site-specific problems, but their perceptions match the claims of those who advocate the use of action research rather than linear-experimental research in schools. Action research takes the dynamic conditions of the school or classroom into consideration; experimental designs do not (Bassey, 1986; Cummings and Hustler, 1986; Mishler, 1975; Pine, 1981).

Team members suggested that because action research projects change over time and address site specific problems, they tend to uncover many other possible researchable issues in the school. As a result, an action research project could serve as the basis for a continuing program of research in a school:

George: In action research ... inevitably you leave many tangential questions, loose ends. ... It might be nice to build in a way that these loose ends or tangents could be systematically addressed. (interview, 12/82)

Brooks, too, noted that part of action research is identifying other questions and ending up at a place from which you can continue your investigations (documentation, 17 November 1982). Their discovery supports the notion that action research could serve as the basis for a program of school change and improvement (Cassidy, 1986; Lieberman and Miller, 1984; Schaefer, 1967).

Team members also defined collaborative action research by comparing it to school processes of curriculum development and committee work. In their comparisons, they suggested that the rigor and validity of research differentiated it from typical school investigations. (This parallels Corey's (1953) comparison of action research and the traditional 'commonsense' approach used in schools.) During one meeting, for example, John pointed out that collaborative action research went on in schools: Brooks' reading program was collaborative — she and her co-worker were always collaborating, and in science they 'get together and decide what will be done, although they don't add research to it'. Ted replied, 'You always collaborate with colleagues to some extent, but it's the research that separates the boys from the men' (documentation, 9 February 1983). In his final interview, John described what usually goes on in schools as 'action inquiry' rather than 'action research',

> Because we were not looking through other books, looking into other schools ... that's what I would call the formalizing process ... We were inquiring within our own building and asking questions and taking the advice of many different people and then coming up with recommendations. (interview, 6/83)

Team members' definitions of action research as dynamic, site specific, providing questions for future research, and more rigorous than typical school-based inquiry evolved from their experience over the two years of the project. In turn, this definition allowed them to explain the process they had used and the many shifts they had made in research problem, question, and design. The 'crooked path' George described the team having taken (interview, 6/83) was consistent with action research as they defined it.

Team members' tendency to define action research as a process rather than a means to specific ends also allowed them to see this process as an end in itself. For some team members, the goal of the project became their own experience of this intrinsically valuable process:

Brooks: There's something mystical or magical about research. The university researcher asked us what do we want to do with the research findings, and I said it doesn't really matter if things don't work out the way we'd like them to work out or they're supposed to work out — I think just that we did it, went through the experience (was important). (presentation at the University of New Hampshire, 5/83)

John: All the end result is going to get you is possibly a change, and so therefore I don't think the end result is so important. I think it's the process we went through doing it, and to be able to possibly go through this process again is going to be the valuable thing. (interview, 6/83)

Changing Self Definition: Teachers as Researchers

Throughout the ARCS project, team members claimed that teachers should be doing research to improve both school practice and educational research. In his initial interview, George noted that if all teachers had been involved in the kind of research he had done in his masters degree program they might be more effective. At the end of the two-year project, he clarified how schools would benefit from practitioners doing research:

> I just think that active collaboration implies that a bunch of people at some school get together and work out a problem, and in that format ... they might have a more tunneled view of possible solutions than if they considered themselves involved in research. Because if they considered themselves involved in research they would necessarily review literature, look at other settings, and in doing so broaden their scope of alternatives in attacking their own problem ... The inclusion of this research point of view multiplies substantially the possibility of coming up with a quality solution to whatever problem might have been in place. (interview, 6/83)

George also said that research could be improved by having 'practitioners, meaning teachers, ... be the ones that do the research rather than people who aren't as actively involved in the classroom situation, such as university people' (interview 9/81).

Some team members suggested that doing research fulfils certain needs for teachers. It provides information which may permit a teacher (rather than a parent or administrator) to 'call the shots' (documentation, 27 October 1982). It also 'gives one a direction and ideas and food for thought, and a beyondness' (interview, 6/83) which can help teachers remain intellectually stimulated and interested in their work.

> *Brooks:* Action research allows the creativity, I think, that teachers generally feel or have a need for. ... I think it enhances their creativity, allows it to really be a part of the research, and ... the research becomes alive and really interesting and interesting for other people to hear about. (interview, 12/82)

Thus action research can help teachers, and teacher involvement can enhance the research which results.

Despite their advocacy of practitioner involvement in research, teachers in the first year of the project suggested that a number of obstacles prevented them from becoming researchers. Several teachers said that their lack of knowledge about research techniques limited their ability to take part in the project. They suggested that the university researcher and research assistant would have to guide them through the research. When working through issues of problem definition in year one, for example, Jack and Ted said, 'No wonder teachers don't do research', and 'This proves what college people think about teachers not being able to do research' (documentation, 31 March 1982). In describing how he saw the project developing in November of the first year, George said that he did not have the language to talk about it so he was making it up. John responded that teachers do not know that language, which is why the research articles they had been reading made no sense to them. Their comments suggest that at this point in the project these teachers did not see themselves as researchers because they lacked necessary knowledge and skills.

Some team members also noted that teachers lacked time to do research, and that other commitments limited the amount of time they themselves could work on this project. Partly because of this pressure, several team members noted that it was important to have a non-teacher, like the university researcher, on the team to help the teachers carry out their project. As George pointed out, 'A group of teachers doing what we're doing doesn't occur in a natural setting' (interview, 12/81).

During year two, as teachers developed a better understanding of their own research project and began to articulate their own definitions of action research, they seemed to become more comfortable in the role of researcher. One indication of this (described in more detail in the following section) was teachers' projected use of action research in their classrooms and school. George suggested, for example, that 'someone who has been through collaborative action research could use some of the skills they learned to do their own project, which could be action research' (documentation, 22 February 1983).

Another sign of teachers' acceptance of the role of researcher was their growing use of the research of others and the language of research. In year one, teachers rejected many of the research articles brought to the team by the university researcher and research assistant because they found the reports confusing or meaningless. Other outside researchers

(Cassidy, 1986; Elliott, 1985) have also had teachers ignore 'relevant' literature presented to them early in a project. During year two, however, ARCS teachers requested, supplied, read, and used many articles related to their project. Teachers also showed a growing facility with research terminology. In the spring of 1982, the university researcher introduced terms such as 'sample', 'reliability', and 'validity' to the team in discussing data collection procedures. By year two, teachers themselves used these terms with ease in discussing their own work and the work of others.

Teachers' growing facility with research gradually allowed them to see themselves as researchers. When asked what stood out for him about the project, Ted responded:

> What stands out in my mind is the idea that the word research is no longer scary ... I think the biggest thing is that teachers can do research. ... In my mind they shouldn't be afraid of it; it isn't something that only people who are at the university level that are divorced from the school, may not have been teaching for years (can do). (interview, 6/83)

Teachers' experiences presenting their work at national conferences contributed to their sense of having gone 'beyond' teaching to become a member of the research community. Brooks explained:

> I thought the highlight was going to AERA in Montreal, and being able to take what we were doing and explaining it to another person and really feeling that excitement and getting the feedback, the recognition ... I think that was really important to know how the outside world was reacting to the research that we were doing. (interview, 6/83)

George also noted that presenting at AERA promoted 'feelings of accomplishment for team members' (documentation, 25 May 1983).

During year two, team members began to suggest that they had become experts in their particular area of research (teacher morale) and on the process of action research. Teachers' sense of expertise allowed them to suggest that their research process could serve as a model for future action researchers. Consequently, the section of their final report entitled 'Implications for future study' included several suggestions and recommendations for teachers and administrators who wished to use the action research process.

Noffke and Zeichner (1987) suggest that action research projects in the United States tend to encourage teachers to learn the skills of social science research. In the ARCS project, teacher-as-researcher did not mean teachers investigating and reflecting on classroom practice, but teachers learning and using research techniques to better understand and perhaps change the school context. This emphasis seems to result from the teachers' own definition of research and the expectation of the sponsoring agency that traditional educational research would emerge from the process.

Team members began the project believing that teachers should do research but lacked the necessary background, time, and motivation. During year two, as they gained familiarity with standard research terminology and techniques and worked through the specific tasks of their own project, teachers exhibited a growing sense of themselves as researchers. This appears in their use of existing literature and the language of research, their feelings of accomplishment and expertise, and their perceptions of how they would use research in the future. The next section addresses this latter aspect of the teachers as researchers in more detail.

Changing Goals: Personal and Professional Growth

By the middle of year two, all but one team member had agreed that the value of their project lay in what they might take from it, personally and professionally, and in how others might use their project as a model in implementing other action research projects. (One team member, Ted, agreed that these were important outcomes, but held to his belief that the project would have been more valuable had it affected school practice.) Team members' goals emerged from their perceptions of what they had gained from the project and how they could foresee using new insights and skills in the future.

Like most teachers involved in action research, all of the ARCS teachers noted that the project had contributed in some way to their personal and professional development (Booth and Hall, 1986; Groarke, Ovens and Hargreaves, 1986; Pollard, 1985). Even in the first year of the project, John and Brooks said that they had become better observers and listeners in the school as a result of school context discussions during team meetings (documentation, 2 December 1981). These discussions allowed them to vent anger about school issues and identify and deal with school problems more calmly. Both felt that team meetings made them more comfortable in the school and able to cope with pressures of the school day.

Brooks: The group is really helping me in that all my bitches and gripes and complaints and tension and pressure is sort of discussed on Wednesday, and I get it all out, and I don't have to carry it with me. (interview, 12/81)

John explained that the project had given him

a lot of peace of mind. ... Some of the things that would really get us upset in September don't bother us now ... because this is the way we're doing things (in the group) ... just thinking, okay, here's the problem, what are we gonna do about it? Well, we can't do anything about it so let's not worry about it right now. This is something that runs through our minds. (interview, 12/81)

During the second year of the project, team members began to identify other ways in which they had benefited from the project. John said that participation had made him sit down and think:

It's something that I try hard not to do most of the time. I have been teaching basically the same thing for ten years and I mean it doesn't matter what room they stick me in, how long the periods are, how many students I have; I manage to keep more or less teaching the same thing. ... This year I've had to think along a lot of lines I'd just closed my mind to. I've always been a firm believer in you can always close your door and teach and let everything around you just go if you want to and I do that from time to time. This year I've had to just constantly be aware of what's going on, constantly be ready to answer questions that other faculty members will ask about what we're doing. Constantly have to be checking with people on the team for different things and even doing research, which I haven't done for probably fifteen years or so. (interview, 5/82)

John also noted that by participating in the project he had gained self confidence in his ability to write and to speak to others about his own ideas. He felt he was an expert with something to offer others in the field:

The project contributed by giving me more self-confidence in speaking to people. When you can stand up there and speak, when you know that four other people sitting there happen to be famous people in the field you're talking about and you can say something and have them come back and comment to you about it gives you a tremendous amount of confidence. (interview, 6/83)

John and others also observed that attending national conferences validated their own experience and provided intellectual and personal satisfaction. When asked what stood out for him in the project, John said, 'Going places and seeing other people and other people's ways of doing things and discovering you're really not that far off the track from everyone else' (interview, 6/83). George, too, found value in this:

> I enjoyed the road trips and found some intellectually interesting things happening on the trips to Syracuse and Montreal ... I guess they weren't even so intellectually exciting as personally exciting. Just being able to hear speakers make presentations who I may have quoted in a paper I wrote somewhere along the line, things like that. (interview, 6/83)

The group process of action research facilitated team members' developmental growth (see Chapter 4). For Brooks, participation in the research project paralleled and reinforced a period of personal self-analysis. When the project began, she was considering leaving teaching. She felt that the project helped provide her with a more positive sense of herself as a teacher:

> I think I have really changed. I was really unhappy teaching. I mean, it seemed like there were things that were affecting me and that were out of my control ... I was feeling really emotionally burned out. I felt I need to keep myself alive and vital. The only way I know is to become active and involved in educating yourself. ... Now that I don't feel trapped and now that I feel I have control — I have skills, I have knowledge, I have the power — I can deal with all the problems that are coming up. I just think if I'm in a situation like that again that there will be resources available to us to take a look at the problem. (interview, 6/83)

Teachers also observed that as a result of participating in the project they had grown in their ability to work with, recognize, and understand the perspectives, limitations, and skills of others. Brooks said,

> I think that I've grown more accepting of people and their differences, and I see more of an ability to compromise and to work with people that I don't necessarily socialize with or philosophically agree with. (interview, 6/83)

For most team members, this understanding applied not only to others in the group but to the school context and the actors and events which comprised it. Teachers suggested that they now understood the problems and decisions faced by the school administration and could try to find ways to work with administrators on school problems rather than become angry or frustrated as they had in the past. This understanding gave Brooks the sense of being more in control of her own individual needs and problems. John saw his new understanding and skill as a possible basis for wielding more control in the school:

> And I know where the real power is within a school structure so I know how to deal with that. Knowing the timing of when to say what I want to say to get across what I think needs to be done, being in this for two years has helped that. (interview, 6/83)

Teachers also had ideas about applying action research to other school problems. By the end of the second year of the project, Brooks had initiated discussions with her supervisor about using action research to investigate a number of issues in the school's reading program. John had initiated and carried out a project to address a school-wide problem of student hall passes. Teachers also talked in more general terms about how action research could benefit the school.

John: I think we each know there are things we can do within the school system in the future that can be helpful. Not just for ourselves, but helping people within the school system. That, to me, is the value of this committee. (interview, 12/82)

Brooks and Ted both suggested that the school could become more research oriented, so that decisions could be based on actual data rather than teacher, administrator, or school board whim. Thus, participation in action research gave these teachers an understanding of how their 'private' concerns reflected 'public' or school issues (Mac an Ghaill, 1988) as well as the ability to become more thoughtful and informed policy makers in the school and system (Griffiths, 1985).

Teachers also valued the action research project and process for its potential value or use to them in their classrooms, even though the research project the team carried out became increasingly separated from school practice. John said that his participation had made him a better teacher:

> If anything it's made me better in the classroom because I'm more conscious of what I'm doing there than I was. I was

sliding on things; I'm not doing that so much. It's made me refocus some of the things I'm doing because we've had to keep logs. ... I think it's made me better in the classroom over the last year especially ... because I've had this to channel some of my anger and frustration. (presentation at the University of New Hampshire, 5/83)

John also planned to use elements of action research in developing future projects which he could carry out in his classroom. He focused in particular on the process of 'documentation', or following students' work in a more systematic way throughout a certain class science project, as an aspect of the research process which he intended to use the following year.

Team members also believed that the project had value in its use for others. One possibility would be for teachers in another school to duplicate this team's research. Comparison of results could lead to a better understanding of factors influencing teacher morale. Another follow-up project on the team's research might include the examination of the relationship between teacher morale and student achievement.

Other teachers and administrators could use the team's research process as a model for carrying out action research. In presenting their research to others and in writing their final report, teachers carefully described the steps they had taken in completing their project so that others could repeat them. Toward the end of the second year, teachers talked about putting together a package of written work, slides, and tapes describing their project which could be used by others interested in trying action research. Although they did not pursue this idea, it illustrates the value teachers placed on their process as a model for others.

Thus, teachers' perceptions of what they gained as a result of participation in the project included personal satisfaction, development of self confidence, control, and an accompanying sense of power, and growth in skills useful to them as teachers or researchers in the classroom or school. They also perceived a gain for others who could build on their research project or emulate their research process. Despite their lack of influence on the school and their sense of the limited importance of the research product, teachers emerged from their two-year experience feeling that it had been valuable both personally and professionally. In Chapter 4, we examine in more detail the developmental outcomes for individual participants in this action research project.

Teachers' emphasis on the process of action research and their understanding of the value of the two-year experience appear to be mutually reinforcing. Because an immediately useful product was unattainable, teachers focused on the process and the value it could have for them and others. Conversely, the gains teachers actually experienced were more related to the process in which they had engaged than to the specific project which resulted from their work. Thus, their feelings of success and personal and professional growth may have helped them see the research process as the most important aspect of action research.

Conclusion

Although all research teams may not experience the same processes and patterns exhibited by this Action Research on Change in Schools team, analysis of these patterns suggests several possible generalizations. First, an action research team must be flexible in carrying out its research project. Attention to the group's interpersonal needs, teachers' inexperience as researchers, their uncertainty as to outcomes, and the school context within which they work may prevent the team from working sequentially through predefined research steps. For example, teachers may begin working with ideas and processes with which they are most comfortable, such as data collection. Allowing recursion to take place in an action research project allows teachers to progress from familiar and concrete tasks to unfamiliar, more abstract concerns about research question and design.

The opportunity to experiment, reflect, redesign and requestion ultimately provides teachers with a project that is meaningful to them. Although the team will move through typical steps in its research: identifying a problem, defining a research question, choosing methodology, designing the project, collecting and analyzing data, and presenting results, it will not always do so in a neat, sequential process. It may frequently cycle back into earlier steps or work simultaneously within several. The process tends be cyclical or recursive, an indication of participants' perception of the interconnectedness of the steps of the research process and of their need to learn and use those steps in ways that best meet their needs.

In the ARCS project, the team tended to work on more concrete aspects of the research, such as designing data collection tools, before they had clearly determined more abstract parameters of research question, design, and the nature of data needed to conduct their research. This ordering of research steps may have arisen out of the general and somewhat amorphous nature of the team's initial research question: 'How can we make scheduling changes to benefit our school?' The team saw data collection as one way of informing themselves about specific areas to investigate within the broader area of scheduling. They also seemed more comfortable starting with concrete data collection procedures than with unfamiliar issues of research design and methodology. Throughout the two-year project, the team cycled back into research planning stages, gradually clarifying their research question and design and allowing the nature of the data needed to determine data collection tools. The cycles of action research not only allow for a project which is responsive to the context within which it occurs, it also helps action research groups meet the personal and professional needs of the individuals involved.

A second generalization which can be made is that a group of teachers working together on a research project will have to address interpersonal as well as research task demands. At times, interpersonal concerns such as trust, leadership, group boundaries and individual commitment may dominate; at others the research task may take precedence. This study suggests that a team will experience a shift in emphasis from interpersonal to task-related concerns over the course of its existence. At the outset of a project, interpersonal concerns include establishing trust, setting boundaries, and developing norms. The group's initial sense of identity may be based on agreement in areas of opinion not necessarily related to the project. After the team addresses concerns of who they are in the group and how the group will operate, it may need to deal with issues of power and leadership. The team gradually coalesces around a common goal or set of tasks. Members who disagree with this goal create a conflict for the group midway through its life, and the group may need to reexamine its professed purpose, its membership, and its boundaries. Finally, the group focuses on completion of its task and may develop strong feelings of cohesion and pride based on common effort and a unified product. Chapter 4 uses theories of adult development to examine issues such as power, leadership, and group interaction which emerge in the phases of the group process.

Third, a team's research project will be influenced by its interpersonal concerns and patterns. In the ARCS project, the team's choice of a school rather than classroom-based research project grew out of their team building processes in phase 1. Their school context discussions led them to focus on school rather than classroom issues, even as these discussions allowed teachers to share opinions and ideas. Shifts in the focus of the project — from scheduling to teacher morale — were influenced in phases 2 and 3 by teachers' initial hesitation in taking control and moving ahead on the project and their gradual growth in understanding the research process. Once they were willing to assume greater leadership in their own project in phase 3, they became very task oriented and moved ahead on the research project. Their positive feelings about the task and group process in which they were engaged in phases 4 and 5 overrode some team members' concerns that their research results would not be used by the school administrator to improve school practice. Questions about the value of the project were pushed aside in these final phases. To some extent, the cohesion of the team, the maintenance of good relations, and the value of learning the process of action research became more important than questioning or changing the project to make it more effective in the school.

Results of this and other collaborative action research projects suggest that the collaborative process provides a rewarding experience for teachers (Elliott, 1977; Florio, 1983; Griffiths, 1985; Lieberman, 1986). Team meetings and projects create an outlet for teachers' frustrations with their school and a sense of collegiality absent in many school settings. Teachers feel that they become better observers of the school context, more skilled researchers, and more able to address problems which arise in the classroom or school. Teachers also gain a sense of professionalism from having worked together to carry out a research project and produced results which are of interest to those outside of their own school community.

Educators leading or engaged in collaborative action research must be able to recognize elements of the process the group experiences in order to make best use of group time, resources, and abilities. An understanding of the interaction between group dynamics and the research project will lead to a more positive professional experience for participants and more successful action research in the schools.

4
Collaborative Action Research and Adult Development

Introduction

When asked about the Principal's role in school change, each ARCS team member spoke from his or her own frame of reference. Brooks said, 'The Principal controls change'. George responded that ideally the Principal 'triggers', facilitates, and organizes individuals around common goals, while Jack said the Principal 'pulls the trigger' and orders unilateral change. Upon hearing George's comment, Brooks agreed with the ideal of the Principal triggering change. The two other teachers on the ARCS team expressed different opinions. John felt least concerned with the Principal in relation to his own planned changes in the school. He said that how teachers are evaluated has changed; it is never constant, and teachers don't know what to expect. John may have focused on the issue of teacher evaluation because it was the only area in which he felt the Principal had an effect on him (documentation, 5 November 1981). Ted wrote in his log, 'Principal seems to have little effect on change. Teachers were in the front when it came to setting policy' (log, 4 November 1981).

Action research team members at different adult development stages had different perceptions of the Principal, and they responded differently to issues related to the group process and the research project. Although all team members contributed to the collaborative research process, each added his or her own perspective. A developmental model provides a framework for understanding teacher behavior in the collaborative research process. In the last chapter we used group dynamics theory to study the group's development over five phases in the collaborative action research project and the resulting personal and professional outcomes for group members. In the current chapter we continue the examination of the ARCS team looking at each individual's patterns of thinking and problem solving, performance and behavior in the collaborative action research group from the perspective of adult development stages. Such an analysis allows us to hear individuals' voices and view interactional behaviors in another way, providing a new lens through which to see the developmental process of collaborative action research. This chapter identifies the characteristics of participants in the ARCS project in terms of their different stages of development and describes the support, conflict, and challenge factors at each of these stages which affect individual satisfaction and the group's accomplishments. In addition, adult development theory provides a framework for examining individuals' attitudes and behavior related to decision-making, change, and authority in the school — all of which affect the group's effectiveness in defining and reaching its goals.

Adult Development Theory

Adult developmental theorists focus on underlying patterns of thought which, they claim, play a central role in determining an individual's approach to the world. They are called cognitive-developmental theorists because they focus on the cognitive basis of thought, interpersonal relations and emotional structures. All of these theorists agree on certain characteristics of development. They posit global, holistic determinants of experience and maintain that human development, personality and character are the result of orderly changes in underlying cognitive and emotional structures. Development involves progression through an invariant sequence of hierarchically organized levels, called stages. Each new stage incorporates and transforms the structures of the previous stages and paves the way for the next stage. Each stage provides a qualitatively different frame of reference through which one interprets and acts upon the world. The sequence of development progresses from simpler to more complex and differentiated modes of thought and functioning. The higher stages of development are said to represent more adequate modes of functioning in the sense that they include adopting multiple points of view, more empathic role taking, and more adequate problem solving.

Adult developmental theorists provide several different frameworks for observing how individuals organize their worlds: ego development (Jane Loevinger and Robert Kegan); moral/ethical judgment in a morality of justice (Lawrence Kohlberg and James Rest) and a morality of response and care (Carol Gilligan, Nona Lyons and Nel Noddings); cognitive/conceptual development (Jean Piaget, David

Table 6: Comparison of Adult Development Theories

	EGO DEVELOPMENT 'Sets of Perceptions Toward Oneself and Others'	MORAL/ETHICAL DEVELOPMENT 'Attitudes of Reasoning About Moral and Social Dilemmas'		COGNITIVE/CONCEPTUAL DEVELOPMENT 'Attitudes Towards Learning and Preferred Style of Learning'		INTERPERSONAL DEVELOPMENT 'Ability to take the Perspective of Others'
		Morality of justice	Morality of response and care	Intellectual development	Women's ways of knowing	Group Relations
Stages of Adult Development	Loevinger (1970, 1976) Kegan (1982)	Kohlberg (1981, 1984) Rest (1986)	Gilligan (1982) Noddings (1984) Lyons (1983)	Piaget (1972) Perry (1970) Hunt (1975)	Belenky, Clinchy, Goldberger and Tarule (1986)	Selman (1979, 1980)
Preconventional	Impulsive Self-protective •Imperial	Punishment-obedience Instrumental egoism and exchange	Primary concern for one's own survival in the face of powerlessness	Concrete operations Dualism	Silence •Denial of self Received knowledge •Dualistic thinking •Powerless	Unilateral relations Bilateral partnerships •Exchange of favors

Conventional	Conformist •Interpersonal / Self Aware transition / Conscientious •Goal oriented •Institutional	Approval oriented / Authority, role, and social order orientation	Goodness in caring for others / Self sacrifice the highest virtue	Multiplism / Concrete/formal transition / Mutual dependence / Relativism	Subjective knowledge •Self awareness / Procedural knowledge •Complex ways of understanding	Homogeneous relations • Converging interests •Common values •Pressure toward uniformity
Post-conventional	Individualistic / Autonomous •Self-defining •Interindividual / Integrated	Social contract Utilitarian legalistic orientation / Universal ethical principle orientation	Recognition of self as a legitimate object of care / Development of an ethic of care	Full formal operations / Reflective judgment (Kitchener and King, 1979) / Commitment in Relativism / Dialectical thinking (Basseches, 1984) / Post-formal problem finding (Arlin, 1975) / Reflection on action (Schon, 1983)	Constructed knowledge •Speaking and listening used equally in active dialogue with others	Pluralistic relations •Differentiated values •Interdependent systems

Hunt and William Perry) and women's ways of knowing (Mary Belenky, Blythe Clinchy, Nancy Goldberger and Jill Tarule); and interpersonal reasoning (Robert Selman). These different theories of adult development are listed in Table 6 (Comparison of Adult Development Theories) and briefly described.

Ego Development

The concept of ego development has played an important role in clinical and theoretical work but it has only recently become a topic for empirical study. A pioneer in this work, Jane Loevinger, draws upon cognitive-developmental theory and H. S. Sullivan's theory of the self-system for her conception of ego functioning as involving 'the striving to master, to integrate, to make sense of experience' (Loevinger, 1966 and 1969). Ego development involves sequential changes in an individual's overall frame of reference. In the course of development the individual comes to regard one's self and others in an increasingly differentiated and complex fashion. Loevinger's conception of ego development must be distinguished from that employed by researchers more closely tied to traditional psychoanalytic theory (Hauser, 1976). For such thinkers the ego's primary function is to find solutions to the problem of instinctual expression which involves the development of coping patterns and defenses (Haan, Stroud and Holstein, 1973). In contrast, Loevinger's conception of the ego is predominantly cognitive; the ego provides a system of meaning which the individual imposes upon experience. Ego development can be understood as an overarching concept that encompasses cognitive, moral, and interpersonal dimensions. Loevinger describes development as a sequential progression through distinctive frameworks of meaning. She identifies seven stages and three transitional phases; each ego stage has its own 'inner logic' which helps to maintain the stability of its structural characteristics through selective inattention to factors inconsistent with the current ego level (Loevinger, 1969). Each of the stages differs along the dimensions of impulse control and character development, cognitive style, conscious preoccupations and interpersonal style; each distinctive meaning framework has an associated character type.

The stages of ego development, as listed in Table 6, are not tied to given ages. Individuals may, and do, stabilize at certain stages; among adults there are representatives of each age who can be characterized in terms of the features specific to the stage at which they stabilized.

Adults at the early stages (impulsive and self-protective) are impulsive and fearful, and have dependent and exploitive interpersonal styles and stereotyped cognitive styles (Loevinger, 1976). They operate from what Kegan (1982) describes as the imperial meaning system. However, when feeling threatened, any individual may temporarily react with some of these pre-conventional stage behaviors.

Most teachers score at subsequent stages of development (conformist, self-aware and conscientious ego stages). Individuals at the conformist stage of ego development or the self-aware transition stage place a high value on conformity to social norms on appearance and social acceptability. Belonging and being helpful characterize the interpersonal style of these individuals while their cognitive style is exemplified in stereotyped thinking and the use of cliches. During the self-aware transition there is an increase in self-awareness accompanied by the beginning development of situational logic and awareness of individual differences. Kegan (1982) describes this stage as the interpersonal meaning system. The self-aware transition level has been found to be the predominant adult ego level (Loevinger, 1976; Hauser, 1976). Further growth in self awareness and a capacity for self-criticism characterize the conscientious stage. Rules are internalized and self chosen standards guide long-term plans. In Kegan's (1982) terms individuals at this stage use an institutional meaning system. An individual operating from the institutional stage is embedded in personal autonomy and self-definition, assuming authority, exercising personal enhancement, ambition or achievement. We have found that experienced teachers predominantly scored at the self-aware ego level or at the conscientious ego stage (Sprinthall and Bernier, 1978; Oja and Sprinthall, 1978; Oja, 1980b, 1984a, and 1988a).

In the ARCS study, as in our previous studies with teachers, the highest ego development score in pretest data was the next, individualistic, ego stage. Individuals who have reached the post-conventional level of development (individualistic, autonomous and integrated stages) value interdependence in interpersonal relations and display a high degree of cognitive flexibility. They are able to cope with internal conflict by drawing upon their well developed self-awareness. People in these stages have been described as 'self-defining' in an 'interindividual' stage context (Kegan, 1982).

Levels of ego development can be compared with levels of moral development, cognitive development and interpersonal development (Table 6). Loevinger claims that cognitive development may be necessary, but is not sufficient for ego development (Loevinger, 1976); there are many cases of individuals whose cognitive development is far in advance of their ego development. Loevinger regards moral development as but one aspect of ego development (Loevinger, 1986). She asserts that moral development in the Kohlbergian sense, is necessary to, but not a sufficient condition of, a parallel stage of ego development. Ego functioning involves the integration and coordination of cognitive, psychosexual, psychosocial and moral strands of personality and must be regarded as a 'master trait' governing the expression of all these other aspects of personality.

Moral Development

A morality of justice

Modgil and Modgil (1986) provide recent consensus and controversy in moral development theory and deliberate moral education practice based on the work of Lawrence Kohlberg. Kohlberg's theory of moral judgment identifies three levels and six stages of moral growth representing qualitatively different systems of thinking that people employ in dealing with moral dilemma questions. Kohlberg's stages move from early self-protective and manipulative stages, called the preconventional level, through those dealing with maintaining the social order, the conventional level, to those stages based on loyalty to universal principles, the post-conventional level. This orientation to moral development has been called the morality of justice. The stages of moral development parallel Piaget's stages of cognitive development (see Table 6). Nevertheless, Kohlberg maintained that moral development was distinct from cognitive development, stating that a given cognitive stage is a necessary, but not sufficient, condition for the corresponding moral stage (Kohlberg, 1984). Rest (1986) describes current moral research methodology using an objectively scored instrument, the Defining Issues Test (DIT) of moral judgment. We used the DIT with the ARCS teachers to determine their usage of post-conventional levels of moral thought, called the percent of principled moral thinking or P% score. As will be shown in table 7, the range of DIT scores from the ARCS teachers is similar to that found in our previous studies with experienced teachers (see studies listed above).

A morality of response and care

Recent research investigating women's development (Gilligan, 1982;

Lyons, 1983; Noddings, 1984) has identified a different morality based on response and care which seems to be gender-related. Gilligan worked with Kohlberg and, over time, began to raise issues about the disproportionate number of women being scored in the conformist stage 3 of his scheme of moral development. She proposed that a predominant belief that men's concern with justice and autonomy is superior to women's concern with attachment and care was based on bias from traditional research which had investigated men's experience and then generalized it to women. She suggested that systematic attention to women's lives in both theory and research would result in a more balanced conception of human development. Gilligan chose a sample of women to study the disparity between women's experiences and the traditional representation of moral development. Her research with women showed that women prefer to discuss moral problems in terms of contextual solutions; they approach moral problems not as an intellectual exercise in abstract reasoning but as human problems to be lived and solved in living. Women define themselves in a context of human relationships and judge themselves in terms of their ability to care for others in the relationship. In Gilligan's developmental model, women spiral through a three-level evolution of responsibility to themselves and others. The first form is characterized by primary concern for one's own survival in the face of powerlessness. This gradually changes to a position where one seeks goodness in caring for others and self-sacrifice is the highest virtue. The final synthesis in the spiral occurs with the recognition of the self as a legitimate object of care. This insight becomes the framework for women's ethic of care. As will be discussed later, Brooks' work with the ARCS team over two years helped her to move through this spiral of care to a point of beginning to care for herself as well as others.

Having worked with Gilligan's study titled *In a Different Voice*, Lyons (1983) went on to study both male and female adults and the relationship of their conceptions of self and morality to considerations made in moral dilemmas. Lyons further defined two perspectives on relationships and morality, one based on response and care and another on justice and rights. Lyons' research documented women's predominant perspective of response and care. Although these differences did not necessarily divide along gender lines, it is clear that more women than men defined themselves in terms of relationships as connected to others. When men did define themselves in terms of connection to others, they also framed their moral judgments in terms of care rather than justice.

In describing a morality of care, Noddings (1984) suggested that women approach moral problems by placing themselves in the context of the situation and assuming personal responsibility for the choices to be made. She said that when individuals behave ethically as ones-caring, they are not obeying moral principles (in the Kohlbergian sense) although certainly moral principles may guide their thinking. Instead, they are meeting the other in genuine encounters of caring and being cared for. There is commitment, and there is choice. Noddings says that the commitment is to those being cared for and to one's own continual receptivity. Each choice one makes tends to maintain, enhance, or diminish the person as one-caring. Noddings discusses the ethics of care in relation to teachers and teaching and asks whether teaching by its very nature becomes an ethic of care. Will women and the men teaching in our schools reflect more the ethic of care? Our work with Ted on the ARCS team suggests the possibility that an ethic of care predominates in his thinking.

Cognitive/Intellectual Development

Piaget (1972), Hunt (1975) and Perry (1970) are among a wide variety of researchers who have studied cognitive growth and intellectual development. The cognitive development theories are based in Piaget's stages of concrete to abstract thought. Hunt (1975) describes cognitive complexity in terms of 'conceptual levels' which are defined by degree of abstractness (ability to separate, integrate, and/or discriminate many conflicting conditions) as well as degree of interpersonal maturity (increasing self-responsibility). A person scoring at a high conceptual level is more complex, more capable of responsible actions, and better able to adapt to a changing environment than is a person with a low conceptual level (*ibid*, p. 187).

Hunt's successive developmental stages range through four levels. Low conceptual level is characterized by concrete negativism, lack of differentiation, overgeneralization and preoccupation with immediate gratification of personal need. The next conceptual level stage represents responses containing categorical judgments (good-bad, right-wrong), overgeneralized and unqualified acceptance of a single rule, and reliance on external standards. The subsequent level represents responses which begin to show signs of self-delineation, express an awareness of alternatives and indicate sensitivity to one's own feelings. The highest level represents responses which demonstrate a clear indication of self-delineation and reliance on internal standards, a sense of self in context or relationship with others, and the ability to take two viewpoints into account simultaneously (Hunt *et al.*, 1973).

Conceptual level is assessed by evaluation of responses to five sentence stems designed to tap the individual's manner of dealing with conflict and response and orientation towards authority and rules, the Paragraph Completion Method (*ibid*). We used this test with ARCS teachers to determine conceptual level. We then observed the relationship between teachers' conceptual levels and their behavior on the action research team. We find Hunt's (1971) 'matching' model helpful; it describes learning environments that should promote development of conceptual level. The matching model builds upon the observation that individuals with low conceptual level prefer highly structured learning environments while those with high conceptual level prefer a lower degree of structure or are flexible with regard to structure in new learning situations. Researchers using conceptual level have been concerned with demonstrating the relation between cognitive complexity and behavior. As a result their research focuses on behavioral outcomes to a far greater degree than that of other cognitive-developmental theorists and 'much of what has been demonstrated is in support of theoretical predictions' (Miller, 1981, p. 80). We were very interested in teachers' behavior on the ARCS team, and we did document differences. For instance, in comparing teachers, Jack, with a lower conceptual level score (see Table 7) preferred more direction and structure than George who was able to function equally well under differing circumstances in the collaborative action research.

Perry's (1970 and 1981) work was also helpful as we investigated teachers' cognitive development on a continuum from dualism, to multiplicity, to relativism, to commitment in relativism. Perry's scheme is divided into nine positions each of which defines an approach to making sense of the world, similar to the way in which Loevinger's or Kohlberg's stages provide a perspective on one's world. Perry organized the positions from longitudinal interviews of Harvard male students; the work traces a progression which reflects our traditional education system and may describe how one learns to be rational and separate. In dualism, one sees the world in polar terms of we-right-good vs other-wrong-bad. In multiplicity, one accepts diversity and uncertainty but remains puzzled as to the standards. In relativism, one perceives all knowledge as contextual and relativistic. In commitment in relativism, one sees the need for and makes commitments which affirm one's identity as a result of multiple responsibilities, and one recognizes commitment as ongoing in repeating cycles. On the ARCS team it matters if a teacher thinks about problems from the dualist perspectives. As shall be seen, Jack often did function at the dualist level and he was disturbed when Ted, who functioned from the multiplist and relativist positions, brought up many legitimate and complex alternatives.

Women's Ways of Knowing

Belenky, Clinchy, Goldberger and Tarule (1986) studied how women from all walks of life think about thinking and about themselves as knowers. Building on Perry's cognitive and ethical scheme, their work positioned women's cognitive perspective on five major epistemological categories: silence, received knowledge, subjective knowledge, procedural knowledge, and constructed knowledge (see Table 6). In constructed knowledge, the final position of women's knowing, speaking and listening are used equally in active dialogue with others, in which knowledge is constructed by persons who experience each other as equals. In constructed knowledge, women 'find a place for reason and intuition and the expertise of others' (p. 133). A retrospective analysis of Brooks, to be presented using this newer theory, illustrated her development over the two-year ARCS project from subjective and procedural knowledge toward constructed knowledge, a very significant shift which helped her to understand better the workings of the school system.

What Belenky, Clinchy, Goldberger, and Tarule have added to our understanding of the development of thinking is the importance of voice, and the difficulty of women's gaining a voice. They have also demonstrated the importance of one's own experience and its significance in learning. They document the critical need for 'connected education' which is based on personal individual experience while acknowledging existing uncertainties and accords respect to and allows time for the understanding that emerges from first-hand experience. In connected education the leader tries to create groups in which members can nurture each other's thoughts to maturity and construct truth through consensus, not conflict. There is a respect for each others' unique perspectives and authority is based on cooperation, not subordination. These qualities describe to us what is important and necessary in the ideal collaborative action research group process.

Interpersonal Development

Robert Selman's (1980) developmental theory of interpersonal understanding identifies five levels of social perspective taking based on an
individual's cognitive capability and the social context. We found
Selman's stages of interpersonal understanding in peer group organization (Selman, 1979) to be very helpful in our analysis of the collaborative research group formation, cohesion, rules-norms, decision-making
and leadership. (See Table 6 for a listing of stages of interpersonal
development in group relations compared to other theories of development.) In group organization, the stage of unilateral relations implies
that people do what the leader says with no awareness of possible
converging thoughts and interests and 'agreements' between members.
In the stage of bilateral partnerships, everyone is supposed to 'like each
other,' and members believe that teamwork occurs through the
exchange of favors based on equal treatment. At this stage the person is
still unable to organize the group as a shared community, common to all
members regardless of their specific relations to one another. In the
stage of homogeneous community, there is increased concern with peer
group relations and a focus on each member's relation to a common
whole. There is emphasis on the group 'working together as a unit',
held together as a shared community by consensus on expectations: 'We
decide on one thing everyone wants to do'. Limitations at this stage are
due to the person's equating community with homogeneity of values
and inability to accept differentiated values. A sense of obligation to the
group is felt but generally in terms of pressures toward uniformity:
'You go along so you are not the odd ball'. At the next stage the group
is viewed as a pluralistic organization. A person understands the group
as a multifaceted system which can accept and incorporate individual
differences: 'A group is a continuing process and it functions for
members to coordinate their activities'. There is an understanding of the
group as a pluralistic community in which individual diversity is not
suppressed but united behind common goals. At this stage the person
becomes aware of the need to compromise in order to integrate the
diversity of interests in a pluralistic group. Teachers' understanding
of the ARCS group, as we observed in team meetings through
this interpersonal development stage lens, did influence both the
group process and the research process in the ARCS project. The
particular effect of each teacher's perception is presented in the cases
which follow.

Developmental Stages: ARCS Participants

Participants for the collaborative research teams were selected to represent a diversity of adult development stages based on their scores on three empirical measures of developmental stage: the Loevinger sentence completion test of ego stage (SCT), the Rest Defining Issues

Table 7: Cognitive-Developmental Stage Scores

	Sex	Yrs. of exp.	Ego Level SCT[a] TPR Score	Cognitive Complexity PCT[b] CL Level	Moral Judgment DIT[c] %P Score	Interpersonal Stage Global Stage[d] Score
Jack[*]	M	17	3	1.8	32%	1(2)
Ted	M	15	3/4	2.3	63%	3
John	M	19	4	2.0	46%	2(3)
Brooks	F	8	4	2.0	40%	4
George	M	11	4/5	2.2	75%	4

[*] Jack left the team after year 1.

Cognitive-Developmental Stage Scores Interpretations

a. The Loevinger Sentence Completion Tests were assigned Total Protocol Rating scores by an experienced rater. Scores indicate the following ego levels:

  Ego level 3 = Conformist
  Ego level 3/4 = Self-aware transition
  Ego level 4 = Conscientious
  Ego level 4/5 = Individualistic
  Ego level 5 = Autonomous

b. Hunt's Paragraph Completion Test of Conceptual Level generates scores that can range from 0 to 3. Scores of 1, 2, or 3 on this test may be interpreted as indicating the following conceptual levels:

  Score of 1 = Categorical judgments, stereotyped thought. Other directed; accepts single rules.
  Score of 2 = Self delineation, awareness of alternatives, and awareness of emotions.
  Score of 3 = Abstract internal principles, awareness of multiple viewpoints.

  Hunt has classified CL scores as follows:

  0.5 to 1.0 = low CL score
  1.1 to 1.4 = moderately low CL score
  1.5 to 1.9 = moderately high CL score
  2.0 and above = high CL score

c. The %P score on Rest's Defining Issues Test represents the percent of principled moral judgment responses (Stage 5A, 5B, and 6) in the person's total responses. Rest and Davidson (1980) have classified scores into quartiles:

  0–38% = low P score
  39%–58% = moderately low P score
  59%–77% = moderately high P score
  78%–99% = high P score

d. Selman's interpersonal stage score represents the global stage score of group organization and process:

  Stage 0: Physicalistic organization
  Stage 1: Unilateral relations
  Stage 2: Bilateral partnerships
  Stage 3: Homogeneous community
  Stage 4: Pluralistic organization

  Transition stages are shown in parentheses.

Test (DIT) of moral judgment and the Hunt paragraph completion test of conceptual level. Since there are no single valid measures, an overlapping assessment was employed with the three tests serving as proximate measures. Each test is viewed as an indicator of how the individual processes or makes meaning from experience. The Loevinger largely assesses how an individual thinks about or conceptualizes about self; the Hunt assesses how a person conceptualizes issues of teaching and learning; and the Rest assesses how a person processes social–justice questions. Because the area of interpersonal sensitivity cannot be readily extracted from the database provided by the three developmental tests mentioned above, a fourth method, the analysis of teachers' reasoning behavior in team meetings using the Selman assessment of interpersonal functioning, was added to the database and used as a cross check in the analysis of teacher's perceptions regarding the issues of change in the context of the classroom and school, group process, leadership, the principal, and goals/outcomes of the action research project.

Table 7, 'Cognitive-Developmental Stage Scores', presents the teachers' scores on each of the four assessments of development and provides information to interpret the developmental scores. As can be seen from Table 7, Jack scored at the conformist stage of ego development, Ted at the self-aware transition, John and Brooks scored at the conscientious stage, and George at the individualistic transition stage. In terms of cognitive complexity, the conformist stage teacher, Jack, had the lowest score, while the other four teachers scored very near each other with high conceptual level scores. What stands out in the pattern of moral judgment scores is Ted's noticeably higher score compared to the scores of the teachers in the developmental stages near his stage; this is also true of Ted's conceptual level scores.

Case Histories: Patterns of Cognitive–Developmental Functioning

We have identified five areas which differentiate teachers at varying stages of development: the individual's perception of *power, decision making, and change* issues in the context of the school and the collaborative action research process; the individual's perception of the collaborative *group organization and process*; the individual's perception of *authority and leadership* and the impact these perceptions have on the working of the team; the individual's perception of the *school Principal* in relation to the context of the school and the process of the research team; and the individual's *goals and expected outcomes* of the project the team undertook. Each of these areas will be described in the cases below; in each case the five areas are introduced by capsule phrases which highlight the teacher's perception. The teachers are described in the order of the stages of development, first, the conformist stage, then the self-aware transition stage, then the conscientious stage, and finally the individualistic transition stage. With each description of a teacher at a new stage, we begin to make comparisons with teachers at previously described stages in order to further clarify qualitative differences between the stages.

Jack: Conformist Stage of Development

In the conformist stage of development change is perceived as a simplistic way to solve problems and as an external process. The person at this stage is more concerned with issues of authority and control, with minimizing controversy, and with maintaining rules and implementing policies than with questioning the purpose of rules.

Change as an external event

Jack perceived of change as an external event which most often resulted from acts imposed by others. Change was viewed as a one shot episode rather than as a process over time. Jack talked, for example, about individualizing instruction and how it was impossible to carry out and that any teacher who claims that they are individualizing is a liar (documentation, 4 November 1981). In another meeting, Jack said that solving the teacher morale problem depended on who came in as Principal (documentation, 21 October 1981). When change is seen as being externally imposed, it can become manipulative. Jack solved problems by resorting to one problem-one answer solutions. If it can't be done one way (often his way), then it can't be done. There was little need for thinking about alternatives or graduations in an issue. He seemed not interested in changing his thinking to incorporate other points of view, and, as his conceptual level score indicated, he was probably unable to do this as readily as the other team members all of whom had high conceptual level scores (see Table 7). Jack frequently tried to minimize controversy in group discussions. He tended to maintain rules and enforce prior school policies and was reluctant to question the purposes behind certain rules and policies.

The group as bilateral partnerships

Jack's loyalty to the group was based on one-to-one partnerships he made with each individual in the group, a characteristic of Selman's stage 2 of interpersonal development in which teamwork occurs through the exchange of favors based on equal treatment. At this bilateral stage of interpersonal development, the ideal group member is someone who treats others as equals. Jack considered himself to be an ideal member if he was seen as 'a teacher, himself', equal to the other teachers, and if he was seen as able to keep their secrets.

> I'm trying to participate as a teacher and have them see me as a teacher, and I know these people well enough so if I sit here and talk about the office ... they understand that I'm not going back down there and say to the office world ... they (the team) say you did this or that. (interview, 12/81)

University researcher should lead the group

Jack saw a leader as one who has more knowledge, a view consistent with Selman's stage 2 of interpersonal understanding. He said that the university researcher should lead the group; he expected her to be the director, facilitator, arbitrator, and organizer because she knew more than the other group members.

> I think there's going to have to be an awful lot of help ... I think you're going to hand guide this team in the actual doing of the processes and methods ... by discovery, maybe, through questioning, not spoonfed, but I still don't see the team doing anything but fumbling as far as actually doing, knowing the processes and steps of the method. (interview, 12/81)

He also pointed out that when team members led the group, they did so because they had more knowledge in a particular area: 'After we identify the problem, I think there will be one, at least one out of the five, that will relate closer to that problem, and probably assume the leadership ...' (interview 12/81).

Principal pulls the trigger

Jack often seemed to take a rather manipulative view of his own part-time administrative role, a perspective which paralleled the ways in which he saw the role of the Principal and others whom he regarded as higher authorities. He described, for example, the way to move a student from one class to another as being 'not to tell the guidance department' because it was easier to do by not explaining the reasons, which would mean 'more paperwork'. He also described how he tried to 'convince teachers it was their idea' to make the change rather than tell them that he or the student wanted the change to another class. When Jack talked about informal changes that he had made, often as house coordinator, he said that maybe he would 'catch hell' if he was found out, but it was worth it (documentation, 21 October 1981). These examples appeared to be methods of making changes without 'making waves,' staying on the good sides of those with whom he interacted in the school. He said that it was a mistake for Principals to ask teachers for their opinions and then do the opposite, that it would be better to just tell teachers what you were going to do in the first place. When George said that the Principal should be one who triggers changes, Jack said, no, the Principal ought to just pull the trigger and order the changes. The Principal at the junior high school did not seem to affect Jack's life as a classroom teacher. At one team meeting, Jack said he'd been through four Principal changes, and:

> The Principal hasn't changed the way I teach in my classroom for sixteen years and hasn't affected me personally per se as a classroom teacher but has affected the overall philosophy of the school, which is where the morale problem exists ... now. (transcript, 10/81)

Jack clearly separated the selection of a new Principal from the collaborative research team's process. At one meeting, Jack read what was in his log, explaining that the team's discussion should not dwell on the Principal selection issue since it was past and not a part of what the team was doing. In addition, Jack said it was not his responsibility (documentation, 28 October 1981).

Goals and outcomes to benefit self

When asked about goals and benefits of the project, Jack said, 'Well, just sitting and talking with other people, getting other ideas, there have to be benefits to yourself. Even if they are accidental there have to be benefits'. When talking about outcomes, Jack also said that the team members should do the project for personal satisfaction, since it was 'fantasy island' to think that the administration would get involved and support the team's efforts. This initial focus on benefits for the self is characteristic of the pre-conformist level of moral development described by Kohlberg as the 'what's in it for me' stage. Jack was not interested in hearing others' personal concerns or what others wanted from the group. In the group Jack emphasized dealing with group issues rather than what he called 'pet peeves'.

> As a member of a team, if there was a problem, I'm the type of person on a team who says, hey, we're off the subject, let's get on to the subject ... I do not perceive of this as being a place where five teachers come to bitch about their pet peeve. I'm the type of person who will say, hey, let's get to the point, that may be important to you but you're off the subject of what we're really trying to do here for the school. If we solve the school's problem, our general problem, hopefully yours will be a small part of that, that will fall into place by solving the overall picture. (interview, 12/81)

By the end of the first year, Jack had just begun to form some deeper interpersonal relationships with the teachers on the team (even though he had worked with most of them in the school for six years or more). A transition from dualistic to relativistic stages of cognitive develop-ment requires interpersonal investment as does the transition from conformist to self-aware and conscientious stages of ego development. Jack was beginning such a transition. Much of Jack's change during the year was a result of working with the team together weekly in the project and spending more social time together at conferences outside of school time. Jack became more helpful as others expressed their different opinions; he listened and let them finish rather than continually cutting them off. He began to find value in the others' opinions and began to invest more in the group goals for the project.

Jack left the school after the first year of the project to become a Principal in another school district. In his final conference with us he continued to urge the university researcher to take more direction with the team. Documentation from the team meetings during the second year indicated that Jack's absence actually enhanced the team's ability for self-direction and achievement of their own group goals. Had Jack stayed during the project's second year, the team interaction of individuals operating at different stages of development may have encouraged development that we saw beginning over the course of the first year: Jack's own development of widened perspectives and his awareness and beginning acceptance of individual differences among the other teachers' attitudes, interests and abilities. Jack was interviewed at the end of his first year as Principal at the new school and he remarked that the teachers in the project would be surprised and pleased — he was listening to some of his own teachers in ways he never had at the old school, and he even let them make some changes he never would have allowed before.

We believe that the collaborative action research team setting was an environment in which Jack began to extend his problem-solving abilities and conceptual development. David Hunt's (1975) research suggests that 'matching' for developmental growth involves placing an individual in a learning environment slightly more complex and demanding than the individual would naturally prefer. Over time Jack began to see that the collaborative action research project issues could be approached from multiple perspectives. This ability indicates an increase in intellectual flexibility and is related to the ability to deal with abstract problems with possibility as well as actuality.

Ted: Self-Aware Stage of Development

At the self-aware transition stage, an individual is moving from the prior conformist stage to the subsequent conscientious stage. In this self-aware transition stage, an individual begins to differentiate norms and goals. One is aware of oneself in relation to the group and is concerned with helping others. Adjustment, problems, reasons and opportunities are conscious preoccupations of the person at this stage, and the cognitive style moves from conceptual simplicity to multiplicity.

Ted scored at the self-aware stage of development. He was concerned about external approval, and he wanted to work in a community where understanding and kindness were supports of the most essential kind. He thought that people 'should care about' the changes that were occurring: 'the gutting of the school-within-a-school program, less teachers ... translating into less individual attention, bigger classes and more and more students in need of special help with less and less resources to meet these needs' (transcript, 11/81). His attitudes toward change depended upon seeking acceptance from others, whether they were parents, administrators, or other team members. Ted exhibited characteristics of both the conformist and conscientious stages; this matched his scoring at the transition stage between them, the self-aware stage. His beliefs, which often sounded like principles for what *should* be done did not match his ability and willingness to act on his beliefs on the collaborative action research team. This difference between espoused beliefs and actual practice seems to be characteristic of the transition stage. Argyris and Schon (1975) and Schon (1983) are helpful resources describing 'theory in practice' and how one becomes a 'reflective practitioner', able to diagnose problems better, decide how to respond, *and* implement solutions.

Change as a process

Ted viewed change as a process, which contrasted with the conformist teacher's definition of change as a product. Ted said:

> The process of change in this school starts with a need. This need is transferred to the administration who, usually in big decisions, appoints a committee to make recommendations ... In the past, the Principal ruled by committees. The school-within-a-school system was a major improvement over past practices at the junior high. However, many faculty members perceive this change now (toward a more traditional junior high organization) as a major reaction to budget cuts, staff reduction, heavier schedules and bigger classes. (log, 14 October 1981)

This log entry illustrates the multiplistic, abstract thinking pattern that was indicated by Ted's high conceptual level scores (see Table 7). He could see many facets of an issue. Ted often posed questions using *should* or *could*. He seemed to be appealing to a more adequate system of thinking, not limited by reality but based on principle. He was concerned with rights and ideals, a concern typical of the conscientious stage of development. Ted also referred to a democratic system of decision making and expressed concern for moral problems and obligations. The word *should* as a moral imperative was always present in his statements and arguments. Typical of Ted's statements was when he said that when he was a Principal that he had more communication with higher administration. He said that people *should* be able to band together, that somehow problems *should* be solved (documentation, 28 October, 1981).

Group as a homogeneous community

Ted's view of the collaborative action research group as a homogeneous community reflects stage 3 of Selman's theory of interpersonal under-standing. Ted's loyalty was based on the concept of homogeneity of values and interpersonal relations based on common ground. Ted saw an ideal group member as someone who was faithful to the group as a whole, someone who was like everyone else in the group and who shared the group's concerns. Ted believed in doing what was required of him in order to stay a part of the group. Although he felt a sense of obligation to the group, this was generally in terms of pressures toward uniformity of ideas. When Ted's ideas differed from others, he gave up on his ideas, but he never really invested himself in the group's common goals. He exhibited little formal obligation to the research task either because he was unwilling to make decisions or unable to accept the responsibilities that came with the duties. There were differences in his capability level and operating level in the group. For instance, at one point, Ted objected to the team's research focus on scheduling because it did not include the issue of working with kids who are not functioning in school, and he felt it should. Brooks, operating at the conscientious stage, listened to Ted's argument and suggested he read some materials she had read and listen to some audio tapes she had which suggested alternatives for such students. She used those outside readings and tapes as an attempt to find a common ground with Ted as the team searched for a research focus. Ted, however, did not follow up on her suggestion. The interaction illustrated Ted's use of the moral imperative *should* and his tendency to back off when he was asked to be more specific. Ted dropped the subject and chose not to make waves nor find a common ground for his ideas with Brooks or the other team members. Making controversial decisions makes one less conforming to the group, and this may explain Ted's unwillingness to carry through (in action) his questions and objections to the research focus at times. Ted didn't feel ownership or investment in the group's research goals.

Unable to act on his ideas or lead the group

Ted was unable to act on his ideas or lead the group in what he thought should be done. This is an example of his not having reached the conscientious stage of development where achievement and self-confidence enable people to take on leadership roles. In part, Ted needed the willingness and confidence to take on new responsibility and risk involvement by taking action on the principles he espoused. It is interesting to note that throughout the project Ted seemed to appreciate conversations with John, who scored at the subsequent (conscientious) stage of development, because John could provide Ted with examples of the patterns and the strategies which John used to operate effectively in the school system. Ted appreciated John's greater experience and success in the workings of the school and John's willingness to take action and operate in the system with the administrators, Superintendent, school board members, and other staff members in the school. Ted was unable to take on his own authority and tended to depend on others' authority, or assign authority to them. In discussing cooperation from the Superintendent for the ARCS project, Ted told the team they should try to get the Assistant Superintendent's cooperation. However, even though Ted sat on the Staff Development Committee regularly with the Assistant Superintendent, Ted did not act on his thoughts. He did not bring up the ARCS group nor did he follow up even after John started a series of conversations with the Assistant Superintendent and made a presentation about ARCS to the Staff Development Committee. John wanted cooperation from the Assistant Superintendent and was able to follow through, keeping the Assistant Superintendent informed throughout the second year of the project.

Ted's focus on other people's feelings, although it was expressed in vague terms, exemplifies a characteristic of the self-aware stage that indicates growth beyond the conformist stage of development. In typical fashion he entered a conversation with Jack, at the conformist stage, by asking a question: 'Do the school board, superintendent, etc., know our feelings?' Jack said it was a question of knowing them versus caring about them. Ted said he could not believe they wouldn't care if they knew. Ted also said that because we live in a democracy, they should care if they knew. Jack answered Ted's question by saying that Ted was interested in his own feelings but that others weren't (documentation, 10/81). Jack dismissed the concern and turned the conversation back to the external realm. When Ted pushed a bit further with other possibilities, Jack was unwilling to defer to him and resorted to his own authority as part-time administrator by cutting off the conversation with the implication that 'something was being done'. To Jack, at the conformist position, Ted's focus on feelings and ideals seemed to add another contingency that upset Jack's simpler world. Jack wanted straightforward and clearcut solutions. Ted was able to see alternatives and look at people's feelings and individual differences as additional facets of problem solving. Ted and Jack had many interactions during team meetings; often their discussions began when Ted directed questions to Jack, perhaps in deference to Jack's experience and authority as an administrator. But Ted's abstract thoughts and relativistic thinking (reflective of his high conceptual level scores) added too much complexity to the discussion. In another instance, Jack said that if he looked at what directly affects you as the teacher, then federal legislation, director of special services, and the Principal have direct effect; others have little effect on you (documentation, 28 October 1981). Ted interjected that the administrative decision-making process also depends on who the people are in each role because persons fill each role differently. Early in the project, when disagreements between Ted and Jack resulted, Jack often used his own authority status to cut off further discussion on the topic. As the first year went on, Jack began to listen more because of a growing interpersonal bond between himself and more of the team members.

Principal has little effect on change

Ted observed that the former junior high Principal had little effect on change, that he was just a middleman implementing policies dictated from above and below him. 'Teachers (committees) were in the front when it came to setting policy' (log, 4 November 1981). Other teachers on the team disagreed with Ted on this. Jack, at the prior (conformist) stage, said it was the Principal who set policy. In agreement, Brooks and John at the next (conscientious) stage believed teachers (even on committees) had little input into policy at the school. George, at the next (individualistic) stage said the Principal acted 'arbitrarily, rigidly, ... paying lip service to teachers'. If one considers the developmental position of each teacher, it is not so surprising that these teachers in the same school (all described to be 'interested, active participators' by the Principal) had such different perspectives of the same events. In developmental theory one begins to notice that the same physical event can, in fact, be seen differently by those affected. Not only do they explain their perceptions of the event differently, they seem to have 'seen' different realities. Persons are constructing reality out of very different systems of logic (Selman, 1980). In Ted's logic system, teachers' committees have an effect on policy in the school, while Jack, Brooks, John and George all see little effect. Could these other teachers influence Ted, by telling him something different? Pointing out their differing perceptions did not swerve Ted away from his own reality. It would take a developmental transformation for Ted to see the Principal, teachers, and school policy making in a different way from what he thought *should* occur.

Goals: fulfilling the needs of others; outcomes: vague

Ted stressed fulfilling the needs of others (teachers and students) in the school as goals for the project. He wanted to do a project 'that all of us have deep caring for', expressing his awareness of the possibility of internal/emotional connections to the project. Both of these ideas reflected his conformist/conscientious transition, in which caring for others and wanting to work on a project in which group members have feelings of commitment and caring are important. Although he expressed these ideas in vague and broad terms, we wonder whether Ted's feelings reflect the quality of an ethics of care, which Noddings (1984) has described in relation to teaching and the field of education. Ted's contribution to the group tended to be what he called 'enthusiasm' because he felt he lacked skills necessary to contribute in more concrete ways. The skills he lacked included confidence in communicating with other teachers, reading research articles, writing, analyzing data and speaking at presentations. His lack of confidence is reflective of the self-aware stage and, no doubt, influenced his participation (or lack of participation) in the group tasks. Ted continually experienced a conflict between his inability (often seen as unwillingness) to take on tasks and his desire to live up to what was expected of him by the team.

Ted's perceptions of project outcomes were vague. He was unable to specify what he had gained from the project, although his general feeling was that the process was beneficial for teachers as a whole. One positive outcome of the project for Ted was a global sense that 'teachers can do research' and that 'research is no longer scary'. Because he expected that the project would meet the needs of all teachers and students in the school, he saw the project itself as not reaching all the initial goals he had set for it. He said the project was valuable 'only for a limited number of people', and not something that would 'affect most of the teachers in the junior high and in their own classrooms'.

John: Conscientious Stage of Development

The conscientious stage is characterized by self-evaluated standards, self-criticism, long-term goals and ideals. Individuals at this stage express intensive interpersonal styles, responsibility, mutuality and concern for communication. They are preoccupied with differentiated feelings, motives and patterns for behavior, self-respect, achievement, traits and expression. Their cognitive style reflects conceptual complexity. John's patterns of thinking in the group exhibited characteristics of the conscientious stage of development: a focus on goals, problems and the tendency to use formulas and predesigned solutions to new problems; idealism and a long-term perspective on change; self-evaluated standards; and recognition of individual growth and change.

Use formulas in decision making for change

John emphasized his assumption that the project would solve specific school problems, 'dealing with students and dealing with teachers within our particular areas — trying to find help with the problems'. While Ted, the self-aware stage teacher, focused on doing a project to address people's needs, John wanted to solve problems within the school as a system. John was very stable and in control of what Kegan (1982) describes as his own self-system in the school. He felt confident and assertive about his opinions. Unlike Ted, affiliation and acceptance were not his ultimate needs from colleagues or authorities. John was always concerned with keeping stable his own patterns of working in the school as a system, which is the crucial limiting factor in the conscientious stage. John's extreme stability at times became a rigidity toward change in general. When his plans, curriculum, and school committees were running smoothly, John was confident of his control over the system and surroundings. But when conflict and new ideas arose that could cause his stable system to be threatened, John's initial reaction was inflexibility, and he used every strategy he had to allay any possible controversies. Although he might have preferred a school decision-making policy that was different from that of the Principal, he did not want to risk his own curriculum with open-ended encounters that may have led to conflicts. John's first choice in establishing a research question was to look at the state laws and the requirements concerning scheduling. This concern is typical of the conventional thinker's reliance on laws to guide future actions.

> John said that to research the issue of scheduling, he would want to look into state laws on class time, required classes, school time; on ideal class length for junior high and the possibility of it being different for different teachers/subjects; and on plans other schools used to overcome problems raised by administrators.

Once he had all that information, John said he would work out two or three schedules and present them to the powers that be. He would also be armed with the information when the issue arose. (documentation, 2 December 1981)

John tended to find and use formulas to solve problems he saw as part of the team's project seeking the rules or laws which governed behavior and interactions. While this allowed him to work on the problems identified by the group and move the team along, it prevented him from thinking up alternatives or seeing subtleties in the problem situations. It is often up to teachers at the subsequent individualistic stage to bring up the alternatives and point out the subtle contradictions.

Group as a homogeneous community

John saw the group as a place for sharing personal feelings about school problems and saw the group contributing to his solutions of and dealing with those problems. Being a part of the group was being a part of a larger whole. In operation, John also seemed to use the group (later in year one and during year two) to gain access to the school administration; not quite seeking prestige but working for his own recognition within the system. John's perceptions of the group process and his actions as a group member indicate some transition from Selman's interpersonal stage 3, the group as a homogeneous community, to interpersonal stage 4, the group as a pluralistic organization. From a stage 3 perspective, he tended to see the action research group in a more singular dimension, i.e. as situation specific. John did not see the team as a static group but was able to see it as more dynamic and self-regulating, a stage 4 perspective. However, he was unable to view the group process from the following additional stage 4 perspectives: he was unable to separate group processes, such as roles and decision making; he was unable to analyze the total process of the team in a variety of contexts; he was unable to see the group in comparison to other groups, using ideas such as leadership and conformity to distinguish and compare groups; and he seemed unable to view the group as composed of a variety of sub-systems, or decision-making processes, which were needed to make the group a whole.

Able to take on leadership roles

John viewed the university researcher in the role of group leader as a catalyst, helping to energize rather than direct the group, marshalling group solidarity as a whole. He said, 'To me it seems that the university researcher is the kind of person who tosses out the ideas or tosses out the things to get us stimulated to say something, to start with' (interview, 12/81). Like the other conscientious stage teacher and the individualistic stage teacher on the team, John felt skillful in his ability to address problems and assume tasks which led to problem solutions. He was able to take on a leadership role in the group, and he felt confident in his ability to approach and talk to other teachers, Principal, Assistant Superintendent and school board members. He was comfortable directing the team as it carried out data collection and analysis. Even though he originally felt he lacked research skills, he continually found ways to bring the skills he had into the working of the team. This approach was very different from Ted who tended not to initiate tasks and not to compensate for skills he may have lacked.

Principal is a benevolent dictator

John said a Principal runs a school and is at best a benevolent dictator. He implied that teachers need to figure out ways of staying out of the Principal's way. John was firmly entrenched in the conscientious stage, with confidence in his own working ideas and little dependency on the Principal, as long as 'he leaves me alone'. In the ARCS project, John actively took on the role of providing the Principal with information on the project during year one. This fit with his belief that one should let the Principal know and, if the Principal is interested, he will make the next move. Midpoint during the first year John said that the new Principal was hoping the team would come up with some ideas, that he was really interested in what it could offer (documentation, 16 December 1981). During year two, John no longer continued in his voluntary capacity of updating the Principal on the team's progress. It became clearer to the team that the Principal was not as interested in the team's research and results as first anticipated. John seemed to be embedded in the school context and the teacher role in the school and acted on his beliefs, being consistent in what he said should be done and what he did. His ideas of what should be done were pragmatic, based on what he had done before; they represented the conventional stages of moral judgment. His own moral code seemed tied to his internal system. He acted more from what is pragmatic and strategic, socially desirable or expected, than what is most fair or just. John tended to change behavior to fit the situation, to do what he called 'the right thing in the situation', primarily defined by his own system orientation in the job and school.

Outcomes: specific skills to solve school problems

John listed a number of specific outcomes which helped him solve school problems as he evaluated his own participation in the project, changes in his own learning, and growth in himself. He said he felt 'more conscious' of what he was doing in the classroom and that a value he had found in the project was the use of logs to vent his anger by writing his frustrations down. He said this helped him 'channel the anger and frustration and get it out of the classroom'. John described how he would use some of the skills he gained from the project in his classroom and said he hoped to capitalize on his increased confidence in writing by working on a paper describing a teacher's view of action research, thinking he might possibly present it at a conference. He emphasized the value of the process the group went through and planned to modify it (to action inquiry) for use with science colleagues and other teachers. Another outcome for John was that his increased confidence and skill gave him greater power within the system. 'Doing this has given me a way to write, which I did not have, to increase that particular power base ... talking at places, conferences, knowing that I can stand up in front of a group and say what I want to say'. The best part of the experience John said was 'being thought of as an expert ... so that when you're meeting (other people) they have the feeling that you know something and you even have the feeling that maybe you know something. That's a good feeling, good experience' (interview, 6/83). John could clearly list his own strengths, weaknesses, and perceived outcomes from the project. John's specificity was in contrast to both Jack and Ted, the conformist and self-aware stage teachers, who were more vague in identifying skills they had or lacked and what they wanted or gained from the project. Participating in the project 'revitalized' John. He liked the contact with other teachers in the school that he had gotten by sharing his log entries with them throughout the project (documentation, 18 November 1981).

Brooks: Conscientious Stage of Development

Brooks scored at the conscientious stage but showed in her inter-personal development the movement to the subsequent stage, the individualistic stage. In addition, there are some aspects of her profile which bring up gender-related issues that are also important to the analysis of the collaborative action research team.

Sees complexity of the change process in schools

Brooks recognized the complexity of change as a process in the school. As a result of her lack of influence on school decision-making, she felt ineffective in resolving problems. Her perception of change as a complex issue encompassed her intrapsychic concerns as well; she wanted to be in control of herself, to have as stable a self-system as John. Like John and Ted, she equated individual growth with change, but she was even more capable of being very specific about personal changes in herself over the course of the project. Beyond changes in her own individual growth, Brooks continued to focus on attitudes as she discussed the school context and the team's research focus. She began to see the psychological causality behind individual growth and change. For instance, when asked about what helps or hinders change for teachers and students, she said:

> The total 'school' (learning) environment, too much real or imagined stress, and an inflexible schedule seem to stand in the way of positive change. Teachers feel uneasy, unhappy, ill-at-ease. This is transmitted directly to students who act out the feelings in adolescent ways. (log, 3 November 1981)

She was able to see behavior in terms of feeling patterns and motives, a characteristic of the conscientious stage. Like John, she resorted to the use of formulas and predesigned courses of action. Brooks, too, had the ability and willingness to act to take on tasks and responsibilities, and she exhibited abstract, reflective thinking in relation to the process of change in herself and the school.

Group as a pluralistic organization

Brooks viewed the group as a pluralistic organization in which members stick together to achieve collective ends. This is an example of Selman's stage 4 of interpersonal development in which a group's collective spirit serves an important function and interpersonal relationships in the group are independent of the collective spirit. It seems that the collaborative group organization and process itself was enough of a challenge for Brooks to elicit her highest level of problem solving.

Brooks was aware of others' perspectives in the group and knowledge-able about and competent in different social contexts. She had more experience in groups than any other teacher on the team. Her inter-personal insights were, however, not always consistent with her actions in the group. Brooks operated in the team meetings at a lower interpersonal level than expected. She talked about recognizing individual differences in the group and still being able to work together toward a common end. But she was intolerant of Ted's differences after he refused her ideas and offers of help to bring his concerns about alternative schools into the research focus in year one, and she saw him 'shirking responsibilities' as he declined more active involvement in year two. She was at times unable to work with him. Selman's stage 4 of interpersonal development assumes that people can have different interests and still build a group process. Stage 3 assumes group solidarity dependent upon shared homogeneous values. Her actions with Ted suggested the lower stage; this indicates the transition in Selman's interpersonal stages of development. Although she was cap-able of the higher stage thinking, she was unable to put it fully into practice.

Group leadership: depends on different interests and abilities

Brooks' thinking in relation to the leadership of the group also represented a transition in growth. She understood that the group leadership was variable in the group; group leadership depended on members' different interests and ability to take on multiple roles. Brooks explained her perspective that team members had initially looked to the university researcher for leadership and direction, and then began to understand their need to develop ownership and take on the project leadership. She (in the second year) saw the university researcher as a colleague, a member of the group who has specific roles just as other members do. At the end of the project in a presentation given by the team to a university class, Brooks shared her belief that the more researchers try to control an action research group, the less successful the group will be. She said she heard examples of this at an AERA conference she attended, but did not feel it had happened in her ARCS team.

Brooks used outside readings as authorities to explain and support her ideas. In March of the first year the university researchers brought in the results of an ERIC search on junior high scheduling issues which the team had requested. The team members took turns reporting on the articles they selected from the ERIC search. Brooks conscientiously read the articles brought to the meeting by the university researcher, and she sought out additional articles, for example, a report on the State of New Hampshire guidelines for junior high schools. At another meeting, she brought in a journal article which reported on parents' ideas and a parent/student opinion poll which investigated junior high school issues. She summarized this article for the team and asked, 'Should we include parents in our study?' Brooks felt skillful and confident in her reading of professional journals and in her knowledge of research design. In April and May when the team was focusing their research question, Brooks brought in a research methodology textbook and summarized nine different forms of research. She briefly described her understanding of hypothesis testing and statistical significance in order to help other team members who were confused. Near the end of this time, she made an appointment with an expert at the University of New Hampshire to find out about his studies of teacher burnout. She returned from the meeting urging the team to continue its focus on teacher stress in relation to school scheduling and to use the Maslach Burnout Inventory as one of its surveys.

Principal controls change ... triggers change

When discussing a Principal's leadership in the school, Brooks at first said the Principal controls change, but she soon agreed with George that the Principal triggers change.

> The Principal triggers the elements of change — number of staff in areas, schedule, budget allocations, tone of interpersonal relations, level of academic involvement. This can be transmitted formally by what the Principal shares with his staff or informally by what the staff 'sees' as decisions that the Principal is able to influence or make. (log, 3 November 1981)

Having been active in school staff development activities before, and having tried to make changes, Brooks recognized the value of the Principal's backing of the team's research idea if it was going to work. Several times during discussions of whether to involve the Principal more in the team's work, Brooks referred to an article on school change and the importance it gave to a Principal's involvement in successful school change efforts.

Because Brooks was in transition to the next stage, the individualistic stage, in some dimensions of her thinking; because she had less experience in the school than John; and because she is a woman, the conscientious stage characteristics were manifested differently. Brooks felt less stable in her own self-system in the school. Although she was confident and assertive interpersonally, she was in conflict when acting with the Principal and with the decision-making systems of the school and district. Her concern for interpersonal relationships had not provided her with power. In contrast, John had been an insider in district decision-making; he had formed the original Staff Development Committee, set policy as a result of that committee work, talked to and influenced school board members and principals of other districts, and had a close working relationship with the Assistant Superintendent of schools regarding the Staff Development Committee. Brooks had been active on committees in the school, in her area of reading and later on the Principal selection committee, but she had experienced little sense of power or control in decision-making. Being a woman in a tradition-ally male-oriented system of authority, she seemed to have participated, yet was without full knowledge of or influence on decision-making processes. Her efforts in the collaborative action research team focused on holding onto and developing her growing sense of her individuality and extending her understanding of the informal and formal decision-making processes in the school and district. For instance, when Ted said that, due to the financial crunch, more decisions seemed to be top-down, Brooks said that there were also outside political groups that influenced change or instigated change. Brooks also said that sometimes the Principal does not control change, that there are political rami-fications. She noted that there was 'a power structure we don't begin to understand'. She had felt that teachers should have more say and yet when she tried to speak up, she 'got (her) little toes stomped on' (documentation, 28 October 1981). Brooks was beginning to be the 'constructed knower' described by Belenky, Clinchy, Goldberger and Tarule (1986) as she tried to make the unconscious conscious, consulted and listened to herself, and became alert to the currents and undercur-rents in the school.

Specific personal and professional outcomes

Brooks said her goal was to 'establish a dialogue within the school — of some concerned teachers, of what's happened to us, where we've been, what has really transpired'. Her understanding of communi-cation, also to be expected at the conscientious stage, may be a gender-related difference that appears at this stage. It is an example of what Gilligan (1982) has described as women's preference to discuss problems in terms of contextual solutions. Brooks defined herself in a context of human relationships and judged herself in terms of her ability to care for others in the relationship. Her concern for others was expressed in an active, specific way; she said, 'It is through communication that caring would take place'. Like John, Brooks felt confident talking to other teachers in the school and taking on project tasks. More than John, she seemed to understand other people's viewpoints and to be looking for her own individuality within the connection she felt with others. This may be another gender-related difference at this stage as described by Lyons (1983). Brooks was able to define both the personal and professional outcomes of the project for herself. One of Brooks' original goals was that the project would 'establish a dialogue within the school'. In this her thinking reflects her movement to the final position of women's ways of knowing (Belenky *et al*, 1986), constructed knowledge, where speaking and listening are prized in active, equal dialogue with others. The collaborative group process made a distinct impression on Brooks: 'I'm absolutely convinced that it was the process that was really important.' She said that the collaborative process was the key (for her) more than the generalizable results, 'especially since everything keeps changing in the school'.

Brooks was moving into post-conventional stages of development. Signs of Brooks' transition to the individualistic stage included her increased respect for individuality of people who were different from herself. Brooks was aware that people hold a variety of values and opinions. She said, 'I think that I've grown more accepting of people and their differences and I see more of an ability to compromise and to work with people who I don't necessarily socialize with or philosophically agree with, but I'm much more able to realize that there is a greater good for being together as a group'. As an example of this growing ability, we note that her actions during the project showed that initially she was unable to work with Ted but did learn to accept his differences, primarily by letting go of her expectation that he would volunteer to take on specific obligations and duties in the group. Instead she grew to see Ted as a person in the group who needed more careful instruction for specific tasks, and at the end she began to provide more of the structure he needed to perform tasks. The confidence she gained and skills she extended through the project, plus her deeper appreciation for individual differences, contributions of team members, and the Principal's role in the school and district, seem to have helped her define herself more clearly in terms of the reality of the school context and decision-making.

At the beginning, Brooks hoped that the project would help her 'cope with all the changes' that had happened at the junior high. In her interviews after year one, she said she had more control over the kinds of things happening to her and that she was actively building her concerns into the research design (focus on stress as related to scheduling issues). At an interview midway through the second year, she said that the research project, the reading she had done, her greater awareness of the school context ('I sometimes see why principals and vice-principals have to make the decisions like they do') had all helped her feel more in control. In Kegan's (1982) terms, Brooks was assuming her own personal authority and her personal autonomy within the system. Brooks said she felt less burned out. She had survived her feelings of powerlessness, moved away from a position of self-sacrifice in caring for others, and was now recognizing herself as a legitimate object of care. These transitions are concepts in women's development which Gilligan (1982) has studied, a three-level evolution of responsibility to oneself and others. In her final interview, Brooks no longer felt trapped but said, 'I have control, I have skills, I have knowledge, I have my power, I can deal with the problems that are coming up'. She also said that if she is in a situation again where she is unable to cope with the changes in her work environment that she knows there will be resources available to deal with the problem. For Brooks, the ARCS project provided such resources. She said that after working on this research project, she realized the issues causing stress in the school were not going to change so somebody had to change and 'it was me'. She was operating from what Kegan calls the institutional stage of development (equivalent to the conscientious stage). The person operating from this meaning system is embedded in personal autonomy and self-definition, assuming authority, exercising personal enhancement, ambition, or achievement. In doing this one leaves behind a dependence on external reinforcement. Brooks was moving toward her own internal standards and developing her own constructed voice (Belenky *et al*, 1986) by integrating her reasoning, intuition, and other's points of view.

George: Individualistic Stage of Development

The individualistic stage is a transition between the conscientious stage and the subsequent autonomous stage of development. In this transition, the individual develops a heightened respect for individuality and, with it, begins coping with conflicting inner needs and toleration of others' individuality. Dependence becomes a conscious preoccupation as the person is growing toward autonomy and interdependence. Increased ability to tolerate paradox and contradiction is reflected at the individualistic stage and, along with greater conceptual complexity, is shown by the person's awareness of discrepancies between inner reality and outward appearances and between process and outcome.

Complexity of hierarchies of school decision-making

George's ability to see the complexity of the school decision-making process and his feeling of lacking power in it had made him somewhat cynical about the possibility of the research team substantially changing the school. At times, his comments sounded like Jack's at the conformist stage, but there was a very clear difference in their meanings, and they both contrasted with Ted at the self-aware position. The different points of view illustrate the three developmental positions: Jack who talked in simplistic terms about personal satisfaction because it was 'fantasy island' to think that administrative involvement could happen; Ted, who said the group 'should' attack the power structure in order to get the administration involved and 'should' make the impact felt, but was unable to take responsibility to do any of this; and George, who was cynical about the possibility of substantial changes being made, but who became more and more involved in the research because it began to address the way teachers felt about decision making and their involvement in school processes.

Group as a pluralistic organization

George saw the group as a pluralistic organization in which a variety of points of view were not incompatible with a sense of community, stage 4 of interpersonal development. Thus, a diversity of interests was tolerated and even welcomed, and conformity was not necessary for him to be comfortable functioning in the group. For George, the individual personalities contributed to the richness of the group as a whole. George saw the group sticking together to achieve collective ends; for him, the team was a working group when each person was willing to work with the others to achieve group ends, despite individual differences. Loyalty was a personal commitment, a decision made by each person to carry out tasks which promoted the group goal. As opposed to the perception that groups exist in order to achieve shared feelings, George felt that the group spirit was a process, like a tool, for unifying the group behind its overall group purpose. George saw group members taking on varying leadership roles, depending on their differing interests and their ability to take on multiple roles to meet the needs of the group as time went on and tasks and focus changed. George, more than any other teacher on the action research team, was able to separate the individual and/or the status of the individual from the functions that he believed the group leaders should perform in the group. Early on, George suggested tasks to the university researcher and research assistant — seeing them as equally responsible for particular role functions in the group process. This was consistent with his concept of the formation of the team as a group of individuals working together to achieve a common goal.

Initiating, leading and accomplishing team tasks

While George's goals were individualistic, he had a sense of obligation to the group, a feeling of contractual commitment which influenced his acceptance of leadership and initiation responsibility for team tasks. He talked about being 'flexible' in the group, so that even when he made objections or questioned aspects of the research project, he said he did so to enhance the overall project, not to obstruct it. This characteristic was very different from the conformist and self-aware stage teachers on the action research team who thought that if they began to question, then they were obstructing the group and causing it to break down. In comparison to the conscientious stage behaviors like using formula solutions to problems, George was able to generate alternatives, project consequences, and to accept conflicting points of view, seeing when they were equally valid. For instance, at the beginning of an important team discussion about whether or not to research scheduling issues, George did not see scheduling as an overarching concept. He at first perceived of scheduling as a more mundane, immediate change, like setting up a schedule. John argued convincingly for a broader picture of scheduling as encompassing many of the team's concerns including teacher morale. Later, George showed his ability to change his mind as a result of the new information gained in this argument. George said he began to see that scheduling is the 'absolute problem;' it was 'foolish' to focus on anything else.

The ability to change one's mind and consider new alternatives when conflicting information threatens to upset one's opinions or beliefs is a characteristic of the individualistic stage. It is interesting to note that as soon as John had convinced George of the value of researching scheduling, John went back to his earlier point of view that a simpler issue, time, was the key concern and priority. John seemed to be able to generate more adequate arguments when pressed or when he had an investment in an idea, and George's initial perception of scheduling as a 'mundane' change pressed John to a more complex argument. This is an example of how interactions of people at two stages of development can actually help both people to come to a more adequate solution. From this point on George helped the team keep its focus on the broader implications of scheduling.

Individualistic stage teachers can stand back from the group and examine the team's process and each member's contributions to the collective goals. Unlike those in transition from the conscientious stage who tend to get caught up in interpersonal conflicts, George, operating fully at the individualistic level, was able to accept individual differences which could have resulted in conflict and work with these differences toward mutually defined goals. So, for example, he continued to work with Ted on pieces of the project while Brooks (at the conscientious stage) tended to ignore Ted in order to concentrate on the team's work.

George's thinking and behavior in the collaborative action research project exhibited characteristics of a transition to the next stage of development, the autonomous stage. He was able to keep his own needs and goals in mind while fulfilling obligations to the group. George felt skillful in setting individual and group goals in the action research team meetings. For example, doing computer programs and data analysis contributed to his own needs to learn more for a course he was teaching while it also satisfied the group's goals and needs. George's balance of personal and group needs contrasted with Brooks' (operating at the conscientious stage) difficulty in maintaining her obligation to the team at the same time in which her own growing sense of individuality was emerging. At the beginning of the project Brooks tended to focus on either her need to address personal issues or on her responsibility to the tasks of the action research. She seemed to dichotomize the two so that her sense of responsibility to the team would not overtake her emerging focus on fulfilling personal needs. George, in contrast, was able to integrate his individual needs with the demands of the team. George was also able to stand back from the group and view it in perspective when needed, whereas the conscientious stage teachers in the foregoing examples tended either to have their values and actions embedded in the group's work (John) or were struggling to differentiate their individual emerging values and perceptions from those of the group (Brooks).

Principal triggers change, facilitates and considers other viewpoints

George said a Principal triggers change by organizing a group of teachers, and taking into consideration the teachers' points of view. This was consistent with George's idea of a leader as someone who should help a group reach a common goal. In a log comment in year one, George suggested that the proper posture for a Principal was that he knows what is wrong and and does not permit it; the Principal should function on the basis of what is right. The 'rightness' equates roughly with what is 'best'. He then noted that 'best' should not be determined unilaterally and that staff collaboration must determine the 'best' system of functions for the total school. George said that in his experience, past Principals have acted arbitrarily, rigidly, by paying lip service, by not considering alternatives to their preferred decisions.

George saw the Principal within the larger context or system, and perceived the Principal's voice as one of many to be considered and his preferences as only one set of those that occur in the school. George said that in order to understand change, one has to understand formal and informal channels of power. Because George saw the Principal as only one part of a larger system, as was the action research group, the system needed to be considered in weighing whether or not to invite the new Principal to join the group. Group cohesion also needed to be considered. The Principal could be seen as a resource rather than a deciding or controlling force (this paralleled George's earlier statement that the Principal triggers rather than controls change).

When George expressed this view in a project meeting in the fall of year one, others' opinions came forth. Ted, at the self-aware stage, said it was valuable to invite the Principal in to give the team ideas, although it should be the team's decision on a project in the end. Ted's desire parallels his view that, on school decisions, the Principal ought to get teachers' opinions for face value alone, even if he did not intend to use their ideas. John's concern with inviting the Principal depended more on who the new Principal would be because that, he said, would determine whether and how to involve the Principal. George was concerned about the action research group's process and said that the Principal should have been involved from day one if he was going to be included as an equal voice on the team. Since George considered the

Principal as one who could offer another opinion, he said that the team might look to the Principal as a 'valuable resource' whom the team could call on at certain points in the research process (but not a full team member).

Involvement of the Principal was an issue that was still unresolved for George at the end of the project. Throughout the project George was very consistent in his understanding and actions in terms of the team's work and group process, all aimed toward merging individual diversity and conflict to achieve common goals. However, George was unable to interact with the Principal in a way that would contribute to the group's goals. George never mentioned discussing the project directly with the Principal, even though the new Principal had been a teacher in the same department with George prior to his taking the principalship. At the end of year one, George took a job in the high school, and thus, during year two, he had no contact with the junior high Principal. It is impossible to predict what would have happened in the project had George stayed at the junior high. Would he have become aware of the possibility of negotiating with the Principal to help bring about the changes the team's research suggested were important and necessary? Would he have been able to act personally on his belief that the Principal should be a resource to the team? On this issue it may be that George's determination not to be controlled by the Principal at times overshadowed his perception that the Principal could contribute to the team.

Outcomes: intellectual and personal excitement

George discussed project goals and outcomes in terms of his own professional growth. He noted that the best thing about the project was the intellectual and personal excitement he felt in the national conferences as he saw and met speakers whom he may have quoted in his written papers over the last few years. He said that in the future he would like to facilitate or be an outside resource for another school's action research team. He thought about the steps the group took in its process and wanted to investigate how a different group could progress under different conditions. He described the research process of the group as 'the crooked path we took in developing research questions and developing our instruments and making our conclusions' and wanted to go through the collaborative action research process again with a different group and study the similarities and differences. In terms of benefits from the project he said, 'Personally, I've developed confidence and also interest in pursuing the topics related to action research and, in general, any topics that would broaden my own experience or bring some sort of recognition to me.' Since the project has ended, George has continued to investigate the possibility of further graduate study. George is actively redefining his career; although he views teaching as his professional career, he is not limited by the definitions of duties, performances, and work roles that the school as an institution gives rise to. As a teacher exhibiting characteristics of the individualistic transition to the autonomous stage of development, he could be viewed as entering the perspective where an interdependent definition of oneself retains primary focus and self-actualization becomes a goal.

Observing Development in an Action Context

Adult development theory posits development of individual self-concept and ego maturity, moral/ethical judgment, conceptual complexity, and interpersonal understanding in a series of stages. However, there is a difference between a person's reflective thought about an issue or experience and the person's action in relation to that experience. Neither interviews nor measures for developmental stage capture teachers in their own settings in which they interact with others in a complex array of pressures, expectations, and roles, seldom displaying the order which the developmental stages imply.

Developmental researchers must therefore use a 'wide angle lens' (as suggested by Selman, 1980) in surveys of human learning and development. This wide angle lens allows us to observe development in action, in an interpersonal context, as we have done with the ARCS team. We have found that the developmental stage approach provides a model for understanding the organization, principles and underlying strategies in ARCS teachers' attitudes as they are translated into action.

We began the project asking how teachers' stages of development influenced their participation on an action research team. Using the action research process of recursion, we modified this question and developed others during ongoing analysis of the data collected during the two years of the project. For example, our analysis led us to ask: When is a teacher consistent or inconsistent in his or her thinking and acting on a particular issue in a particular situation? To what extent do situational factors in the team or school context cause variability in thinking and acting? A person's functioning at positions lower than the highest he or she is capable of must be examined in relation to the demands of the situation and the interpersonal context. It seemed important to gain some sense of how stable a person's developmental understanding is across a range of issues and experiences in action research. Does the person think about each issue at roughly the same developmental position? Are there individuals with fluctuating stage patterns across issues? In what ways does gender make a difference? What happens for the individual whose stage of development is very different from others on a collaborative action research team? The cases above suggest some of the answers we found in the ARCS study and illustrate the range of patterns of reasoning and behavior exhibited by team members.

We investigated a critical area in need of study, the longitudinal, week-to-week interactions of teachers in the group situation of a collaborative action research team. The idea of teacher as researcher is new to most schools and may be a stimulating experience to interested teachers. Collaborative action research may challenge some teachers to new learning; it can overwhelm others. By observing the natural process of the collaborative action research team, we have begun to examine how we can best provide opportunities for teachers to grow within the process of action research.

Methodological Issues: Capability, Operating and Minimal Levels

In this study, we investigate how a teacher's developmental stage affected the dynamics of the collaborative action research process and how the process affected the teachers' development. The ego, moral judgment and conceptual assessments of developmental stage were used to help explain participant's thinking and functioning, and Selman's stages of interpersonal functioning were used to cross check our observations of teachers' patterns of thinking and behavior in the collaborative action research group. The findings suggest that the type and quality of collaborative action research is dependent upon the developmental stages of the teachers involved.

Our work also investigates the interaction of a teacher's developmental 'capacity' and the teacher's ability to 'function' at his or her most competent level under a range of circumstances in the context of the collaborative action research group. Developmental scoring of the Rest, Loevinger and Hunt tests is based on assigning scores to an individual's written responses to predesigned rating and ranking checklists, sentence stems, and paragraph stems. Developmental scoring of one-on-one interviews is based on assigning scores to an individual's verbal responses to predesigned interview questions and probes. The scores that result from both are called the competency or capacity score. The ARCS study additionally used the collaborative research team's meetings and transcripts as the natural real-life context in which to investigate interpersonal understanding and functioning.

There is difficulty in scoring transcripts of collaborative research team meetings for cognitive-developmental thinking and interpersonal reasoning in that analysis of the data might underestimate the individual's capacity. In order to address the questions of reliability and validity of scoring individuals' responses in team meeting interactions, this study has followed Selman's (1980) suggestion of identifying individuals' minimal, operating and capability levels. Many statements recorded in natural discussions do not necessarily represent low level understanding even if they appear to do so. These responses or ideas appear to be evidence for a person's *minimal* developmental level in interpersonal understanding and problem solving, i.e. the individual can think at least at that level. Other verbal responses seem to indicate a typical style of *operating* regardless of the person's minimum or maximum level of reasoning. If probed, an individual's response could indicate the highest level the person is capable of and thus be called the 'competency' or *capability* level (*ibid*, p. 293). A one-on-one interview may probe interpersonal reasoning to get the highest capability response, but in a team meeting discussion specific probes may not be given, and so the individual's responses do not necessarily indicate his or her capability level. However, by analyzing a series of team meeting interactions, the individuals' patterns of reasoning emerge and their operating levels over a period of time can be examined and compared.

In discussing methodological difficulties with measures of ego level, Loevinger, too, makes it clear that there is no straightforward relationship between ego level and behavior (Loevinger and Wessler, 1970). Behavior has multiple causes and is only probabilistically related to ego level. Behaviors which might characterize specific ego levels of functioning could also be found at earlier levels in more tentative or embryonic forms. Furthermore, since every individual displays behavior at more than one level 'every behavior sample must be assumed to be diverse with respect to ego level' (p. 9). This is why it is so important to consider patterns of behavior rather than single occurrences. Documentation of two years in the ARCS project has allowed the analysis of individual teachers' behavior patterns over time during the normal operation of the collaborative action research process.

Conclusion

Cognitive-Developmental Theory and Action Research

A teacher's cognitive-developmental stage perspective defines a context or meaning system through which he or she interprets and acts on issues related to the school environment and the workings of the action research team. The findings of the case histories of teachers on the team, who represented of different stages of development, suggest that the same basic structures which shape a teacher's meanings and attitudes toward change also operate in that person's conceptions and behavior in terms of group dynamics and the collaborative research process, team leadership, the role of the school Principal, and goals and perceived outcomes for the research project. In particular, at the conformist stage of development, we have documented a teacher's tendency to conform to external rather than self-evaluated standards and to have little self-awareness and little appreciation of multiple possibilities in problem-solving situations as well as in the resulting effects of the collaborative action research project. At the conscientious stage, we have documented teachers' tendency toward self-evaluated standards, intense sense of responsibility, focus on achievement, and deepening recognition of individual differences in the attitudes, interests, and abilities in others. At this stage we have also found little toleration for paradox, contradictions and ambiguities. At the individualistic transition to the autonomous stage of ego development, we documented a teacher's ability to assume multiple perspectives, utilize a wider variety of coping behaviors in response to school and team pressures, employ a broader repertoire of group process and change strategies, and be highly effective in many collaborative action research decisions because of the ability to be self-reflective, self-evaluative, and interpersonally sensitive.

Collaborative Action Research as an Intervention for Development

The ARCS collaborative research team became a temporary system in the school (Pine, 1983; Oja and Pine, 1988) that differed from the permanent system of the school in a number of significant ways: climate, norms, processes for decision-making, shared experiences, possibilities for communication, collegiality, experimentation, expectations and rewards. The newer temporary system of the collaborative action research team became self-sufficient and as such provided a positive context within which teachers could try out new patterns of thought and behavior. A school-based team cannot, however, exist in a vacuum. As part of the permanent system it has to find mediums of co-existence if the team's research results are to have an effect on the permanent system. Balancing the need for self-sufficiency in the temporary system and co-existence with the permanent system is a difficult yet primary task of the school-based collaborative research team (see Chapter 6).

Even though the collaborative action research team becomes a temporary system which can support new thinking and behavior, there is a general consistency or stability in each teacher's conceptions and attitudes, based in the stability of his or her developmental stage. At times the action research group supports new teacher attitudes and behavior; at times it challenges old familiar attitudes and behavior. Teachers' unique perceptions and abilities enable them to take on different roles and tasks according to varying needs of the action research team over time. We have found that the framework of developmental stages enhances the understanding of the context of how teachers' individual abilities are woven into the team's task, research and group process.

Knowledge that a range of stages of development exists in adulthood may help to address an issue raised by Ebbutt (1985) about the processes in action research, in particular, how new data in some action research teams becomes analyzed and integrated into the recursive process while in other teams new data stays at the level of fact finding. In Kemmis' Planner (1982), Elliott's Framework (1981) and Ebbutt's Cycles of Action Research (1985) (see Figures 1, 2 and 3) and our own Recursion Diagram (see Figure 4), new data is fed into and consequently affects the action research process. But for the team member who is thinking at concrete stages of cognitive development, the new data does not necessarily change one's mind or thinking about an issue, rather it remains at the level of fact finding, and thus limits the recursion process. At the more abstract, reflective stages of cognitive development, new data does get analyzed and consequently affects change throughout the action research process. An action research project cannot automatically assume that participants have attained high conceptual levels and abstract thought. Our research suggests that efforts need to be made to aid adults in the transition from concrete to abstract modes of thought. In some contexts, like the collaborative action research team, an appropriate goal would be to foster development beyond formal operations as in a stage of problem-finding (Arlin, 1975), to foster a parallel development of divergent, dialectical thought (Riegel, 1973; Basseches, 1984), and to investigate the alternative path of women's intellectual development (Belenky, Clinchy, Goldberger and Tarule, 1986).

In the context of school settings, the ability to clarify instructional problems, to determine alternative solutions, and to plan new courses of action all demand abstract thinking. It appears that teachers who possess such problem-solving skills, and who can judge the consequences of alternative actions, are more effective in meeting the needs of others. Likewise, educators who have not developed such abstract thinking ability are limited in discovering alternative solutions or in defining new courses of action, both of which are important in collaborative action research.

The collaborative action research team operating as a temporary system within the more permanent system of the school can provide the general *supports and challenges* needed for individual teacher growth. First, it gives teachers the opportunity to apply new learning and to examine and reflect on experiences in team meetings, at conferences, and in regular entries in logs or journals. Second, it allows teachers to try out more complex roles and responsibilities which focus on learning to take more fully the perspective of others. Third, ongoing on-site collaboration, supervising, advising and consulting among teachers and university researchers in action research provides a supportive environment within which teachers can deal with the times of cognitive conflict in the challenges of new learning and experience. These focus points for development were originally discussed in Oja (1980a) as necessary for continued adult development within school staff development opportunities.

Our work with teachers suggests that the process of collaborative action research in schools is both a vehicle for stimulating adult cognitive development and a process for linking theory with practice. According to the research of Kohlberg and Turiel (1971) the stimulus for helping people move into higher stages of abstract reasoning comes primarily from the interaction with others who are functioning at more advanced stages. The assumption is that at more advanced stages, people can promote the conditions, set the environment, offer the support, and provide the probing questions or ideas to stimulate and challenge the thinking of those at other stages. The research among pre-service and in-service teachers, however, suggests that the higher abstract conceptual thinkers either leave teaching or regress to operating at lower cognitive stages within the confines of the school context, while those at lower levels do not increase their abstract thinking ability (Kohlberg, 1971; Harvey, 1970; Higgins, 1983).

Kohlberg (1984) discussed the necessary conditions to promote an upward shift to post conventional, principled moral stages. 'Principled moral judgment (Stage 5)', he wrote, 'is a genuine adulthood stage based on personal life experience, first of a relativistic questioning, and subsequently of personal experience of responsibility and its conflicts' (p. 480). 'Personal experiences of choice involving questioning and commitment, in some sort of integration with stimulation of cognitive-moral reflection, seem required for movement from conventional to principled thought' (p. 493).

Collaborative action research team discussions can provide the kind of environment which will encourage adult development in schools. These discussions frequently draw on teachers' deeply held values about students, teaching, and curriculum and have a moral/ ethical dimension which encourages teachers to think in more encompassing ways. Previous studies indicate that moral judgment development can be fostered in teachers with the use of certain developmental education strategies (Oja and Sprinthall, 1978; Oja, 1980b, Sprinthall and Thies-Sprinthall, 1983). Collaborative action research can be a teacher development strategy even as it contributes to improved theory and practice in the schools if: participants on the collaborative action research team represent diverse stages of development; they experience choice, questioning, commitment and cognitive reflection; the team focuses on issues which relate to teachers' deeply held values and perceptions of the teaching-learning-schooling process; and facilitators on the team recognize developmental characteristics and provide the support and the activities which promote individual and group development.

5
Collaboration: Roles and Leadership

Introduction

Just as the group and research processes of an action research team change over time, so do the roles played by the individual participants on the team. On the ARCS team, individuals' roles developed over the two years of the project, reflecting shifting research needs and patterns of group interaction and teachers' changing perceptions of themselves as researchers. Team members themselves noted the process:

George: I think that team members tried to share information, especially where they had individual expertise. ... Each individual seemed to feel responsible to offer his or her input, especially where it might be unique. ... Whenever an aspect ... came up that one or another group member was especially familiar with then that group member would somewhat take charge of that phase of the discussion. (interview, 12/81)

Because action research draws on participants' abilities and perspectives, each person's role or function changes as the group works through interpersonal and research tasks. Having examined individual team members' developmental differences in Chapter 4, we now analyze how those differences interact with the group and research processes.

A key role in the group, noted both in group dynamics and action research literature, is that of the leader. Because action research demands a democratic group process which allows all voices to be heard, a leader in action research must be a facilitator who can empower other participants. Outside researchers often provide group leadership in action research, despite the fact that perceived differences in power and status between outside researchers and teachers may influence the group and research process. An important group task therefore involves building trust and establishing roles to respond to these differences.

Although much previous work in action research suggests that leadership falls to one person in the group, some group dynamics theory describes a distribution of leadership functions among group members. Given the notion of parity which guides collaborative action research, it seems likely that any team member can assume leadership when he or she has the confidence, skill, and knowledge to do so. Thus, leadership may shift over time along with other roles; it is not the sole domain of the outside researcher, although he or she may have special tasks to fulfill.

This chapter examines the roles individuals may take on an action research team, focusing particularly on the issue of leadership. It begins with an analysis of roles taken by participants in problem solving groups and examines group leadership as it is described in prior studies of group dynamics, adult development, and action research. The ARCS project is used to illustrate both the roles taken by group members and the concept of developmental leadership in collaborative action research. Such an analysis allows us to see the interplay between the individual and the group: how they affect one another, and how their interaction affects individual satisfaction and growth and the group's effectiveness in reaching its goals.

Roles: An Overview

In theories of group interaction, the group's task and interpersonal interactions are generally discussed in terms of individuals' roles in the group. In the process of group interaction, differences among group members may arise in the areas of power, status, and function. These differences stabilize into generalizations about each individual's actions which are based on the person's past activity and serve as expectations for his or her future behavior. In every act, the individual may reconfirm the expectations of others about his or her position or deviate from it in a way which modifies the position or role in the group (Bales, 1951; Hare, 1976).

Several theories of group dynamics define roles in terms of function rather than power or status, describing roles as 'clusters of norms providing for a division of labor or specialization of functions among the members of the group' (Thibaut and Kelly, 1986, p. 148). A member's role thus consists of a number of functions or behaviors which in some way serve the group. Roles may fulfill task or maintenance functions. Task functions lead toward goal achievement and include initiating group action, predicting outcomes for various actions, training group members with needed behaviors, keeping members' attention on the goals, clarifying issues, evaluating work done, making expert information available, and fending off interference from the environment. Maintenance functions include keeping interpersonal relations pleasant, arbitrating disputes, providing encouragement, giving minorities a chance to be heard, stimulating self direction, and increasing interdependence among group members (Cartwright and Zander, 1968; Leary, Robertson and Barnes, 1986; Schein, 1969; Thibaut and Kelly, 1986). Because individuals at lower stages of development tend to have stronger goal (task) orientations while those at higher stages are more comfortable with a process (maintenance) orientation, it is important to have people with a variety of developmental stages on an action research team. A team without some members at higher developmental stages may begin to move along on its tasks but experience conflict and setbacks if no one can assume group maintenance functions.

Any given function may be served by several different behaviors, for example, encouragement may be provided by direct approval or by showing the group how their work compares to others. Conversely, a particular behavior, such as providing expert information, may serve a useful function at some times but not at others. Also, one action may serve both task and maintenance functions — an individual's enthusiasm for a task may encourage the group (maintenance) *and* initiate group action (task) — or an action may serve one function at the expense of the other (for example, the eager member spurs the group on in ways that lead to project success but also conflict among team members; thus the goal may be achieved but the group may suffer).

Individuals in the group may assume both task and maintenance functions or they may specialize in one set of functions. Thibaut and Kelly (1986) suggest that a group may have different people serve as task and maintenance 'specialists' because the functions may require different abilities and/or be incompatible. For example, a task specialist may have to keep members at work on the task while the maintenance specialist provides the reassurance that keeps group members content. Yet Bonner (1959) points out that an individual may assume a variety of roles which, together, create a pattern of behavior:

The distinct character of individual roles is normally obscured by their strong tendency to form networks of interrelated roles. They act in sets or patterns. The network conceals their strongly individual nature. The sets or patterns themselves, furthermore, tend toward individuality; they are characteristic of the person. We thus come to identify a person, not by a single or isolated role, but by the pattern in which the roles are integrated. (pp. 384–5)

To some extent, the nature of the group, its goals, and the environment within which it operates all help determine which functions are needed when and who will perform them (Leary, Robertson and Barnes, 1986). 'The specific requirements of the group's tasks demand that members possess certain skills in order to serve the appropriate functions. If the task changes, different behaviors are required, and the same person may or may not be able to perform in the new way' (Cartwright and Zander, 1968, p. 306). Thus group members may adopt roles that continue over the life of the group or their roles may shift to meet the group's interpersonal and task demands.

Group dynamics theory explains that roles or functions should correspond to the abilities of the individuals who perform them and that the different roles each individual assumes should be compatible if he or she is to be effective. The organization of roles and functions in a group may, however, be affected by group members' pre-existing expectations and perceptions of natural patterns or combinations of functions. Typical formations borrowed by groups include family or classroom role organizations (Thibaut and Kelly, 1986). These accepted role patterns, like the adopted status and power structures, influence group norms and decision-making processes. The demands of the situation and the interpersonal context also help to explain discrepancies in participants' developmental capacity to understand the need for certain roles and their ability to perform the tasks required to fulfill those roles (see Chapter 4). Thus, both group dynamics theory and theories of adult development provide insight into the evolution of an individual's role on an action research team.

Roles in Action Research: ARCS

One way to differentiate team members' contributions to action research is to define them as being primarily task or maintenance related. Some team members may assume task roles, initiating and implementing important elements of the research project. Others may provide maintenance functions, supporting other team members and facilitating communication within the group and between the group and the rest of the community. Although most people on an action research team will take on a combination of task and maintenance roles, at certain points in the process we may see individuals fulfilling specific functions in the group. Individual roles will change during the project as the team faces the different interpersonal and task demands described in the earlier analysis of phases (see Chapter 3).

During the first phase of the ARCS project, team members all initiated, clarified and added to the statements of others, and summarized when they felt they had something to contribute. The school context and problem identification discussions in this phase allowed each team member to support and challenge one another, move the discussion along, or provide new information. Because the task remained undefined in phase 1, so did specific roles. As a result, team members contributed fairly equally, fulfilling similar functions in the group while providing different perspectives. George noted, 'Everyone seems to fill voids created by the other ... kind of like we complete the jigsaw puzzle' (interview, 12/81).

As the team moved through its other four phases, individuals began to assume more differentiated positions in the group based on the skills each brought to the research task and group process. Developmental stage capabilities also influenced when and how each individual became involved in fulfilling certain roles. Some team members assumed task-oriented roles, identifying and carrying out research tasks; others assumed maintenance roles, facilitating communication and providing clarification of the team's purpose; and some team members carried out both sets of functions. Team members noted that change in roles depended on individual familiarity and ease with shifting task demands.

John: I think that changes occurred with each of us as we went along, and it was probably due to our growth in the project — whether we felt more comfortable then we felt we could contribute more. (interview, 6/83)

Brooks: I know people have changed, but also it depends on the task that we're doing, really, like who feels comfortable with it and who has the time and who gets involved with a certain aspect of the research. (interview, 12/82)

Assumption of roles therefore depended on a combination of factors including individuals' skill and knowledge, their developmental concerns and needs, and the demands of the research in each phase.

Two ARCS team members' experiences illustrate how individual roles in a group change over time. Although one, Brooks, primarily took on task functions in the group and the other, John, assumed more of a maintenance role, their experiences show how each fulfilled some of both kinds of roles while incorporating personal insights, skills, and needs into the process. It is not surprising that Brooks and John, both at the same stage of development, provide good examples of the range of roles taken by participants on an action research team. As conscientious stage teachers they had confidence in themselves and their ability to act within the system and a willingness to take on the new challenges and tasks offered by the ARCS project. Their stories suggest the complexity of a group member's role and the relationship between role, group process, and research task.

Brooks

During the first two phases of the project, Brooks participated in two ways. In discussions of school context concerns, she tended to contribute general ideas accompanied by personal anecdotes from her recent experience. Brooks' general comments often seemed to provide her with a vehicle for sharing personal experiences, a process which allowed her to work through the particular stresses and concerns she was feeling (see Chapter 2). Brooks found that participation on the team helped her release and channel some of the anger and frustration she accumulated during the school day.

Brooks also made some attempts to focus the team on the research project during these first two phases. On several occasions she repeated the idea that she was 'task oriented' (documentation, 28 October) and suggested that the team think about where it was going. She also called the team's attention to ideas presented in articles provided by the university researcher, such as the importance of finding a research problem to which everyone would be committed. Her suggestions and comments were accepted but not often used at this point in the project, the result of the team's unreadiness to confront its task and Brooks' lack of dominance in the group.

A shift occurred in Brooks' behavior and position in team meetings from phase 2 to phase 3. She initiated, to a large extent, the team's concentration on its research question and design in phase 3 by bringing some information on null hypothesis testing to a meeting in March of the first year. Throughout phase 3 she tended to control team discussions, asking questions, initiating topics, and bringing the group back on task. During a team meeting in May, for example, the university researcher wrote the agenda and asked if there was anything to add. Brooks replied, 'That's a lot — okay, let's get started.' During several meetings at this time she also asked questions to introduce new tasks or ideas, the pattern initiated by the university researcher in phase 1.

As a result of her control over the team's process at this point, Brooks also directed the research project. Teacher morale was one possible research problem discussed by the team in April and May of year one. Brooks showed special interest in this area, partly because of her personal frustrations with teaching. She did some outside reading on the topic and spoke with a professor at the University of New Hampshire who had done research on teacher burnout. Her strong interest in the issue motivated her to encourage the team to investigate teacher morale. Her leadership in the research topic and group process came at a time when the team needed a focus. As a result, her impetus to move forward on the issue of teacher morale carried the team through the clarification of its research question and design and into the implementation of data collection procedures in phases 3 and 4.

Brooks saw her increased participation and control during this phase of the project as the result of her familiarity with research. A greater knowledge base seemed to give her the self-confidence and the recognition from others needed to direct the project at this point.

Brooks: When we were trying to hammer out what kind of research design, I felt more comfortable with that having had that as part of my educational experience. ... Where it was seen as railroading from other people's standpoint I sort of felt at times like ... there's a decision to be made, let's get on with the show. Here's the information, okay, let's make a decision. (interview, 6/83)

At the beginning of phase 4, Brooks continued to be more directive during team meetings, explaining what needed to be done and getting the team to focus on agenda items and research tasks. Her task orientation and position in the group contributed to the increasing tension between Brooks and Ted which resulted in the confrontation described in Chapter 3. Even here, Brooks controlled the interaction, choosing to initiate the argument when Ted reentered the room and effectively ending it by returning to a specific research task. Although the confrontation was a maintenance or process-oriented event, it clearly arose from Brooks' task orientation and her involvement in the research project. At this time, she was less concerned with opening communication in the group than with completing necessary research tasks.

Brooks began to move out of a task leadership position in the group during the middle and end of phase 4, partly as a result of the stress she felt from teaching but partly because the team was moving into data analysis and presentation of results, areas in which she felt less proficient. In late November and December of year two, Brooks almost left or did leave three meetings early, saying she was tired and unable to work. During phase 5, she frequently mentioned her exhaustion, sometimes using it to explain why she had not completed a task she had agreed to do. Other team members provided less support for Brooks' personal issues raised during team meetings in phase 5. Her comments about having had a bad day or feeling burned out or unwell elicited fewer responses from team members as they concentrated on data analysis and report writing. When such statements were unacknowledged, Brooks tended to involve herself in the task at hand, often shifting from a negative, somewhat self-centered mood at the beginning of a meeting to a more positive, task-oriented perspective by the meeting's end.

Brooks herself noticed the shift in her position in the group over time:

> I think that from my own standpoint there were times when I felt more on the inside and as a driving force and there were times when I backed down and felt more on the outside, felt more like wherever the group goes I'm going with them but I'm not directing and I'm not active but I'm there as a part of the group and supportive. (interview, 6/83)

She saw herself in this less active role during the last phase of the project:

> I felt that it sort of fizzled a little bit ... in terms of my feeling in control of what I was putting into the group. I felt that I just didn't have much to give. ... I felt that I was too distracted by what I was doing in my class, all of the other things that were evolving around the end of the school year. (interview, 6/83)

Despite her less prominent position in the group during the second half of year two, Brooks finished the project feeling that she had benefited from it. Her roles in the project and the use she made of team meetings contributed to her perception that the experience was valuable to her personal and professional development as a classroom teacher.

Brooks' experience was that of a conscientious stage group member who used her prior knowledge of research and her personal and professional interest in teacher morale to help the group proceed with its research project, especially during the middle phases of the project. She did perform some maintenance functions, such as soliciting the reactions of other team members to her idea of investigating teacher morale and scheduling, but her actions were primarily task-oriented. Brooks also used the group process and two-year project as a vehicle for her own self-exploration, drawing on the support and encouragement provided by other group members. Both her task role and her use of the team as a personal sounding board stem in part from Brooks' transition from the conscientious to an individualistic stage of development. Initially, Brooks tried to differentiate her needs from those of the group, but she often submerged herself in the group's work. In her gradual transition to the individualistic stage, she began to develop a sense of personal authority and control which allowed her to see herself as working within and yet autonomous from the group and the school. Looking only at the role she played in terms of task and maintenance functions may be somewhat limiting; we must see what she took from as well as what she contributed to the group to get a complete view of the group process.

John

John himself described his role during the first two phases of the project: 'As far as my role's concerned, I just like to talk and discuss, so that's what I do' (interview, 12/81). John, also at the conscientious stage, willingly participated in school context and problem identification discussions and survey preparation, administration and analysis during the first five months of the project. He freely discussed his views of school issues from the vantage point of an eleven-year veteran of the junior high school and occasionally initiated topics of interest. In his log, John wrote short position papers on school issues which concerned him (such as 'Junior high school: Junior to what?') and shared these writings with other teachers and administrators in the school.

John later claimed that he was confused about the team's purpose and the part he would play in it during the first two phases of the project, although his discomfort was not apparent during team meetings. In February of year one, he offered to do a brief history of the school documenting changes which had occurred in the last ten years. The history would provide a basis for whatever research project the team chose and would clarify much of what they had discussed over the past few months. John saw the school history as useful to the team even if it did not immediately contribute to their project goals. For John, doing the history marked his real entrance into the group process.

> I mostly did that because I felt I should be doing something, and that part I knew ... It was mostly my way of doing something besides just comments at meetings. (interview, 5/82)

> I got all the way up to February before I felt I was part of the team. I was there, I was doing some logs, I was listening to other people, and I had no feeling of belonging to that group, because although I would say things I just felt I wasn't contributing. And then I said to Sharon, I think I'm going to write a history ... and then I felt like I was part of things. (presentation at the University of New Hampshire, 5/83)

Thus, early on, John described tasks he assumed in terms of group process; he took on the historical description not necessarily to promote the research project (at least not directly) but to engage himself in the group. Given his maintenance approach, he tended to assume tasks which helped to promote group interaction and communication, just as Brooks' task approach led her to address only those maintenance functions which directly affected completion of the research project.

During discussions of research design and methodology in phase 3, John listened to others and asked questions about research procedures. On several occasions, he suggested that the group postpone a decision about the research, saying he needed time to digest all of the new ideas presented at a meeting. This phase appeared to be one in which John gained a greater understanding of research in general and the team's particular project. His learning in this phase allowed him to feel more comfortable with the project and to assume a more active role in phases 4 and 5, although at the end of year one he continued to see his activity in terms of maintenance or support:

> I think I'll probably be mostly backing people up who are actually writing the testing material that we're going to use, helping them more. Not that I'm going to be in the forefront

developing stuff, but mostly helping people who are developing stuff. (interview, 5/82)

John provided Brooks with support in phase 3 and throughout the project. They frequently discussed the project, teaching, and the school (their rooms were across the hall from each other), and their shared perspectives and opinions, influenced by a common stage of development, often carried over into team meetings. In phase 3, John supported Brooks' direction of the research topic and design. At one meeting, for example, John agreed that the team should investigate teacher morale as measured by the Maslach Burnout Inventory (MBI). He then said to Brooks, 'And now do you want to explain why we have to go with evaluation research?' (documentation, 5 May 1982). In other phases John provided support for Brooks by empathizing with the difficulties she had as a special needs reading teacher. He noted, for example, that her class was an 'exceptional group of students' (documentation, 27 October 1982) and pointed out to Ted that Brooks' situation was more stressful because she had no opportunities to meet with other teachers (documentation, 10 November 1982). John's support both during and outside of team meetings gave Brooks some of the recognition she needed to stay with the project and to value it as a positive experience.

John's growth in understanding, confidence and sense of having contributed to the group during year one culminated in his presentation at the National Staff Development Council conference early in year two. John experienced the conference as a validation of what he and others had done, and he brought back from it a more all-encompassing vision of the team's research project. As a result of his broadened perspective and increased confidence about himself as a researcher, John assumed a more directive role in the group in the last two phases. His direction continued to be more maintenance than task-oriented, often focusing on communication between group members and between the group and the school or school system. He described his behavior on the team in years one and two in terms of group interaction and the research process:

I think that my purpose on the Committee is representing lots of people, getting their view across to other members. ... Also, I think that I see some of the long term things that we are doing and can kind of push in that direction. (interview, 12/82)

I was probably more outspoken in the second year than I was in the first year. ... I thought, well fine, nobody else seems to know what's going on so I'll say what I want. ... In the second year it didn't bother me to express an opinion because sometimes I could express an opinion and nobody else had thought of that and therefore it was okay because it stimulated ... a good discussion. (interview, 6/83)

Because he perceived that he lacked skills in data analysis and writing, John's leadership in year two did not consist of identifying and carrying out specific tasks. Instead, John provided the 'bigger picture' of the project, often, for example, answering George's and Ted's questions in phase 4 about the value of the project and the use of particular data collection tools. He also frequently established processes for carrying out tasks during team meetings. In one team meeting, for example, he took computer printouts from George, gave them to Brooks to identify, looked them over, and passed them to the university researcher to analyze. He contributed his analysis of the data whenever he felt it was appropriate, often speaking from his perspective as veteran teacher.

John also served as the team's liaison to the school and school system administration in year two. He noted that as a result of participating in the group he had become more active in the school, in part because he had taken on this liaison position. This role began in phase 1, when John shared his logs with other school colleagues, but became more formalized in phase 4 when he initiated a meeting to discuss the project with the Assistant Superintendent and subsequently presented a description of the project at a system-wide staff development meeting. Because of his familiarity with the school and system and his willingness to carry out this role, John became the team's spokesperson in the school. Although he resisted input from the Principal on the final report, John ultimately volunteered to invite the Principal to a meeting to discuss the team's findings and conclusions.

John's increased feelings of competence and skill, his process leadership in year two, and his position as team representative at conferences and in the school and system all contributed to his strong feelings of project ownership and his positive valuing of the project. At the end of the two years he had plans for continuing to use pieces of the project (documentation, teacher collaboration) in several ways. He also planned to use his new skills to try to change aspects of the school which concerned him and to write about teachers doing research.

John's experience illustrates a maintenance role on this team, although he sometimes carried out task functions. It is important to note that in this role, John supported both individuals and the group research process. A maintenance role requires more than empathetic support; it demands that the individual facilitate the group process in ways which contribute to the success of the research project as well as to positive feelings for individual group members. John's role assumption also reflects his developmental stage. John, like Brooks, is in a conscientious stage of development, which accounts for his confidence in interacting with others in the school and system and his willingness to help the team establish working patterns and norms.

Leadership

Theorists in the area of group dynamics agree that leadership is one of the most problematic areas in their field (Bonner, 1959; Cartwright and Zander, 1968; Crosbie, 1975; Richardson and Piper, 1986; Thibaut and Kelly, 1986). Research in this area sometimes has difficulty separating value assumptions about what leadership ought to be from research into what kinds of leadership promote certain group outcomes. Empirical studies of leadership in small groups often provide inconclusive or conflicting results. Given these theoretical uncertainties, group dynamics theorists note that any definition of leadership must consider the context within which it occurs:

> ... it is apparent that the nature of leadership behavior chosen for the performance of group functions will be influenced by situational factors both inside and outside the group. (Cartwright and Zander, 1968, p. 306)

Some of these factors include the group's channels of communication, group members' geographical location and possession of resources, the nature of the group task, and individual group members' feelings of worth, acceptance and expertise (*ibid*). In describing a situational leadership approach, Hersey and Blanchard (1982) explain the need for a match between a leader's actions and the circumstances within which they occur.

There are several approaches to the study of leadership. The 'great man' or trait approach, prevalent in the 1930s and 1940s, tried to identify the physical, intellectual, and personality traits of those who were effective leaders (Bonner, 1959; Cartwright and Zander, 1968; Crosbie, 1975; Hare, 1976). Researchers used a range of criteria to define effectiveness, including high morale, high productivity, popularity, egalitarianism, and authoritarianism (Cartwright and Zander, 1968). Not surprisingly, later researchers found this approach inadequate; it was difficult to identify consistent leadership traits across the studies, and most of the so-called leadership traits appeared in group members who were not designated as leaders.

More recently, work has focused on the behavior of leaders. This functional approach parallels the analysis of roles provided earlier in this chapter and is the most useful way of analyzing leadership in an action research group. According to this approach, the leader is a group member who shares with others the responsibility for moving the group toward its goal.

> The group leader does not primarily control others but initiates acts that cause others to perform certain acts that result in satisfaction to the group as a whole. He leads others in the sense that, in playing his roles, he enables others to play theirs, so that together they achieve a common goal. (Bonner, 1959, p. 173)

The functional approach sees the leader as a 'super' group member, one who performs many of the task and maintenance functions required by the group and/or enables other group members to do so.

> More specifically, leadership consists of such actions by group members as those which aid in setting group goals, moving the group toward its goals, improving the quality of the interactions among the members, building the cohesiveness of the group, and making resources available to the group. In principle, leadership may be performed by one or many members of the group. (Cartwright and Zander, 1968, p. 304)

Theories of group effectiveness tend to emphasize the value of a democratic group process in which all group members share responsibility for the organization, maintenance and productivity of the group. This self-determined distribution of functions is believed to be more flexible, allowing greater participation, satisfaction, and productivity within the group (Bonner, 1959; Cartwright and Zander, 1968; Hare, 1976). The question then arises: Is democratic leadership shared by all group members, or does a democratic process require or benefit from a single leader?

> In some groups, the members are expected to take over as much of the responsibility for leadership functions as condi-

tions will allow. At the other extreme, groups may concentrate all leadership functions in one person and punish any member who appears to want to usurp any of these functions. (Cartwright and Zander, 1968, p. 313)

Although arguments exist to support the effectiveness of leadership that is concentrated in one person and leadership that is distributed across the group, there is little empirical evidence in group dynamics literature that either form is consistently better (Cartwright and Zander, 1968; Richardson and Piper, 1986; Thibaut and Kelly, 1986). A more inclusive definition of democratic leadership might, therefore, include the assumption of leadership functions by any and all group members as well as the reservation of certain organizational, symbolic, task and maintenance functions to a particular leader when necessary to promote the group's goal. This tentative balance would capitalize on group members' abilities, help them remain motivated and involved in the group's work, and yet ensure group cohesion and progress if and when no group member (other than the leader) can assume functions necessary for progress.

A developmental perspective suggests that the leader will consider both the individual's stage of development and the situation when choosing the most effective actions for stimulating the group and research processes. Oja has described a developmental approach to teacher education (Oja and Sprinthall, 1978; Glassberg and Oja, 1981), staff development (Oja, 1980a), collaborative action research (Oja and Ham, 1984) and supervision (Oja and Ham, 1987) in which the leader takes a developmental perspective and the goal is to provide support and challenge for continuing adult development.

Those who describe effective leadership in action research (for example, Hord, 1981) imply a form of developmental, democratic leadership. To some extent, collaborative action research groups tend to espouse the idea that leadership is a matter of degree rather than a distinct category: 'Any (and every) member of the group can be considered as exhibiting leadership insofar as he exercises power effectively, performs various functions, promotes organization along functional lines, or has symbolic value' (Thibaut and Kelly, 1986, p. 289). As suggested, this definition of leadership parallels notions of collaboration and parity that characterize action research. And yet, an outside researcher or school administrator may play an important, distinctive role as a group leader in an action research project (Carr and Kemmis, 1986; Ebbutt, 1985; Threadgold, 1985). The rest of this chapter will use the ARCS project to illustrate first the democratic, distributed nature of leadership among team members in action research and then the unique developmental leadership role of the outside researcher.

Leadership in Action Research: ARCS

The descriptions of Brooks and John provided earlier in this chapter show that group leadership on the ARCS team emerged as a role carried out by whoever had the confidence, knowledge or skills most useful to the team at any given time during the two years of the project. For example, Brooks provided task leadership, especially in phases 3 and 4, and John fulfilled maintenance (and some task) leadership functions, especially in year two. Team members themselves saw leadership as shared and dependent on the needs of the group and the project.

Jack: I think pretty near everyone within the group were leaders at one time or another depending on the particular chore or activity that they felt comfortable with. (interview, 12/82)

Ted: I think people become the leader because they just picked up the ball and ran with it. (interview, 6/83)

It is interesting to note that, until the team began to clarify its task and goals late in phase 2, most leadership functions were shared by Jack, a team member who was part-time teacher and part-time administrator, and the university researcher. Group dynamics theories explain that external factors, including status, power, and prior experience may influence group leadership (Hambroff *et al*, 1984). The university researcher maintained the role of developmental leader throughout the project, but Jack's authority waned as the group task and process demanded leadership functions which he was unable to serve. External forces may therefore diminish as the group establishes norms and behaviors focused on its project goals. Because we have described the leadership functions filled by Brooks and John, we will now examine Jack's case, in which leadership took a very different form. We then provide a brief comparison of the roles assumed by Ted and George which illustrates how teachers at different stages of development approach leadership and how the assumption of leadership affects participants' experience of the project.

Jack

Jack was in the unique position on the team of being both a teacher and an administrator (house coordinator) in the school. As a result, he faced the distrust of some team members and felt he had to let his colleagues know that he shared their concerns and merited their trust: 'I talked to them and I told everybody, I'm a teacher number one first, my contract and my feelings and all' (interview, 12/81).

Jack's position and his many years of experience at the school allowed him to take on several leadership functions during the first two phases of the project. He may have assumed these tasks because he was comfortable in a position of authority in relation to a group of teachers. Other team members may have accorded leadership to him as a result of his status and access to information outside the group. For example, Ted, at the self aware stage, perceived of Jack as the leader at the beginning of the project and deferred to his authority.

Ted: Jack's personality, I think — he's outgoing, he's been here a long time, he was house coordinator, Assistant Principal. I mean, I guess he's down to earth, people just accepted it. He was the highest ranking member there I guess. ... It just evolved (from his) being house coordinator. I don't know if he would have been leader through the thing, but I think at the beginning this was his role. (interview, 6/83)

Others, Brooks, for example, may have deferred to Jack because she did not completely trust him. Tacit acceptance of Jack's assumed leadership during the first two phases of the project allowed Brooks and others to wait and see how Jack might use the team as an administrator. They could then decide how they wanted to act and interact on the team.

As leader, Jack often provided the team with information available to him as a school administrator. During discussions of the school context and possible research problems, questions, and designs, Jack offered his 'insider's' knowledge about the new Principal, forthcoming additions of department chairpersons and advanced English and math classes, changes in the guidance department and scheduling changes planned for the coming year. Because he had access to otherwise unavailable information, other team members often accepted his opinion or point of view without question. His position in the school coupled with his conformist stage of development and authoritative style meant that he did not readily accept challenges, and teachers knew this. When asked if he felt his position in the school allowed him to bring a different perspective to the group, Jack responded,

> Yeah, I see me as adding a different perspective ... I feel that I can possibly relate some of these other things to the group as to how it might affect the total running of the school ... seen from the office aspect. (interview, 12/81)

In phase 2, Jack took on the task of collating the results of the Staff Opinion Survey and presenting them to the team. Carrying out this task seemed to increase Jack's perception of himself as the team's task leader although he was unable to go further to analyze the data beyond the summary tallies he presented to the group. Throughout phase 2 he questioned the team about what they would do next and where they were headed, often repeating the phrase, 'What is the question?' He provided few answers to his own questions, believing that by being a 'devil's advocate' (interview, 12/82) he could move the team along. He felt he served as the team's leader in challenging or testing the power of the university researcher, described as an aspect of phase 2. Although not all team members agreed with Jack's position or approach in this interaction, he may have represented, or believed he represented, their feelings about the university researcher's role on the team.

As the team began to focus on its research question and design in phase 3, Jack exerted less control over the team. He himself noted that he knew little about research, and as the team became more research oriented he participated somewhat less and was no longer seen as an authority by others. Because he left the team in September of year two, Jack's role on the team cannot be followed beyond phase 3. In the first year, however, his role appeared to stem from his status and access to information outside the team and his belief that the leader is someone who has more information (see Chapter 4). When his insider's status became less useful to the team and the research and analysis became more complex, leadership shifted from Jack to those with other skills and insights required by the team's growing emphasis on the research task.

Ted and George: A Comparison

Individuals' assumption of leadership functions will influence their perception of the group process, the research task, and the value of the project. Only one team member, Ted, did not assume a leadership position at some point during the two-year project. He was, in fact, only peripherally involved in much of the team's work, although he attended most of the meetings. Throughout the project, the only research tasks Ted performed were those carried out by all team members: administering surveys, interviewing colleagues, and writing up a section of the research proposal. When asked about his part in the project, Ted noted that he contributed 'ideas and suggestions' and enthusiasm. As explained in Chapter 4, Ted could conceptualize a range of abstract issues but was often unable to act on his ideas. His minimal involvement in the research task created problems in the group's interaction and resulted in Ted feeling less positive than other team members about the value of the project for himself and the school.

George assumed a variety of research tasks (such as drafting the initial school survey) during the first year of the project, but he remained somewhat reserved. He noted that his participation was low key,

> ...because other people began to be more confident and seemed to understand better what the goals were and what they contributed in relation to the goals, so that contributions on my part weren't needed. (interview, 5/82)

In part because of his lack of involvement and ownership in the project, in phase 4 George questioned the validity of the project and whether or not he would stay with it. Resolution of his concerns and commitment to the project allowed George to emerge in phase 5 as the task leader, creating computer programs for data analysis and pushing the team to outline and begin work on its final report. He also fulfilled maintenance functions for the group, helping team members focus on the value of the research experience for themselves and for others interested in action research as they moved further away from their initial goal of creating change in their own school. Like John and Brooks, George emerged from the two years with very positive feelings about the research project and group process, and he continued to work on and present the group's findings after the team had officially disbanded.

In this project, it was teachers at the later stages of development (conscientious and above) who assumed effective leadership roles as the project progressed. In particular, George, at the individualistic stage, had a cognitively complex and abstract world view, more empathy and social understanding, and a higher tolerance for diversity and ambiguity which allowed him to provide group leadership toward the end of the project. When he resolved his concerns about the project, he did so in a dialectical way, integrating his awareness that the Principal had not provided significant support and that the project would probably not have an impact on the school with the positive views that other teachers' feelings about the school had been expressed and documented and that team members themselves would benefit both personally and professionally from their experience.

A comparison of Ted's and George's experiences on the team suggests that taking on leadership functions indicates a commitment to the group that results in positive feelings about the project and one's own participation in it. A group member who is unwilling or unable to take on some responsibility for helping the group achieve its goal will not experience the personal or professional growth and satisfaction usually expected from action research. Followers may gain some insights, but leaders appear to engage in the planning, acting, and reflecting that lead to a greater understanding of themselves as practitioners.

The University Researcher as Leader

Recent reports and analyses of action research have begun to examine the role of the 'outsider' in an action research project. Many of these studies note the problems inherent in having an outside researcher work with teachers. First, teachers and researchers may use different languages, focus on different problems, and may therefore have trouble communicating (Cummings and Hustler, 1986; Threadgold, 1985). Second, outsiders (particularly those from the university) tend to have higher status which can lead to intimidation or resentment. This may limit the group's ability to address necessary interpersonal and task demands (Cassidy, 1986; Threadgold, 1985). Finally, because of their greater knowledge of research, their status, and the research framework they may bring to the project, outside researchers may have too much influence on what issues the group addresses, how they collect, analyze, and reflect on their data, and how their findings are used and reported (Carr and Kemmis, 1986). An outside researcher may, therefore, work against the democratic processes which lead to the exploration of teachers' theory and practice.

Despite these problems, many reports of action research see an outsider as an essential facilitator of the process and method, someone who serves many of the task and maintenance functions of leadership outlined in the literature of group dynamics. Hustler, Cassidy and Cuff (1986) write that 'some form of dialogue with an "outsider" is not only desirable for action research, but almost one of its defining characteristics' (p. 15). They and others see the outsider as performing several key tasks in action research. First, the outside researcher — or an in-school person who plays a similar role — activates the process. Ebbutt (1985) notes that educational institutions lack a 'collective dynamic' or an imperative for change. Someone must take the responsibility to initiate change, activate the cycles of planning, acting and reflecting. Activation may require persuading teachers to become involved (Cassidy, 1986); asking questions which challenge the existing frameworks or theories that shape teachers' views and actions (Desforges, Cockburn and Bennett, 1986); and convening meetings to begin the group process (Ebbutt, 1985). Teachers are busy with their daily tasks; they are also fairly comfortable within established patterns of thinking and behaving in their schools and classrooms. An outsider can provide the impetus, the energy, and the initial framework to question what is.

Second, the outside researcher may bring a variety of resources to the action research project that would not otherwise be available to the participants. These resources include time, specialized knowledge of research methods, and theoretical knowledge, which, if well-used, can support teachers' developing understanding of their own practice (Elliott, 1985; Grundy and Kemmis, 1982; Nixon, 1981). Elliott explains:

> One of the facilitator's roles is to mediate theoretical resources in a way which enhances rather than constrains teachers' capacities to develop their own theoretical understandings. So long as the introduction of external ideas constitutes a support rather than a substitute for teachers' own thinking, it can speed up the process of aims clarification and consequently the process of problem identification, analysis, and the formulation of strategic action. Given this supportive rather than controlling context, the introduction of external ideas also gives teachers greater opportunities for making original contributions to the development of pedagogical theory. (p. 253)

Elliott found that when teachers were provided with theoretical literature before they had begun to examine their own concerns, they dismissed the theory as irrelevant. But when theory was provided after teachers had themselves begun to question, articulate, and experiment with their own understandings, the teachers found theory useful in helping to explain and analyze their own actions.

Third, the outside researcher may provide what Carr and Kemmis

(1986) describe as a 'sounding board against which practitioners may try out ideas and learn more about the reasons for their own action as well as learning about the process of self reflection' (p. 203). In this role, the outsider provides process leadership that helps teachers define their concerns, plan strategies for change, observe the effects of change and reflect on their results. Carr and Kemmis (*ibid*) see this outsider role as leading, when possible, to 'emancipatory action research', in which the participants themselves take on full responsibility for the process. While some of those involved in action research continue to see a process and task leadership role for the outsider, Carr and Kemmis (*ibid*) believe that a model of shared leadership which requires no single leader is most congruent with the requirements of action research.

A fourth role for the outsider is that of organizer. He or she can coordinate the work of individual teachers, keep records of plans and meetings, negotiate relations between team members, other teachers, and the administration and arrange for the dissemination of action research reports (Ebbutt, 1985; Grundy and Kemmis, 1982; Nixon, 1981). Although this may be a fairly technical role, it is one that teachers are often unable — because of time and scheduling constraints — and unwilling — because of school structures and hierarchies — to take on. Coordination may also include helping the group develop a common language that reflects practitioners' concerns and assisting in the development of a group process in which power is distributed. 'Since facilitators are usually regarded as "expert" they must consciously encourage the group to take power for themselves' (Grundy and Kemmis, 1982, p. 71).

An additional role, suggested by the ARCS project, is that of the outside researcher as a developmental leader. The case history analyses of ARCS teachers who worked in the same school and interacted weekly for two years on the same team, reveal qualitative differences in the way these teachers identified research problems and conceptualized solutions in the action research process. Knowledge of the characteristics of adults' systems of logic at each developmental stage can help the facilitator on a collaborative action research team recognize the patterns in team members' decisions, actions, and attitudes which affect research and group processes.

Awareness of adult developmental stages also helps a facilitator actively respond to team members in ways which support individual and group development. To function at more comprehensive stages of development an individual must be supported and challenged according to the characteristic needs of that stage (Oja, 1980a). An outside researcher can provide the opportunities and support necessary to stimulate teachers' development of new ways of inquiring, perceiving, and reflecting on their experiences. By recognizing the developmental stages of participants, providing opportunities for them to take on more complex roles, and encouraging reflection on their actions, a developmental leader cultivates in participants an increased capacity for learning and understanding new knowledge and skills. Through these processes, the outside researcher contributes to an effective group process, establishes a norm of support for risk-taking and role-changing, and broadens individual perspectives. A leader-as-developer approach requires that the leader have the ability to see and value other viewpoints and to be flexible in his or her responses in order to meet the developmental, professional, and context specific needs of the teachers involved (Grimmett, 1983; Joyce, 1980; Oja and Ham, 1987; Thies-Sprinthall, 1984).

It is important for facilitators to recognize that their perceptions are filtered through their own developmental stages, exhibited in their interactions and relationships with teachers on the team. The university researcher working as a facilitator in collaborative action research must be aware of his or her own stage of development and its implications for dealing with the needs, cognitive styles, and concerns of teachers at various stages of development. For instance, a teacher with individualistic and autonomous ego development characteristics may perceive complexities and issues which a university researcher operating at another developmental stage, the conscientious stage for instance, may not recognize as immediately important. Or a university researcher functioning at the individualistic or autonomous stage may try to introduce issues in a particular phase of the group process which seem unimportant or unrelated to a teacher at the self-aware stage. Developmental stage theory thus provides a lens for understanding and analyzing what happens in a collaborative action research project and a perspective which helps a facilitator to support action research participants' personal and professional growth.

The Researcher Role: ARCS

In the ARCS project, the university researcher worked to guide individual development, the group process and the research project. Many of her actions contributed to all three. For example, as she supported Brooks' attempts to focus the research project in phase 3, she helped Brooks develop confidence in her growing sense of competence and leadership while promoting the team's clarification of its research task. When she worked with George on computer programs for data analysis, she supported his ability to work independently on the task while helping to move the team along in the final phases of the project.

The university researcher came to the project with the ability to see, hear, and value others' perspectives; she also had a long range overview of the process of action research. The combination of her awareness of individuals and her broader vision of the project allowed her to withstand pressure from team members to be more directive when a non-directive stance more effectively contributed to individual, group, and research processes. At the same time, she could promote group and individual development by respecting and encouraging the skills and insights of team members and planning for their incorporation into the team process.

The role of the university researcher on the ARCS team changed in accordance with the interpersonal and task demands which characterized each phase. Her roles, even more than those of teacher team members, reflected both her actions and the position accorded to her by others in the group. Figures 6 and 7 summarize the researcher's roles during the two years of the project.

Throughout the project, team members consistently saw the university researcher as a group leader. Even when they identified themselves or other teachers in leadership roles, they explained that the university researcher ensured that the team completed its project. As a developmental facilitator, she led by guiding, directing, and delegating.

John: I think she's been more or less the organizer to see that we've met and had stuff there, that we got stuff done if we said we were going to get it done. She's been the leader in that fashion. It's sort of leading by pushing rather than leading by being in front. I think that's the way (she) has led us, by pushing us slowly and steadily toward our goal, which is good. (interview, 6/83)

Brooks: As the research group went on, (her) role — sometimes it was directing, sometimes it was 'okay, we need to do this and this' just from the standpoint that this is the timeline, these are the nuts and bolts of the research. ... But the content of the meeting, more or less, was our input. (interview, 6/83)

In phase 1, the university researcher convened the group and provided agendas for the first four meetings. Team members perceived of her as the group's teacher and, given her status, assumed she would fill the expected role of university professor. They referred to the questions she asked them to address in their logs as 'assignments', and Jack suggested that she could collect and evaluate their logs after a few weeks and tell them 'what was missing, what you want in them' (documentation, 21 October 1981). Team members looked to the university researcher to run each meeting and occasionally asked her permission to raise issues: 'So what would you like us to start on? Talking about these questions?' (documentation, 21 October 1981). They also mentioned their expectation that the researcher would guide their research process and project:

George: Well, the group has met and nearly overcome the first obstacle, selecting a research topic. Next we must plan our research. I hope (the university researcher) has concrete guiding suggestions in this regard. An approach assigning group members to read and report on various secondary sources would be appropriate. (log, 20 November 1981)

YEAR 1

Phase 1	Phase 2	Phase 3
Runs meetings	Disseminates written	Questions
Sets agendas	information	Clarifies
Raises school context	Questions	Summarizes
issues	Organizes agenda/tasks	Explains research
	Summarizes	process
	Refocuses discussions	Facilitates individual
	back to research task	teacher roles
		Provides information on
		research design
	Shifts some responsibility	
	for setting agendas and making	
YEAR 2	decisions to team members ---	

Phase 4	Phase 5
Serves as research	Questions
authority	Clarifies
Models researcher role	Summarizes
Questions	Suggests alternative
Clarifies	approaches
Focuses group on task	Initiates and directs data
Suggests alternative	analysis
approaches or solu-	
tions	
Facilitates individual	
teacher roles	Shifts some research authority
	to other team members ---
	Edits final
	report

Figure 6: Role of University Researcher

166

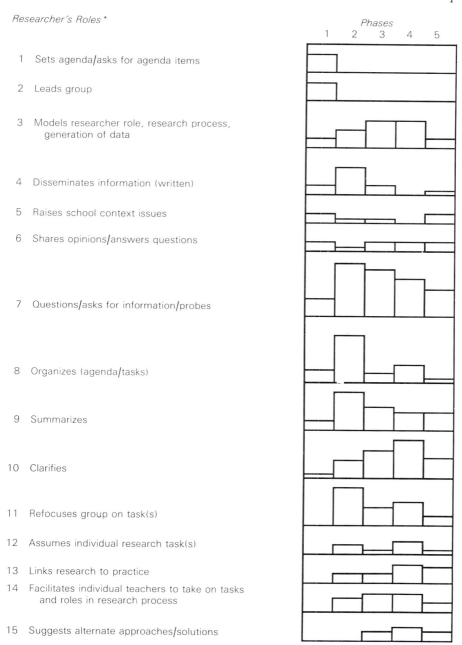

Researcher's Roles *

Phases
1   2   3   4   5

1   Sets agenda/asks for agenda items

2   Leads group

3   Models researcher role, research process,
    generation of data

4   Disseminates information (written)

5   Raises school context issues

6   Shares opinions/answers questions

7   Questions/asks for information/probes

8   Organizes (agenda/tasks)

9   Summarizes

10 Clarifies

11 Refocuses group on task(s)

12 Assumes individual research task(s)

13 Links research to practice

14 Facilitates individual teachers to take on tasks
    and roles in research process

15 Suggests alternate approaches/solutions

* Roles are listed chronologically according to when the role was introduced or assumed by
the university researcher.

Figure 7:   Frequency of University Researcher's Roles

Jack: I don't know how the process is going to work. ... I think you're going to have to lead and guide this team in the actual doing of processes and methods. (interview, 12/81)

Expectations and prior group experiences influence the roles individuals assume in a group (Thibaut and Kelly, 1986). Teachers' expectations of the ARCS researcher role in phase 1 grew out of the project structure, their previous experiences with university faculty, and their individual developmental stages. Because the university researcher convened the group, team members expected her to direct it. Given their feelings that they knew little about research, several team members expected the researcher to teach them or guide them, 'by discovery maybe, through questioning, not spoonfed' (Jack, interview, 12/81). In previous interactions with university faculty, teachers had found that the professor conducted a class of some kind, and they assumed that this 'course' would be similar. Several expressed pleased surprise that this was not true. Ted, for example, said that he originally questioned his participation in the project,

> ...because I thought it was going to be the same type of thing. You would run the thing and we would just sit here, and you were the university teacher and we were the junior high teachers. ... We were going to have to agree to everything. But I'm glad to say I haven't found that ... I think all of us feel equal. (interview, 12/81)

During phase 1, the university researcher gradually moved away from a directive role and into a more facilitative role. She no longer established agendas; she asked team members what the agenda should include. In this and subsequent phases she turned questions directed to her as group leader back to the team. For example, during a discussion of whether or not to meet the following week, Ted asked her what she had planned for the team for next week. She replied that she had no plan; the team set the agenda. When deciding whether or not to replace Jack, Ted suggested that the university researcher would know better than the team about the needs of the research. She suggested that they as a team needed to evaluate task demands and the issues involved in adding a new person to the group. When John asked what she would like him to cover in his presentation to the National Staff Development Council, the university researcher responded that she would like to hear what other team members thought. If asked by a team member to make a decision for the team, the university researcher more and more frequently raised the question as a team issue.

The university researcher's shift away from direction and toward facilitation in phases 1 and 2 made some team members uncomfortable. Both at the time and in retrospect, some team members noted that they would have liked her to take on a more directive role, despite their appreciation of being able to 'have their say'.

Ted: The only negative thing is that some of the time we spend on Wednesday ... we fool around too much, we get off the subject. Maybe a little tighter rein is the only thing. (interview, 12/81)

John: I think there was, in the first year, a mistake was made in not getting us organized a little bit quicker into what we were doing. I think we dragged on too long and then had to make a lot of hasty, fast decisions. ... I think that it should have been at least pointed out that we've got to start to make some decisions ... and maybe that could have been the focus from the research people, saying, 'Okay guys, this is it; you're going to need to come up with something for now.' (interview, 6/83)

Brooks, too, noted that the team wanted the university researcher to be 'leader' early in the project and that they became frustrated at times when she would not assume that role. Brooks and others ultimately saw the university researcher's facilitative role as the best one possible for the team, however, because it allowed teachers to learn about research and have ownership in the project. It also challenged people at a range of developmental stages to take on tasks and responsibilities they might not have otherwise attempted.

George: The five teacher researchers need to have feelings of involvement, and strong-armed or even coercive ... leadership in those early times might have been comforting to the teachers but they needed to feel involved. (interview, 6/83)

Ted: I was new to the idea that all of us had an equal say in the thing. I thought it was going to be run by the university researcher. At first I thought ... she had let us go too far, that we were at a lot of meetings that seemed to go over and over the same things. But I think as it evolved it produced the idea that we were equal and a lot of people had a lot to say. (interview, 6/83)

In phase 2, the university researcher increased her use of questions to probe teachers' knowledge and experience. Such probing is necessary to clarify research problems and to determine that team members define these problems in similar ways. Through probing questions, researchers learn about the contexts crucial to teaching and learning, while teachers learn to specify their problems in more systematically researchable terms. During this second phase, the university researcher's facilitation consisted of redirecting school context and other far-ranging discussions back to the agenda or the research task. At times her comments attempted to link tangential discussions back to the team's research problem. In this phase, however, team members tended to disregard the university researcher's attempts to refocus the team on its research project.

Occasionally, the university researcher directly moved the team to its next task, saying, for example, 'I feel we should go on', and raising another agenda item for consideration (documentation, 24 March 1982). In most cases, the team followed her to the next task, although they often used it as a way of continuing previous discussions. Despite some team members' desire for more direction at this time, they did not always recognize or accept it from the university researcher when she offered it directly or indirectly. Until the team was ready to concentrate on its research design and question, the university researcher could only help them maintain a sense of what they had done to that point. Neither she nor other team members could direct the task until the team had chosen to address it.

In phases 1 and 2, and at the beginning of phase 3, the team depended on the university researcher to focus meetings, keep the team on task, and dismiss the group. If the university researcher missed a meeting or engaged in conversation with one team member during a team meeting, discussions among other team members tended to be non-task related. If the university researcher had to leave a meeting early, team members left soon after, even if she had suggested other tasks they might think about.

A shift in this aspect of the researcher's role occurred in phases 3, 4 and 5 as other team members and the research project itself began to control team meeting time. If the university researcher missed a meeting, the team made an agenda and continued to work on research tasks. In phase 5, they even scheduled one all day meeting when all team members except the university researcher could attend. As the team established and became comfortable with operating norms and developed a clearer understanding of their research project; they did not need the university researcher to direct the group process. Instead, the researcher could be used by the team as a resource person who could provide knowledge and direction in research methodology and research standards.

Grundy and Kemmis (1982) describe a similar process of 'hidden compromise' followed by facilitators in the Deakin University Action Research Group in Australia. These facilitators allowed group members to treat them as the experts while they worked on developing equality and distributing power. They let the name of expert stand as the temporary basis for group leadership, but once they had established 'symmetrical communication' (p. 91), the facilitators showed the group that their focus had been the group process. Then they turned those processes back over to the group and assumed a co-member role.

As we have mentioned, phase 3 of the ARCS project began when team members asked the university researcher to bring in model research designs. This marked the first time the team had requested the university researcher's help as a researcher. In phases 3 and 4, the university researcher's role tended to be that of research authority, a role based on her greater knowledge and experience in the field of educational research rather than on her status as university faculty member.

During phase 3, the university researcher presented the team with information about kinds of research (qualitative versus quantitative) and research designs (research and development, comparative research, evaluation research, and so on). Because she provided the content of team meetings, the university researcher also directed the process at the beginning of phase 3, moving the team from one issue to the next and openly pulling tangential discussions back to the task. She said, for example, 'I want to come back to the research' (documentation, 14 April 1982) to close a discussion unrelated to research design or research question. Team members began to ask the university researcher questions about reliability and validity of data collection tools and about the external validity of their project as a whole, indicating their perception of her as research authority.

The university researcher retained the role of research authority throughout the rest of the project. Team members continued to ask her about techniques for data analysis and expectations others would have of their work. As teachers became more confident researchers and began to assume task and process leadership in the group in phases 3 and 4, the university researcher shifted some of her research authority to others, just as she had previously shifted control of group processes and decisions back to the team. Again, her actions contributed both to individual growth and group and research task needs. For example, she asked Brooks to talk to a faculty member at the University of New Hampshire about research on teacher burnout, allowing Brooks to become the team expert in that area. During year two, when George suggested that she should work on the findings and conclusions sections of the final report, 'picking out trends and significant findings based on the analysis of the information', the university researcher agreed to run some statistical tests. However, because the group had done so much work on the surveys, she said she was reluctant to do the rest of the analysis herself (documentation, 9 February 1983) and helped team members learn to do the analysis themselves. As a result, the team analyzed the surveys and wrote those sections of the report together. Team members assumed positions of authority in phases 4 and 5 in part because of their greater understanding of the project and developing ease with research. The university researcher's actions provided them with the opportunities and encouragement to take on those tasks and positions.

At the beginning of phase 5, the university researcher took on a more directive role, similar to the one she had assumed at the onset of phase 3. In January of year two, the team had collected all of its data, and George had begun to create computer programs to aid in analysis. The university researcher began some of the data analysis on her own, specifically the statistical analysis of significant change in levels of teacher morale from year one to year two. During several meetings in January, she presented her findings and directed the team into analysis of pre- and post-test results of the School Survey administered with the MBI. Her directive role at this point in the project provided an impetus for the team to assume responsibility for data analysis, just as her direction in phase 3 gave the team the background it needed to make decisions about their research design and question. In both cases, once she had provided the catalyst, she stepped back into a less directive position, working with the group rather than leading it. Her intervention at these times served to move the group forward on its task. Because roles in the group had become fluid and because the university researcher had indicated her desire for the team to arrive at its own decisions in phases 1 and 2, her direction at the beginning of phases 3 and 5 was accepted as natural and helpful and not as an imposition of power or an attempt to control the group process.

As a result of her tendency to facilitate rather than direct (except when her knowledge of research was needed by the team), her encouragement and acceptance of other team members as group leaders, and her tendency to redirect group process decisions and questions about the research project back to the team, other team members described the university researcher as a colleague. Team members appreciated this new form of interaction with a university professor:

Brooks: You became a colleague, as an equal, and it didn't seem that you had any difference in terms of status in the group than anyone else. ... Just because you were there didn't mean that ... your ideas were ... more important than anyone else's. (interview, 6/83)

Ted: It's nice that we can sit at equal stations and sit and talk and derive some solution instead of having it told to you or jammed down your throat. (interview, 12/82)

John: As a group of teachers, it was best we had to do it this way ... if it's going to be valuable to us as individuals, not just valuable because we have a paper done and a few recommendations. (interview, 12/82)

George pointed out that 'when university people go out and work with teachers it breaks down the ivory tower concept' (AERA presentation, 4/83). Team members agreed that collegiality with a university faculty member was a valuable part of their experience.

The university researcher's role changed to meet individuals' developmental needs and the team's interpersonal and research task demands. As team members began to get to know one another, establish trust, and develop norms during phase 1, she provided an agenda and a meeting structure. As they worked to identify a research-able problem and appropriate data collection tools in phases 1 and 2, she occasionally summarized what they had done and refocused discussions. When the team indicated their readiness to concentrate on research design and research question in phase 3, she provided information and direction, but as other team members assumed task and process leadership in phases 3 and 4 she followed them. In phase 5, she again led the team into data analysis, providing the impetus needed to focus on that set of tasks.

Throughout the project the university researcher shifted maintenance and task responsibility to other team members whenever possible. She herself described her role as sharing the skills she had, contributing to some standardization of research results, and facilitating the team working together so 'it's not just me doing the research' (presentation at the University of New Hampshire 4/83). Her description reflects the dual nature of democratic leadership: stimulating shared leadership and, when necessary, taking on task and maintenance functions that help the group achieve its mutually defined goals. The university researcher's understanding of leadership reflected the notion of collaboration in which each individual contributes his or her insights and abilities to the group. It also drew on her understanding of developmental stage theory and her ability to use that knowledge to work with individuals and the group. She believed that it was her responsibility as team leader to provide the opportunities and support which encouraged each individual to assume roles benefiting both the team and that individual. The university researcher's decisions and actions allowed team members to become comfortable with themselves in the role of researcher, to assume the process and task responsibilities which arose in each phase, to recognize the possibility of alternative definitions for problems, and to appreciate the value of collaboration with their colleagues. Thus, while many of the university researcher's actions and roles arose out of the interpersonal and task demands of each phase, they also affected the process the group experienced and contributed to the personal and professional value team members attributed to that process.

Conclusion

Analyses of group process, roles, and leadership on an action research team are necessarily interrelated. Once we see that a group moves through a series of interpersonal and task-related phases, we realize that the group's demands are both constant and changing. Individuals serve the group by assuming roles, or ways of acting which have some consistency over time. Roles may shift to accommodate shifting individual and group needs. And yet, there are limitations to analyzing action research groups through the perspective of group dynamics theory. Descriptions of roles imply that each individual serves only as a cog in the group machine, acting in ways which allow the machine to function smoothly and complete its task. The individual cases presented above show a different picture; an individual action may serve a purpose in the group, may satisfy a personal or professional need, or may fulfil both functions.

If action research is to meet its combined goals of personal and professional growth, improved practice, and increased educational knowledge, then the individual and group demands and processes must be closely synchronized. If individual needs are met but the group is unsuccessful in meeting its goals, we may see personal and professional growth without change in theory or practice. If the group completes its task but participants remain unsatisfied, there may be a change in practice without the accompanying sense of empowerment or professionalism expected for those who work in action research. When participants' actions fulfill both individual and group needs, then the group is most likely to achieve the goals of action research.

Leadership for this type of action research group involves a democratic process which encourages others to lead the group when they have the skills and confidence needed to do so. Leadership is a collaborative effort; team members share the task and maintenance functions which allow the group to meet its goals. The outside researcher may, however, have a unique place in this process, often providing the initiative, questions, and support necessary to keep the group moving on its task. Using a developmental approach to leadership, this outsider may also help address the needs of the group and its individual members by offering developmentally appropriate guidance, support and challenge.

An awareness of developmental stage characteristics can help the leader or facilitator on a collaborative action research team understand individuals' attitudes and behavior as they interact in the collaborative action research process. We have found that the teachers on the ARCS team valued the team's group process most highly and perceived changes and growth in themselves as a result of that process. Teachers' emphasis on their individual and group experiences suggest that leaders who consider issues of adult development as they work with the action research group can most effectively contribute to the goals of action research.

6
Issues in Action Research

Introduction

Collaborative action research is a powerful and yet 'messy' process, one that must account for the individual participants and the context within which they work if it hopes to reach its goals. Each report of educational action research shows a somewhat different collaborative process, a different approach to practical problems, and, as a result, a different set of outcomes. Despite these differences, we have suggested that certain lenses, in particular theories of group interaction and adult development, help explain what occurs on a collaborative action research team. There are patterns among the different projects that, when discovered, clarify the processes and outcomes each experiences.

Several educators engaged in second-level analysis of educational research suggest that variations in action research result from each project's resolution of dilemmas endemic to action research (Cohn and Finch, 1987; Elliott, 1985; Rapoport, 1970). Cohn and Finch (1987) define dilemmas as 'pulls in opposing directions, each of which has certain compelling advantages and disadvantages' (p. 14). Elliott (1985) describes a dilemma as:

> A situation which appears to require two equally desirable but mutually inconsistent courses of action. ... Whereas technical problems can be resolved simply by discovering the effective means, it is not so easy to see how dilemmas can be resolved. In some cases, the 'solution' involves a reconceptualization of the nature of the problem situation. Here one's conception of the situation shifts so that it no longer appears ambiguous. In other cases no satisfactory solution is discovered; the dilemma persists and one is forced to opt for a course of action which satisfies one value but denies another. (p. 240)

Lieberman (1987) suggests that it is more appropriate to talk about 'issues' rather than 'dilemmas' in action research. Dilemmas imply an either–or construct which minimizes the possibility of discussion and compromise. In practice, however, action researchers tend to make decisions that best meet their situations and goals and that include rather than exclude a variety of perspectives. In many cases, decisions made in action research require a balancing of divergent needs or views rather than a mutually exclusive choice of a single option.

This chapter focuses on three key issues in collaborative action research. The first issue is the relationship between the action research project and the school or schools within which it is carried out. Choices made about this relationship often determine project topic, longevity and influence on school practice. Within this issue we will examine the relationship between school climate and an action research project; the role of the school administration in the project; the value of team and/or whole school involvement; and the institutionalization of action research processes and outcomes in a school.

The second issue involves questions of project control and leadership. Choices made about the role of the outside facilitator or agency influence the group process and participants' conceptual control and ownership of the project. The third issue is the choice of project goals. Collaborative action research traditionally aims to improve practice, contribute to theoretical understanding of that practice, and provide a professional development experience for participants. In fact, many action research projects struggle with meeting all three goals and find that they emphasize one at the expense of others. This choice may not be conscious at the project's inception but becomes more apparent as a team makes decisions that allow some goals to be reached but not others.

This chapter examines these issues in relation to the ARCS project and several other recent action research projects. Our goals are to clarify the issues, illustrate the range of choices possible within each issue, and examine the implications of choices made for the processes and products of collaborative action research.

Issue: School Context and Collaborative Action Research

School Climate and Action Research

Many of those studying collaborative action research indicate that the school climate affects teachers' willingness to be involved in action research and their ability to carry out a successful research project (Corey, 1952; Elliott, 1977; James and Ebbutt, 1981; Pine, 1981). These authors suggest that teachers will be more receptive to action research if the school allows frequent communication among staff and between staff and administration, encourages teacher experimentation and change, and involves teachers in decision making on policy and curriculum.

The ARCS project provides a different perspective on this issue. During the first few meetings, all five teachers on the ARCS team described the school as lacking in communication and collegiality, closed to experimentation and extremely hierarchical in policy and decision-making. These characteristics of the school environment would be expected to inhibit teacher participation in an action research project (Little, 1981). Instead, several teachers explained that they had joined the team with the hope of changing these conditions, and the team ultimately focused its investigation on one element of the school climate. Therefore, teacher willingness to participate in collaborative action research may be seen as an opportunity to have some impact on elements of the school climate which teachers find unproductive.

There is more evidence that existing school structures affect an action research project's questions, designs, methods, and outcomes. Griffiths (1985) notes that 'the specific context and the specialized knowledge which the teacher has will determine how the research situation is approached' (p. 211). In the Danforth Foundation Improvement of Instruction Project (Cohn and Finch, 1987), six schools were asked to define an instructional goal and plan actions to reach it. Two of these schools were unsuccessful in their use of action research because the school context forced teachers and administrators to focus their energy on problems other than instruction. Cohn and Finch (*ibid*) explain the concerns of these two schools:

> The project is, in essence, providing some answers to the question, how can a school involve its faculty in selecting an instructional goal for the entire school and develop strategies for achieving the goal? These schools, however, are asking different questions: how can we get students to attend school?; how can we keep order in the school?; how can we get parents to care enough to pick up students' report cards? (p. 14)

Cohn and Finch imply that action research would not help these practitioners address their questions because their schools lack the organizational structures needed for reflection and experimentation.

They suggest that the school context can determine the questions teachers need answered and their subsequent success in using action research to answer them.

ARCS: School context and the research project

In the ARCS project, the research topic, process and goals were clearly influenced by the school context at several different points during the two-year period. During their first eight meetings in year one, team members discussed school context issues as a way of ensuring that the action research project they carried out would be school-based. During these early meetings, the team pointed out that decisions were made unilaterally in their school and system. Even when administrators occasionally asked for teacher opinion and input, they tended to proceed with their initial plans. Team members also discussed low levels of teacher morale in the school, revealed in teachers withdrawing to their own classrooms, not communicating with one another, and performing minimal job requirements and no more. The team attributed low morale to the number of policy changes that had occurred over the past ten years in the school and suggested that perhaps the new Principal would be able to improve the school's teaching and learning conditions. They decided that because teachers lacked the time needed to meet students' needs and communicate with colleagues, the team should investigate scheduling issues. Thus their research problem emerged from school context concerns.

During the first year, the team tried to take school givens into consideration in planning their project so that their results would be usable in the existing context. By the end of the first year and into the second year, they were also noting that a number of school context variables beyond their control shaped their research design. At a team meeting near the end of year one, Ted said, 'We can't do R and D (research and development) because there are too many obstacles: administration, time, etc. ...' George replied that R and D required total institutional commitment and Ted pointed out that the Principal would not abdicate that much responsibility and power unless they could get a commitment from the superintendent (documentation, 14 April 1982).

In retrospect, team members saw the shift in their research focus from scheduling to teacher morale as the result of changes made by the Principal and their own lack of power as school policy makers. John said:

We came up with six things on the Staff Opinion Survey that

were teachers' concerns and we dropped two because the Principal changed class length and department chairs were appointed. We dealt with the other four — we thought of dealing with them on the scheduling basis but we couldn't do that, and since the changes took place we thought we could measure the effects of the changes on the teacher burnout we saw.

George agreed:

> We had the sense that our recommendations wouldn't be followed anyway, and on the burnout issue, no matter what changes they made we could measure the results of those changes. (documentation, 27 April 1983)

The team's perception of the school context thus influenced their initial choice of research topic and the ways in which they refocused that topic over the two years of the project.

The team also based their decisions of when to interview other teachers and which team members would interview particular colleagues on their perceptions of the school environment. For example, despite their sense at the end of year one that they should interview a sample of teachers at that time (before changes were made in September which might influence responses), team members chose to postpone these interviews until the fall. Their reasons included end-of-the-school year demands on their own time and their perception that the same demands would make their colleagues unapproachable and uncooperative. When they did interview teachers in November of year two, each team member interviewed those staff members with whom he or she felt comfortable. One team member pointed out that this was necessary because, 'There are some people in the school who won't talk to me' (documentation, 3 November 1982). Thus, the school context influenced many of the decisions teachers made about the shape of their project — their research question, their data collection, and, ultimately, their project goals.

ARCS: School context and project goals

All of the team members began the project expecting to work on a problem with the goal of reaching a solution which would benefit teachers and students in the school. When asked in initial interviews what goals they saw for the project, four out of five hoped for direct gain for the school:

Ted: I hope when we focus on something it will be something that all of us can bring back into our classrooms. At least meet some of the needs of the pupils here and not be something that's going to be filed away.

John: I would assume it would be on our daily dealing with students and dealing with teams within our particular area ... where these problems come up and trying to find help for the problems.

Brooks: Hopefully it would establish a dialogue within the school — of some concerned teachers, of what's happened to us, where we've been, what has really transpired. There's a lot of things that have happened that need to be talked about.

Jack: (The goal is) to look at some of the problems that maybe are unique to this school but also affect junior high education throughout the country. (interviews, 9/81)

George, too, saw gains for teachers and students, but felt those gains would be limited to those who had participated in the project.

As team members discussed a research problem and design during the first year, they reassessed their project goals. In every discussion of goals, team members raised the issues of their lack of power to implement change in the school and the unquestioned authority of the Principal. Despite their interest in creating a change to improve the school, some team members began to advocate goals of personal satisfaction instead. When Ted suggested, for example, that they should attack the power structure or get the administration involved in order to have a greater impact on the school, Jack told him they should do the project for themselves because they were unlikely to get administrative involvement. John later told Ted that it would be nice if the project was used but that 'it's not necessary'. John noted that the contacts he had established with other teachers through sharing his logs had already made the project worthwhile for him (documentation, 18 November 1981).

During discussions of research goals in year two, teachers shifted away from a desire to make specific recommendations for school change. They began, instead, to emphasize the value the project had for them as individuals and for the school system and its use as a model of the action research process for teachers and administrators in other schools. During the second year of the project, John had several conversations with the Assistant Superintendent of schools about the project and presented a summary of the team's work to the system's Staff Development Committee as an example of an effective staff development project. In planning their presentations for the American Educational Research Association (AERA), teachers decided to include a description of the process they had experienced, 'So that other people can see how to get where we have gotten ... also so people wouldn't give up when they got to a hard place — they could see it could be done' (documentation, 9 February 1983). Teachers emphasized the importance of modeling the process of collaborative action research for others:

John: The project has an effect on the school other than what the Principal does with it. It could have an effect on the supervisory union as a whole, through the staff development committee ... It's likely the administration will do what they want regardless of our report.

George: We never had any promises they would listen ... we're working to further the cause of educational research.

Brooks: It doesn't bother me if it isn't used — no one listens to research — but it's good to keep collaborative action research going. (documentation, 22 February 1983)

When the university researcher asked, 'Why did the group choose an issue like scheduling rather than a classroom issue over which they had more control?' team members stressed the value of the process of action research. Brooks claimed that the schedule would be whatever the administration wanted, but that 'even if we don't impact our school, we may affect other schools'. John agreed and added, 'Way back, we three said it would be nice if it counted but it doesn't matter ... It's going through the process from here to there that matters' (documentation, 22 February 1983). At AERA, Brooks said that as a result of her participation in the project, 'I now sense I have some respect, some importance not only as a classroom teacher but beyond that. ... Research is an important part of my life now — the process more than the product' (documentation, 13 April 1983). Team members' changed goals seemed to occur as a result of their questions, raised in year one, about their ability to implement or control school change. By abstracting the goals of the research from the school and focusing on the value of the project to themselves and others, team members no longer had to try to create changes in school policy over which they had no control.

The school climate, in particular decision and policy-making structures, can have an important impact on an action research project's process and product. Teachers doing collaborative action research will consider the school environment as well as their colleagues' interests, needs and attitudes as they plan and carry out their research. If they do not consider themselves to be a part of the school's decision-making processes or if they feel that their work is undervalued, they may withdraw the project from the school, shifting to research questions, processes, and outcomes that lead to personal satisfaction rather than immediate school change. Some teachers might withdraw from such a situation completely; others may find enough reward in the process and collegiality to continue. Because the school Principal plays such an important role in designing and maintaining the school structure and climate, we turn next to the role of school administration in collaborative action research.

School Administration and Collaborative Action Research

Most collaborative action research in the United States, United Kingdom and Australia has emphasized the importance of teacher, rather than administrator participation. The goal is to involve teachers in observing, reflecting on, and investigating practice; interestingly, few action researchers call on school heads to use the process to examine administrative practices. But because of the central role of administrators in supporting action research, several studies have begun to examine what roles school administrators might play in collaborative action research.

During the past ten years, the literature on school improvement has emphasized the role of the school Principal in creating a positive school climate and implementing school change (Blumberg and Greenfield, 1980; Edmonds, 1979 and 1982; Rutter *et al*, 1979). Initially, this literature stressed the role of the Principal as a managerial and instructional leader who should, seemingly unilaterally, set high expectations for students and teachers and develop an environment conducive to student learning and staff development. Oja and Pine (1984) reflect some of these ideas when they explain that,

Whether a member of a collaborative action research team or

not, the Principal can foster effective inquiry and school improvement by striving to:

— Create new patterns of communication, collegiality and sharing.
— Develop an environment that supports inquiry and is professionally rewarding to teachers.
— Create a climate for teachers to interact with each other and to draw on each others' knowledge and skills.
— Improve teaching and learning conditions by consulting with teachers about what needs to be done and working with teachers to bring about change. (p. 29)

More recent calls for teacher empowerment and professionalism have led some who study school change to advocate teacher-Principal collaboration in school improvement. While each may take roles most appropriate to their skills and interests, the participation of both is crucial. Lieberman and Miller (1984) note:

Posing the problem (of school improvement) as strictly managerial puts the focus only on the leadership. But looking to teachers to create and sustain improvement efforts puts the focus only on teachers. It is the sustained support from the leadership by facilitating time, a focus, resources and protection from additional responsibilities coupled with the organization of continuous, practical, hands-on, classroom support that builds commitment, sustains improvement and makes real improvement work in the classroom. (p. 8)

Questions about the role of school heads in action research parallel, to some extent, concerns about the role of the outside researcher (see Chapter 5). For example, Principals engaged in collaborative action research may be working within their own agendas rather than listening to teachers' concerns. Judith Whyte (1986) points out that in the Girls Into Science and Technology (GIST) project, some school heads made a verbal commitment to the project but were unwilling to push for real change. She sees school heads as the 'gatekeepers' who control communication, information, and options available to teachers.

If the change or innovation advocated is incompatible with the personal beliefs and attitudes of the gatekeeper, then he or she is likely to produce a barrier to the introduction of change into that social system. (p. 172)

There is also concern that a school Principal might dominate a collaborative action research team, interacting with teacher participants through existing hierarchical patterns. Cohn and Finch (1987), who asked school administrators to serve as team leaders in the Danforth Project, note that the Principal's attitude influenced each individual project's success or failure as measured by teacher professional development and instructional change.

> In cases where the Principal was a strong leader or had self-oriented needs to 'use' the project for other purposes, the Principal appears to have made a major contribution to the success of the project. In cases where the Principal refused to lead or failed to get teachers to feel they could risk saying what they felt, the instructional or process goals were largely unrealized. There were, in fact, Principals who were uncomfortable or impatient with a process that involved teacher input and consensus, Principals who could not step out of their traditional role. (p. 18)

Administrative domination — or perhaps even administrative presence — on an action research team may minimize teacher reflection and leadership which contribute to the professional growth expected from action research. Only a Principal who can establish a collegial relationship and the collaborative or democratic processes of leadership described earlier will be a successful participant in action research. Little (1984) describes how Principals who assume these roles can shift from being 'gatekeepers' to 'change-agents' in the school. 'Such a pattern of leadership, however, also calls for practices for which most Principals are neither prepared, selected, nor rewarded' (p. 100).

Oja and Pine (1984) suggest that a Principal need not be a member of a collaborative action research team as long as he or she plays a supportive role. Support includes granting the freedom to examine a range of issues and adding administrative perspectives when they influence the team's project.

> In collaborative action research efforts, it is important for a Principal to recognize that teams may choose to investigate 'touchy' issues which require freedom of inquiry for the team and security on the part of the Principal. Principals and other school administrators can express strong support for action research teams while helping teachers understand administrative perspectives of the school system and local community. (pp. 29–30)

The Principal's role in collaborative action research may, therefore, be somewhat paradoxical. An action research team may choose to investigate issues which influence the instructional and managerial processes for which the Principal feels ultimately responsible. The Principal's involvement or support may be crucial to the project's success, and yet that success may lead to teacher empowerment and changes in practice which challenge the Principal's traditional role. The school Principal may be faced with integrating action research, his or her own control of school change, and teacher cooperation and investment in the school. Teachers involved in collaborative action research may feel that administrative involvement undermines their ability to define, reflect on and experiment with practical issues of concern to them. As they make decisions about the extent to which they involve the school Principal in their project, teachers may have to balance concerns for project ownership with the direct or indirect administrative involvement which could lead to more successful school or classroom change. The ARCS project illustrates an action research team's decisions around these issues.

ARCS and the school Principal

As noted, the ARCS team debated the Principal's role in their project several times during year one. The Principal was a former teacher in their school, appointed in October of the first year of the project to replace the Principal who had left that summer. The project had been negotiated the previous spring with the former Principal; the new Principal knew of the project and seemed to be supportive of it. Cohn and Finch (1987) discovered, however, that new Principals may face issues that require more of their time than an ongoing action research project:

> New Principals who had not experienced the project from the outset and who found themselves in a position where the establishment of their own authority took precedence over any other school activities, were not able to be as effective in regard to the project as their predecessors. (p. 18)

Early in the first year of the ARCS project, the team decided not to invite the new Principal to join the team. They based their decision on two factors: first, the group had begun to develop a coherent sense of itself and did not want to introduce a new person to the process. Second, they were concerned that the Principal would make the project his, and they very much wanted to make their own choices. The team did, however, recognize the value of having the Principal's support and sanction. For example, in deciding how to go about investigating their problem during year one, teachers considered the Principal's key role in making policy decisions and changes. In December, John noted that they should consult the Principal before choosing specific issues to investigate.

> Ted said, 'So you're saying to fit our project to what the Principal wants?' John replied that if we're working with the assumption that what we do will work here we have to ... We can come up with ten things to research, take the list to the Principal, and spend our time on the ones which are possible. (documentation, 16 December 1981)

In the first year, the team showed a draft of its Staff Opinion Survey to the Principal and solicited his suggestions for modifications and additions. They later gave him the results of the survey and believed that he considered those results in making policy decisions for the following year. John explained that 'the Principal was pretty sure he knew the answer, but now he's got a survey telling him the answer. ... He can use our survey to back up points, points which he might have already had but at least he's got a survey to prove it now' (interview, 5/82). In an interview, the Principal corroborated this view, explaining that survey results 'reinforced what I was hearing about scheduling. ... It's nice to say everyone feels this way; it's not just a few people' (interview, 2/83).

In May of year one, two team members decided to interview the Principal about his definitions of some of the terms (teams, grouping, house coordinators) being used in the school. Ted asked again if that would cause the team to base their research on what the Principal wanted. Brooks replied, 'We have to start where we are and then build something to change it' (documentation, 5 May 1982). During year one, the team clearly worked to keep the Principal apprised and even peripherally involved in the project while maintaining their own ownership and control of the process. In interviews, the Principal noted that he felt adequately informed about the project through these contacts and said he was satisfied with his level of involvement in the process.

During the second year the team moved away from including the Principal and his ideas in the project. The Principal's input was not sought after September 1982, and the team debated at the end of the project whether or not to invite him to a team meeting to respond to their final report. During this debate, Brooks pointed out that she did not think the Principal had any ownership in the project; she felt less comfortable sharing the research results with the school administration than with people outside of the school. The team had gradually limited their interaction with the Principal, partly because of increased time spent on research tasks and partly because of their de-emphasis on school-oriented goals.

Team members also expressed respect for the Principal's domain and a desire not to infringe on his territory. Throughout the two years, they debated whether or not to make specific recommendations to the Principal at the end of the project. As they began to write the final report in the spring of year two, they faced a final decision on this issue. Several teachers said they could not tell the Principal how to run his school. They agreed to report their findings without making suggestions or recommendations to the Principal. Brooks described the final report in her last interview:

> I really thought that it came out good. I really felt that it said what we wanted it to say without stepping on anyone's toes, without negating all the time and energy that we had spent on the research and without getting into anyone else's personal space. (interview, 6/83)

The team's goals as reflected here suggest not only a perceived lack of power to create change but also a recognition and acceptance of given domains of teacher and Principal. Team members felt that if change was to result from their project, it had to take place within accepted patterns of power and responsibility in the school.

The team did finally invite the Principal to attend a meeting and respond to their report, although they agreed in advance that they would not make major revisions as a result of their conversation with him. The Principal indicated to the team that he was glad they had done the research and said that he hoped some of their findings which correlated low teacher morale and lack of teacher participation in decision-making would change in the next year or so. He did not, however, suggest acting on the team's conclusions in any specific ways, thus reinforcing their feeling that their work would not lead to school change. According to John:

> I feel he has too many preconceived notions and he's very firm and set in them. And I think even the minor, little points are explosive coming out of that report but I think he will sidestep them. (interview, 6/83)

In an interview at the end of year two, the Principal explained that it was good that these teachers had been involved in the project because 'they're the type of people that want to be involved so it was good for them. It was something they really enjoyed doing and it was a lot of work for them. I think that the materials they put out were very professional; everything was done very nicely. It's a credit to the school. They really did a good job' (interview, 7/83). He also noted his surprise at some of their results, for example that teachers felt they lacked input into policy decisions, because he believed he had made teacher input a high priority in his administration. He did not foresee changes in school policy or process resulting from the project, although he did appear to be open to future school-university collaborative teams working on school issues. Several members of the ARCS team noted in retrospect that more administrative involvement of some kind might have led to greater project impact in the school, but they continued to believe that it was better not to have the Principal as a team member.

George: I'm saying that thinking over again what happens I guess if you don't directly involve the authority figure then at least you have to build a wide base of power so that the authority figure needs to come to you to become involved, even if it's involvement on some secondary level, not as a member of the team but as somebody who is being continually advised as to what is going on. If that had happened here, then the Principal would have been more conversant with the possible values of what we found out and what we did. (interview, 6/83)

In the ARCS project, as in many other collaborative action research projects, teachers and administrators face decisions about their respective roles in the process. Teachers may want to maximize their independence in order to pursue a project that is meaningful to them, and yet they may recognize the need to maintain ties to the administration if they hope to have any impact on school change. Emphasis on the process of collaborative action research rather than change in school practice in the ARCS project may have resulted in part from the negotiated and accepted patterns of team and administrator interaction. The team, having assessed school and administrative structures, chose to emphasize their group and research processes rather than proposing changes based on their research findings. Especially when a project focuses on issues which involve the entire school, teachers and administrators must find ways of balancing support for the questions and processes of action research with Principals' views of school needs and teachers' need for autonomy. Teachers and Principals must negotiate answers to the question, to what degree should a school Principal be involved in action research so that teachers experience growth and the school experiences positive, enduring change?

Whole School vs Team Involvement

Just as teachers involved in collaborative action research must develop a relationship with the school Principal, so must they negotiate their interaction with the other teachers in the school. James and Ebbutt (1981) explain that teachers may experience role conflicts when they do research that requires interviewing students and colleagues with whom they work. Teachers involved in classroom or school-based action research need sympathetic understanding and encouragement from colleagues in order to maintain the open climate conducive to both research and effective teaching.

Doing action research in small teams benefits the individuals involved and may increase the project's effectiveness. In his initial use of action research in the social sciences, Lewin (1952) advocated a group approach that provided collegial support for reflection and experimentation. Only a small group can develop the collaborative processes which allow the group to act and reflect on common goals. In school or system-based action research, team members may include representatives from several groups in the school process; the team provides a forum in which perspectives can be shared and strategies developed which satisfy all parties. Once such a representative group reaches its decisions, it can have a powerful impact at the classroom, building and district levels (Cohn and Finch, 1987).

If it hopes to influence school or classroom practice, however, the action research team must find ways of maintaining its group processes while creating a relationship with the rest of the school. Cohn and Finch (*ibid*) note that the most difficult problem the Danforth Project teams faced was how to 'disseminate the knowledge, enthusiasm, and commitment generated at the monthly large group and team meetings throughout the whole school' (p. 27). Inability to do so may result in a project that has personal significance for those involved but has little effect on school practice. James and Ebbutt (1981), for example, explain that their two-person project was valuable only to them:

To suggest, however, that the impact of our research was

either widespread or deep would be misleading. Whilst it absorbed us for some considerable time, our colleagues regarded it as no more than a peripheral activity of marginal interest. ... In the end we had little evidence of whether it made any real difference. (p. 94)

Carr and Kemmis (1986) describe similar results in a project done by a group of teachers who tried to change the means of assessing low-achieving students in their school. While these teachers succeeded in their own classes, they discovered that teachers who had not been involved in the process of action research were not convinced of the value of new forms of assessment, and the general school assessment policy remained unchanged. Carr and Kemmis explain:

The situation did not change as radically as the teachers involved had hoped, but they learned something about the change process itself: that they needed to involve others in the learning process they had gone through, and to involve them early. (p. 170)

Little (1984) points out that some changes will only be effective when 'used on a large enough scale to alter the entire pattern of teaching and learning in a school' (p. 87). One of the teachers engaged in Little's collaborative staff development project noted: 'I think that it would be a disadvantage not to have the whole school behind the project. ... I don't see how a few people ... in one school can have much impact on the whole school' (p. 86).

Action researchers make the same error as traditional researchers if they expect to impose their findings on other teachers. All work in collaborative action research describes the importance of being involved in the cycles of planning, acting and reflecting; involvement leads to understanding and commitment. It is not enough, therefore, to inform colleagues of the work of an action research team and expect them to accept the results; action research teams must find ways to develop cohesive collaborative processes and yet gradually involve others in what has been a small group experience.

As an action research process develops, it is expected that a widening circle of those affected by the practice will become involved in the research process. For this reason, action researchers are inevitably concerned with the politics and processes of innovation and change. (Grundy and Kemmis, 1982, p. 84)

In the ARCS project, the team made a number of influential decisions about its relationship to the rest of the school. During the first year, team members showed a concern for informing colleagues of their work. For example, they chose to administer the Staff Opinion Survey to all teachers rather than a sample, so that no one would feel 'left out'. Brooks noted that 'other teachers have to have input too in order to own it; otherwise they would ignore it' (documentation, 16 December 1983). The team saw the survey as 'good public relations' as well as a data collection tool. They posted the survey results and several team members described discussions with colleagues about their work at this point.

During year two, team members were less concerned with including colleagues in the process as a way of gaining staff acceptance of the project. This parallels the shift away from including the Principal in the project, which also occurred during year two. When writing a cover letter to teachers for the second administration of the Maslach Burnout Inventory (MBI) and School Survey in December of year two, one team member asked if they should include a statement about looking for changes from spring to fall. Another team member said, 'No, don't tell them any more than they need to know ... if they want to know about it they'll ask' (documentation, 1 December 1983). The team eventually posted MBI results, distributed the final report to the faculty, and held a full staff meeting to explain the report. Few of their colleagues came to the meeting, perhaps, as the Principal explained, because it was 'a June meeting, after school' (interview, 7/83). But teacher apathy may have also been the result of other teachers' lack of direct involvement in the team's process of action research. Although team members collected information from their colleagues and provided them with collated results, they did not engage them in the process of action research, perhaps because the team wanted to maintain control over its process and product, and perhaps because they perceived their colleagues' lack of interest. As a result, the team, like James and Ebbutt and the teachers Carr and Kemmis described, gained personal and professional satisfaction from the project but little collegial support for the changes they advocated.

Institutionalizing Collaborative Action Research in Schools

The relationships negotiated between a collaborative action research team, its school administration and its colleagues influence whether or not the process of action research or its products will become a part of the institution. Will the team continue its work after outside support (people and/or funding) is withdrawn? Will other action research teams form in the school to address classroom or school concerns? Many studies of collaborative action research end with these questions, implying that they have not created and left behind structures which will sustain the process once the central team or outside facilitator withdraws from the project (Elliott, 1985). Teachers who have invested so much in such projects may experience feelings of disappointment when a project ends without any mechanisms in place for continuation (Jacullo-Noto, 1984).

Decisions the team makes about the role of the school administration and the involvement of the rest of the school faculty affect institutionalization. Administrative and collegial support of the process of collaborative action research as a problem solving tool may lead to future projects initiated by practitioners rather than outsiders. Support for a particular product of action research (for example, new methods for assessing low-achieving students) may lead to changed practices. But, as we have seen, such support requires some level of involvement, and an action research team will have to balance its own group needs and its need to include others in order to assure project longevity.

In the ARCS project, the team made few decisions that would allow it to institutionalize its process or its findings. The Principal, in his final interview, said he would be open to other collaborative groups, yet he made no attempt to make action research a method of school problem-solving. The faculty, fairly uninvolved in ARCS, could not advocate a process they had not experienced. And the team's findings which correlated low teacher morale and lack of input into decision-making and school policy seemed to remain unconnected to future administrative and teacher actions. The project influenced the teachers involved in it, but neither its process nor its product became an integral part of the school as an institution.

It is difficult to change schools; institutional structures carry layers of expectations and norms which impede attempts to create and maintain change (Lieberman and Miller, 1984; Lortie, 1975; Sarason, 1971). Action research teams may consciously or unconsciously recognize these impediments and opt for projects and intra-school relationships which allow for smaller changes and/or personal and professional growth and satisfaction rather than large-scale change and institutional commitment. However, we now know enough about collaborative action research — its processes, its problems and its possible results — to begin to look for ways of legitimizing and perhaps institutionalizing action research projects from their inception, rather than waiting until they are winding down to ask what will happen to them. Decisions about the project's relationship to the school can be made from the outset and along the way that will allow the cycles of action research, the group processes, and the teacher-defined areas of research to become an integral part of the school environment. Those who initiate collaborative action research need to use new understandings of its processes and issues to make action research the way in which a school conceptualizes and addresses issues and problems which arise.

Conclusion

Each collaborative action research project will resolve the issues involved in the relationship between the school and the project in different ways. Decisions made consciously or unconsciously will affect this relationship, which will in turn influence the processes and outcomes of a project. Despite the differences, several patterns seem to emerge from this issue, principles which may help guide future action researchers.

(i) The school climate may influence teachers' willingness to participate in collaborative action research. It will certainly influence the questions they choose to ask, the data collection tools they use, the analysis they undertake, and the use they make of their findings.

(ii) Administrative support is needed to legitimize and institutionalize the processes and products of action research, but administrative participation on the team may interfere with the goals of collaborative action research. If administrative support includes administrative involvement on the team, participants must acknowledge and deal with possible conflicts between collaboration and control.

(iii) Collaborative action research teams which work in isolation from the rest of their school may have a positive group and professional experience but they will be less likely to have an impact on school practice. Only by gradually involving colleagues in the process of action research can a collaborative action research team influence policy and practice beyond (and sometimes even within) their own classrooms.

(iv)   If collaborative action research is to survive in schools when outside facilitators and funding withdraw, participants must develop structures that allow the method and the products of action research to endure. Explicitly addressing issues of school climate and administrative and colleague involvement in collaborative action research may be the first step in this process.

Issue: Project Control

Most collaborative action research projects in the United States, United Kingdom and Australia are initiated by university faculty working either independently or through public or private funding agencies. Their goals fit the action research model: they want to learn more about and perhaps improve some aspect of school or classroom practice, provide teachers with the opportunity for personal and professional development and perhaps study the process of action research itself. Because these projects tend to be externally initiated, however, they face a second major issue: balancing the demands of the externally-originated project and the expectation that in collaborative action research, practitioners will control the project content and process.

Collaborative action research, as described in Chapter 1, has several requirements if it is to lead to improved practice, greater theoretical understanding, and professional development. One of these require- ments is that the project should focus on practitioners' concerns, specifically on problems or practices that could be improved. A second requirement is that those concerned with this problem or practice should be involved in every phase of the research activity. A third requirement is that the project should draw on each participant's skills and insights, using a democratic group process which allows all voices to be heard. An externally defined and funded project may have difficulty in satisfying these requirements.

Two sets of questions about project control in collaborative action research emerge from analysis of a range of projects. The first group of questions addresses project focus and design: Who defines the overall focus of the project? If the focus is established before teachers join the action research project, how will the project accommodate teachers' concerns and issues that differ from the project focus? Can collaborative action research reach its goals if teachers are not involved in problem definition from the outset?

The second set of questions deals with project leadership. What is the role of project coordinators? Are they evaluators, facilitators, team members? When is the perspective and guidance of project coordinators useful in helping an action research team reach its goals and when does it interfere with the teachers' processes of planning, observing, and reflecting? Each project will resolve these issues in ways which best meet its own situation, but certain patterns seem to emerge from an examination of several projects in the sections which follow.

Project Focus and Design

In order to get funding for collaborative action research projects and/or to gain entry into schools or systems, outside researchers may need to choose a focus for the project they propose. In some cases, the focus is a clearly-defined topic; in others it is an umbrella concept under which teachers can identify their own problems for investigation. Each case presents project coordinators and teachers with a different set of issues, as the examples presented below illustrate.

The Girls Into Science and Technology (GIST) project (Kelly, 1985; Whyte, 1986) was initiated by two university researchers and coordinated by them through a project team. The team worked with eight co-educational comprehensive schools in Greater Manchester on three goals: advancing understanding about girls' avoidance of science and technology in school, encouraging girls to continue their studies in these areas and influencing teachers' attitudes and behaviors in regard to girls' participation in school subjects (Whyte, 1986).

Because the problem under investigation came from the project team rather than from teachers, the coordinators noted that, 'Our first task was to convince teachers, many of whom had never consciously thought about the situation, that this was indeed an educational problem which could be tackled in schools' (Kelly, 1985, p. 135). The coordinators emphasized their desire to involve teachers in examining the issues in their own schools and planning change strategies that met teachers' needs. They found that this did not always occur:

> In practice, this took a long time and most of the ideas came from the project team. Teachers did select which of the possible strategies to adopt. But because the impetus for the project came from us, and our commitment was, at least at the beginning, greater than theirs, the choice was certainly guided. (*ibid*)

Both Whyte (1986) and Kelly (1985) note that despite their need to maintain external control in order to meet project goals, the dominant role of the project team created some problems. There was some teacher resistance to the project, attributed in part to anti–feminism and in part to feelings that outsiders didn't 'understand the problems faced by the classroom teacher' (Whyte, 1986, p. 184). Because change in teacher attitude and behavior was a project goal, teachers may have felt they were being evaluated — feelings which prevent open participation and risk taking. Whyte (*ibid*) notes that strong external control might not have been the best approach: 'More rapid change might result from an approach begun within schools, in which certain members of the staff have clear responsibility for promoting the innovation' (p. 162).

In this project, the given focus provided by the outside team often took precedence over teacher involvement in the process of action research. As a result, the project met its first goal of providing more knowledge about aspects of schooling which discourage girls. It also succeeded, at least in the short term, in providing some practical solutions to the problem: changing curriculum materials and approaches; developing teachers' awareness of language use, patterns of girl/boy participation and subject choice; and using speakers and programs to provide girls with role models in science and technology. But choices made about project control led to more mixed results in reaching the goal of changing teachers' attitudes and behaviors or providing a professional growth experience that would allow teachers to become more reflective and effective practitioners. Studies of teachers' attitudes showed as much resistance and ambivalence as change in new approaches to their own teaching and in their feelings about the project (Whyte, 1986).

In other action research projects, the outside project initiators provide an overall focus without defining the specific topics teachers will examine. In the Teacher-Pupil Interaction and the Quality of Learning Project (TIQL), initiated and coordinated by John Elliott through the Cambridge Institute of Education in England, participating teacher teams were told to define projects related to the overall problem of 'the apparent dilemma between teaching for understanding and teaching for assessment' (Elliott, 1985, p. 244). Early on in the project, central coordinators faced several problems related to project control. First, some teachers who agreed to be in the project wanted assurance that they would be able to focus on their own problems; they did not want to be required to do something for the Institute. The central team provided a mixed response: they assured teachers that in action research, teachers should address their own concerns, but that the central team did expect teachers' problems to be linked to the general idea of teaching for understanding. The second problem arose when teams began to define the problems they would investigate. As they looked at the issue of teaching for understanding in relation to their own concerns, teachers came up with a wide range of problems, diverse both within and across schools. Some members of the central team felt a need to clarify the general focus so that teachers would be investigating more related and useful issues. Elliott, as project coordinator, worked to address both problems by allowing teachers to investigate chosen topics while helping them find connections to the overall theme. He described his role as follows:

> In citing a specific problem area in our proposal for funding prior to extensive discussions with teachers, I created a dilemma for myself and my colleagues on the central team. On the one hand, we saw our role as a facilitating one, yet on the other, I had made the project team accountable to the Council for ensuring that teachers addressed the specific issue of 'examinations/assessment'. My way out of this particular dilemma was to opt for facilitation rather than control. (*ibid*, p. 247)

In GIST, project coordinators maintained control of the research project and design, while in TIQL, project coordinators shared project definition with participating practitioners in order to meet, as much as possible, the requirement that action research draw on teachers' immediate concerns. The GIST project succeeded in meeting two of its three initially-stated project goals. Although TIQL may have been somewhat less successful in reaching the theoretical goal of helping teachers examine the relationship between teaching for understanding and teaching for assessment, the project seems to have been more successful than GIST in helping teachers learn the processes of observing, acting, and reflecting that are the keys to action research.

The ARCS team also began its project with an externally provided focus on school change. During early team meetings the team addressed questions provided by the university researcher about school context and school change: How were changes made in their school? What changes had the school experienced? What changes were to come? From this initial focus, problems and concerns emerged for the team to investigate, including scheduling, student ability grouping and teacher morale. The focus on school change led the ARCS team to concentrate on school rather than classroom topics and suggested that they should aim for school change — a goal which proved to be difficult to achieve.

Throughout the project, the university researcher had to decide when to let teachers pursue their concerns and when to intervene with ideas, materials, and project designs which might be more effective in achieving school change. For example, when teachers chose to investigate teacher morale, the university researcher asked if, based on their results, they planned to act on their concern about teacher morale, perhaps by forming teacher groups or asking the Principal to involve more teachers in decision-making. The team was reluctant to take such actions and chose instead to study teacher morale and report on its findings without instigating specific changes in the school. In this case, the university researcher accepted the teachers' choice. The project met the action requirements that teachers be involved in defining problems of concern to them, but it was somewhat less successful in achieving school change through action research. Again, decisions about project control involved balancing externally defined goals and the processes required to meet teachers' needs in collaborative action research. Choices made about project definition and control influenced the success of a project as measured by teacher satisfaction and growth, improved practice and a contribution to knowledge in the field.

Many collaborative action research projects, of necessity, start the project and begin to define research problems without the key participants: the teachers. The external initiator often presents teacher participants with an overall goal or focus and asks them to identify their own particular topics of investigation within it. Outside coordinators must then deal with teachers' different interpretations of the focus as they choose research questions. The issues of most concern to teachers may in fact be far removed from the centrally provided umbrella concept or topic.

Whose issues should be pursued? If project coordinators suggest that externally-defined ideas should remain the focus, then teachers have lost the opportunity to explore their own interpretations and concerns. If, however, teacher participants are completely free to define their own questions, they may lose the advantage of working together and exploring a shared topic, a process that can lead to more profound understanding of a given issue than the separate, piecemeal approach. If teachers pursue their own problems, outside coordinators may also face the displeasure (and withdrawal of support) of the funding agency or school system which expected teachers to investigate the pre-established topic.

Although there is no one way to resolve this issue, the examples presented suggest that emphasis on an externally defined focus will lead to success in achieving greater understanding of the given topic but less success in helping teachers see collaborative action research as a method for examining problems of concern to them. If the external focus is flexible enough, it may guide teachers' work while still allowing them to participate in all aspects of the cycles of action research. Thus, choices made about project control will influence project outcomes, perhaps determining whether the project will emphasize theory, practice, or staff development.

Project Leadership

Questions of project control continue through a collaborative action research project as outside coordinators define their roles in relation to action research teams. To some extent, the leadership provided by an outside coordinator will depend on the clarity and strength of the predefined project focus. In the TIQL project, for example, Elliott described himself as a facilitator, addressing both the needs of the teacher teams and the demands of the central team. As the project progressed, the central team had to balance its own desire to focus the project and teachers' needs to clarify their own ideas through observation and reflection. Some teachers did not want the central team to interfere, but others wanted clearer direction, feeling that the emphasis on the process of action research kept them from addressing specific questions that would lead to useful outcomes. Elliott, and others on the central team who met periodically with the teacher teams, had to exercise a form of democratic leadership which would allow teachers to own the project while it kept the project within a certain framework.

Jacullo-Noto (1984) describes a similar issue in the Interactive Research and Development on Schools project carried out in three different sites. Although the university researchers did not bring an agenda or focus to the teams in this project, Jacullo-Noto found that teachers began the project very concerned with 'doing it right'.

> The teachers involved in IR&DS repeatedly looked to the university for direction. Deciding when to provide direction and how much to provide was critical in this process. ... Knowing when to provide help and when to encourage teachers to struggle with a problem on their own can greatly affect how much teachers learn from this experience. (p. 218)

The approach taken by the outside coordinators will influence the processes and outcomes of an action research project. In the Danforth Foundation Improvement of Instruction Project, for example, the two coordinators (university faculty members) asked teams in ten schools in St. Louis, Missouri, to identify an instructional goal and decide on strategies for reaching and evaluating that goal. As schools defined their projects, some chose school climate and morale rather than instructional goals and others chose instructional issues and strategies that appeared either too broad or too narrow for effective investigation and change. The coordinators chose to take what they describe as a 'laissez-faire' attitude, giving them feedback in the form of questions and suggestions but allowing each team to pursue its own design.

In retrospect, the coordinators saw pros and cons in their approach. One positive outcome was a genuine trust that developed between school participants, teacher educators and project coordinators. Teachers found that the project did indeed allow them to make their own decisions and pursue their own courses of action. On the other hand, project coordinators believed that more external direction toward a common set of principles would have focused the overall project and improved the quality of individual projects at certain schools. Thus, the coordinators found that leadership decisions about when to allow participants to learn through experience and when to offer an outside perspective or relevant information which would move the team toward its goal influenced both group interaction and what each team was able to achieve (Cohn and Finch, 1987).

Many of the leadership issues addressed in the ARCS project have been described in Chapter 5. It is important to note, however, that this project differs from those described above in two important ways. First, it included only two teams rather than eight or ten. As a result, it faced fewer problems of coordination and focus among disparate teams. Second, in ARCS, each university faculty member/coordinator was also a team member. In most other collaborative action research projects, the central coordinators remain outside of the team structure. This may allow teams more freedom to define and carry out their own projects, but it may also contribute to the problems of project control described above. As team members, the project coordinators in ARCS still had to balance externally defined project demands and teachers' concerns and needs, but they were there to do so on a weekly basis. The relationships they developed with the teams over the course of the project allowed them to voice project concerns as team members rather than as external authorities. Given their understanding of teachers' stages of development, their participation also allowed them to provide the supports and challenges needed to encourage individual team members to assume leadership roles. The university researchers' use of a developmental approach to leadership encouraged teachers to take on leadership roles from the beginning of the project. Thus, the process of democratic leadership (described in Chapter 5) could emerge unencumbered by a hierarchy of external coordinators who were not a part of the ongoing group process. Although not feasible in all collaborative action research projects, inclusion of project coordinators on action research teams seems to help minimize some of the conflict between project control and the requirements of collaborative action research.

Conclusion

This section has focused on issues of project control and leadership in collaborative action research projects which begin with a given framework or topic. Action research which starts with teacher-defined problems, whether initiated by teachers or outsiders, will face different issues of control and coordination. Elliott (1985) suggests, for example, that teachers may resist going beyond the stage of solitary reflection on their own concerns to sharing their insights with others and comparing them to an existing body of knowledge. In this case, an outside consultant may be able to help teachers see where their work fits into other studies and find acceptable ways of communicating their findings to other teachers and researchers.

Again, each project will find its own balance in the issue of project control, and each chosen balance will have its effect on group processes and research outcomes. Given that there will be differences, some general principles seem to emerge from an examination of project control:

(i) Funding agencies and school systems will continue to demand that projects have a focus before they begin. Sometimes that focus can be defined by outside coordinators, especially, perhaps, when a problem emerges with which teachers have little experience. The best example of this is the GIST project. In many other cases, however, it seems possible for outside coordinators to meet with interested practitioners in advance, allowing them to share in decisions about the project focus from the outset.

(ii) In order to meet the requirements of collaborative action

research, any project focus or theme must be flexible enough
to withstand the cycles of action research. Within these
cycles, participants must be free to address immediate
concerns and modify their actions and goals when
observation and reflection suggest this is necessary.

(iii)   Project coordinators must be sensitive to team needs,
providing information and ideas when they will be useful to
the group. Withholding information and ideas for fear of
swaying the group seems contradictory to the collaborative
process. Yet, if such information is to be seen as a
contribution rather than a mandate, project coordinators have
to establish a collegial, trusting relationship with the team
that makes them a part of the democratic process. Elliott's
(1985) concept of facilitation and the developmental
support/challenge model presented in this book are keys to
such a relationship, as is the coordinator's frequent participation in the group process.

Issue: Project Outcomes

Previous research suggests that the mutual participation of teachers and
researchers in collaborative action research will lead to theory grounded
in practical realities, improved practice, and teachers' personal and
professional growth (Elliott, 1977; Hord, 1981; Little, 1981; Tikunoff,
Ward and Griffin, 1979). In the past few chapters, we have demonstrated that, in reality, a research team's emphasis and outcomes may
depend on a number of variables: project control and focus; the
relationship of the team to the school or system; the interests, developmental stages, and skills of participants; the choice of a particular
research topic; and the processes of interaction and leadership which
emerge in the group. The integration of these elements may lead to a
collaborative action research project which succeeds in meeting one or
two of the expected goals, but not necessarily all three. In this section
we examine some of the conflicting demands of the goals of action
research.

Theory and Practice

In Chapter 1, we discussed how collaborative action research reemerged
in the 1970s and 1980s as a method which addressed both researchers'

needs for school-based study and teachers' desires to be involved in more effective staff development. Both university researchers and teachers were looking for an alternative to linear models of research and development in which theory and practice remained unrelated and therefore unaffected by one another. The participation of both teachers and researchers on an action research team was expected to lead to a connection between theory and practice through which theory would be enriched and practice improved.

Action researchers in the 1970s and 1980s had to defend their methods against critiques of action research made in previous years. Thus, they had to prove that teachers could produce research that measured up to social scientific standards and contributed to more effective school or classroom practices. In their report on the Interactive Research and Development on Teaching study, for example, Tikunoff, Ward and Griffin (1979) clearly emphasize that teachers involved produced 'rigorous' research based on problems in practice.

And yet, many collaborative action research projects during the last two decades have had difficulty in producing both improved practice and contributions to educational theory (Adelman, 1985). Kemmis (1980) notes that traditional educational theory did not emerge from many of his studies:

> Preliminary analysis suggests that the theoretical prospects for action research are only moderate, if 'theoretical' payoff is measured in terms of the literature of educational researchers. ... If the theoretical payoff is defined in terms of the development of critical communities of practitioners, then the results are more encouraging. (p. 13)

Some action researchers found that the choices they made about their projects led to an emphasis on practice rather than generalizable theory. James and Ebbutt (1981), as noted earlier, explain that because they had not interacted with the rest of the school, their action research was useful to them but not to a larger audience. Florio (1983) discovered that teachers in her action research group, the Written Literacy Forum, were primarily concerned with using research data to produce classroom materials for their colleagues. They had less interest in analyzing the data, comparing it to other studies of writing, and producing general ideas which contributed to the larger body of knowledge on writing instruction. In both the Danforth Project and TIQL, project coordinators' decisions to de-emphasize the centralized project focus led teachers to address more immediate concerns that may or may not have contributed to broader understanding in the areas of instruction or teaching for understanding, respectively.

In the ARCS project, decisions made about school-project relations and project focus led the team to a study which contributed to theoretical understanding of the relationship between school organization and teacher morale but had little impact on school practice. One key reason for the lack of impact on educational practice was the school-based emphasis of the team's project. Most recent collaborative action research teams have been classroom-based and have focused their investigations on specific curricula or teacher behaviors over which they had some control. In New York, for example, the three teams in the Interactive Research and Development on Schools project (Lieberman, 1983) studied a writing curriculum, teacher interventions with disruptive children and qualities of teachers which lead to positive work attitudes. Teachers involved in the Teacher Initiated Research project (Evans *et al*, 1981) all investigated issues of concern in their own classrooms.

In the ARCS project, however, teachers focused on school-based problems of scheduling which were beyond their immediate realm of control. To change scheduling practices, elements of the entire school organization would have to be restructured. Teachers felt that they lacked the power to do this and indicated an unwillingness to challenge given domains of responsibility in the school. Instead, they concentrated on producing research which would be acceptable to others in the research community and which contributed to an understanding of factors involved in teacher morale and school scheduling practices. Because their project was school-based, the team's study fulfilled the expectation that collaborative action research leads to theory which is grounded in the complexities of the teaching and learning environment. Given their choice of research topic and their relationship to the school context, however, they could not use the project to create immediate changes in school practice.

Conscious and unconscious decisions made about project emphasis and process will influence the outcomes of a collaborative action research project. It may be difficult to produce traditional educational theory and change classroom or school practice all within the same project; the two outcomes may depend on different choices. The most effective way to change practice, for example, may be to have teachers working in small groups on issues of concern to them. Generalizable theory, on the other hand, may require larger numbers of teachers investigating similar issues, sharing their work, gradually expanding their involvement and impact. The two goals are not mutually exclusive, but they may be difficult to achieve simultaneously.

Perhaps some of the difficulty lies, however, in our approach to educational theory. A first step in addressing the theory/practice issue may be to redefine educational theory to include teachers' understanding of the problems and practices in their classrooms and schools (Cummings and Hustler, 1986; Street, 1986). At present, as Carr and Kemmis (1986) point out, much educational theory is produced by people outside of the school community who use the 'straightforward application of the scientific disciplines to educational problems' (p. 124). Elliott (1985) describes this as research for products rather than understanding; Carr and Kemmis (1986) claim that it produces a body of knowledge unrelated to practical situations. More recently, qualitative methods have provided new ways to look at classrooms, report findings, and connect theory to practice (Burgess, 1985a, 1985b and 1985c). Action research in particular offers a different kind of educational theory, one which is 'grounded in the problems and perspectives of educational practice' (Carr and Kemmis, 1986, p. 122) and made up of the insights of practitioners as they use a range of social scientific, intuitive, and practical methods to address their concerns. If this theory is recognized as legitimate, then action research will be closer to meeting its goals of producing both improved practice and educational theory.

A second step may also be required. Some action researchers do not seem to go far enough, taking the time to experience the many cycles of action research needed to develop general understanding or theory. If a project goes through a single cycle of action research — planning, acting, and reflecting — it may only be problem solving. This 'single loop' (Carr and Kemmis, 1986) process may lead to either change in practice or some general ideas which could be applied to practical problems, but it will probably not produce enduring improvements in practice and useful, generalizable theory. In the ARCS project, for example, while the team did experience several cycles of planning, acting and reflecting, it stopped in a reflection stage. The ARCS team produced new ideas about teacher morale, but it did not take the next step of planning actions to address or test out the ideas it generated. The cyclical process of action research demands that it be ongoing, addressing emerging concerns. Teachers in the ARCS project recognized this, but lacked the project structure and institutional relationship that would have encouraged them to continue the process.

John: Action research is research that is ongoing, and as the answers to your questions come up or a shift in what you want to research comes up, you just keep right on researching, whatever direction. (interview, 12/82)

George: In action research, inevitably you leave many tangential questions, loose ends. It might be nice to build in a way that these loose ends or tangents could be systematically addressed. (interview, 12/82)

In action research, which emphasizes the teacher as researcher, teachers must be encouraged to move beyond the stage of solitary self-reflection to sharing their ideas, relating their new understanding to other information on the topic under investigation, and writing up their findings (Anning, 1981; Desforges, Cockburn and Bennett, 1986; Elliott, 1985). While self-reflection may lead to the professional development of an individual teacher and perhaps some improvement in practice, it may not contribute to useful educational knowledge which can and should be a part of action research (Elliott, 1985).

Thus, while it may be difficult for collaborative action research to produce theory and practice, it is not impossible. It may be necessary to redefine acceptable theory to include the understanding of practice which emerges from teachers' work as researchers. Action researchers will also need to make choices about their projects which allow them to push beyond individual or group reflection to more continuous cycles of action research. Then we will be better able to evaluate how successful collaborative action research is in contributing to both theory and practice.

Personal and Professional Development

Previous work in collaborative action research has proposed that teacher involvement leads to teachers' personal and professional growth (Jacullo-Noto, 1984; Mosher, 1974; Oja and Pine, 1981; Pine, 1981); greater school staff collegiality and experimentation (Little, 1981); and improved practice among project participants (Booth and Hall, 1986; Hall, 1975; Elliott, 1977). Teachers engaged in action research emphasize that personal and professional growth result from participation in the *process* of collaborative action research. They frequently suggested that their understanding of the process was ultimately a more valuable outcome than the research project itself. For example, teachers participating in the Ford Teaching Project (Elliott, 1977) said that the value of their project lay as much in the opportunity to come together and examine practice as it did in the research product. A teacher involved in Florio's (1983) Written Literacy Forum said:

> I wonder if it's not so much what we found out but the whole process we went through (that was important). For people to accept what we found out, they have to go through the process, too. (p. 10)

Teachers on the ARCS teams also noted that the action research process emerged as the most important and meaningful aspect of the experience. One teacher commented:

> I think being introduced to action research as a process has been the most valuable part of the project for me. I think if more people sat down and went through the process the way we did, they would recognize the fact that there isn't always a black and white for everything that you deal with and that there are reasons why things are done the way they're done. (interview, 12/83)

For ARCS participants, the collaborative action research process contributed to confidence in their own ability to identify, confront, and solve classroom and school-based problems. Two teachers in the project described some modification in their classroom teaching, and in both cases they suggest that the changes arose out of new, more positive feelings about themselves as people and professionals. The project provided the opportunity, time, and support for these teachers to explore and examine themselves and their practice. Given the project's school-based focus, however, changes in classroom practice appeared to be indirect rather than immediately apparent.

Through participation, teachers became more familiar with research language, methodology and design, a familiarity which seems to have made them better consumers of educational research and, perhaps, more skilled researchers. Some teachers in the ARCS project have suggested that they would like to use their new confidence, skills, and understanding to carry out other action research projects, to write about their experience as researchers, and to present papers about action research at local and national conferences.

The expectation that collaborative action research leads to professional development may, however, require further investigation. Although teachers themselves note that they have changed and say that they foresee future projects or actions which build on newly-acquired competencies, no longitudinal studies exist which investigate the actual use of new skills or the permanence of change in self-perception or behavior which results from participation in an action research project. We can say that teachers involved in this, and other, collaborative action research projects experienced positive professional growth, but further study is needed to document the longevity of changes in classroom and school practice.

In Chapter 4, we explain that teachers' stages of development influence the form and quality of their participation on an action research team. Teachers at different stages may assume different roles on the team, contribute different perspectives to the project, and experience the group process and research project outcomes differently. Teachers appear to benefit in different ways from their participation in action research depending on their conceptual, interpersonal, ego and moral stages of development. Further study is needed on the connections between teacher stage of development and the personal and professional growth experienced by participants in collaborative action research projects.

Conclusion

An examination of the proposed outcomes of collaborative action research — contributions to theory, improved practice, and professional development — illustrates their interconnections. If participants in action research aim to improve practice, they will plan, act and reflect in ways which lead to greater understanding of teaching and learning. Improvements in practice will then be based on systematic investigation of a number of issues and alternatives. If participants aim for greater understanding of ideas about teaching and learning, they will develop a stronger theoretical basis, grounded in the reality of the classroom or school, from which to plan enduring change in practice. If they work through cycles which allow them to experiment with practice and begin to generalize their insights, they will experience personal and professional development which will help them to become critical, reflective practitioners. Thus the pursuit of all three goals in collaborative action research is crucial if any one of the three is to be achieved.

A collaborative action research project may be more successful in reaching one or two of these goals as a result of decisions made about the project's structure, control, and place in the school context. Thus, a project may succeed in helping individual teachers improve classroom practices without contributing to a broader understanding of the pedagogical issues involved, or it may produce general ideas without translating those ideas into practice. To call such projects unsuccessful would minimize the value of the goals they did reach. And yet, given the connections between the three goals, a project's inability to reach one will influence the effectiveness of other outcomes. Theoretical ideas that are untested by practice are less useful than those which have been examined in action. Improvements in practice may not endure and cannot be easily transferred to other situations unless teachers understand the underlying concepts.

Although there is no one right way of conducting collaborative action research, the examples provided in this chapter suggest that a project which involves teachers in creating a focus, establishes a working relationship with school administrators and colleagues, uses outside researchers as democratic leaders and developmental facilitators and plans to carry out continuing cycles of action research will be most successful. Action researchers must therefore aim for improved practice, contributions to theory, and personal and professional development as they balance decisions about the key issues of school-project relationships, project control and preferred outcomes.

Guide to Further Reading

Collaborative Action Research

BURGESS, R. (Ed) (1984) *The Research Process in Educational Settings: Ten Case Studies*, Lewes, Falmer Press. Presents ten first person accounts of how research is conducted in schools, focusing primarily on how research project question and design develops over time to address the needs of the participants people and the demands of the classroom or school setting.

BURGESS, R. (Ed) (1985) *Field Methods in the Study of Education*, Lewes, Falmer Press. Uses first-hand, self-reflective analyses of ethnographic research in classrooms and schools to illustrate themes such as the relationship between research and theory, gender and research, and research and policy.

BURGESS, R. (Ed) (1985) *Issues in Educational Research: Qualitative Methods*, Lewes, Falmer Press. A collection of essays on the relation of research to theory, policy and practice by individuals using qualitative methods in educational projects.

BURGESS, R. (Ed) (1985) *Strategies of Educational Research: Qualitative Methods*, Lewes, Falmer Press. Essays on the strategies and issues involved in the use of qualitative methods in educational research.

CARR, W. and KEMMIS, S. (1986) *Becoming Critical: Education, Knowledge and Action Research*, Lewes, Falmer Press. Examines and redefines the relationships between educational theory, research, and practice and presents action research as a critical educational science.

Collaboration for Change (1986) Special issue of *Educational Leadership*, 43, 5. Describes and analyzes several school-community and school-university collaborative projects in the US.

HUSTLER, D., CASSIDY, T. and CUFF, T. (Eds) (1986) *Action Research in Classrooms*, London, Allen and Unwin. A set of essays by those engaged in action research illustrating the possibilities, problems, and resources available for those interested in carrying out their own projects.

KEMMIS, S. and MCTAGGART, R. (1982) *The Action Research Planner*, Victoria, Deakin University. A 'how to' guidebook for conducting action research in classrooms and schools.

NIXON, J. (Ed) (1981) *A Teachers' Guide to Action Research*, London, Grant-McIntyre, Ltd. One of the first collections of essays describing teacher-based research in the United Kingdom by the practitioners who carried out the projects in their classrooms.

Peabody Journal of Education (1988) 64, 1 and 64, 2. A double theme issue on action research which examines critical issues and processes of action research using examples of projects from the US, UK and Australia.

School Improvement: Research, Craft and Concept (1984) Special issue of *Teachers College Record*, 86, 1. Articles in which researchers involved in many recent studies of schools in the US reflect on their work and suggest new ways of approaching school improvement.

SIROTNIK, K. and GOODLAD, J. (1988) *School-University Partnerships in Action*, New York, Teachers College Press. Provides a general model for effective collaboration between schools and universities and supports and illustrates that model with case studies of successful school-university partnerships.

WHYTE, J. (1986) *Girls Into Science and Technology: The Story of a Project*, London, Routledge & Kegan Paul. Documents and analyzes a researcher-initiated action research project in Manchester, England aimed at encouraging girls to continue work in science and technology.

Adult Cognitive-Developmental Stages

BASSECHES, M. (1984) *Dialectical Thinking and Adult Development*, Norwood, NJ, Ablex. Investigates the meaning and measurement of dialectical thinking with chapters on the developmental significance of adult life crises and work as a context for adult development.

BELENKY, M. F., CLINCHY, B. M., GOLDBERGER, N. and TARULE, J. (1986) *Women's Ways of Knowing: The Development of Self, Voice, and Mind*, New York, Basic Books. Based on interviews with women, describes five cognitive patterns unique to women: silence, received knowing, subjective knowing, procedural knowing and constructed knowing; introduces a view of connected teaching and connected education.

DALOZ, L. A. (1986) *Effective Teaching and Mentoring: Realizing the Transformational Power of Adult Learning Experiences*, San Francisco, CA, Jossey-Bass. Describes developmental growth that can occur in adult lives as a result of higher education and includes a description of teaching as care.

GILLIGAN, C. (1982) *In a Different Voice: Psychological Theory and Women's Development*. Cambridge, MA, Harvard University Press. Describes the differences between moral development in women and men and proposes an ethic of care and response.

HUNT, D. E. (1975) *Matching Models in Education*, Monograph Series No. 10, Toronto, Ontario Institute for Studies in Education. Provides background in Hunt's conceptual level stage theory and the developmental education strategy of 'matching' teaching method with student conceptual level characteristics.

KEGAN, R. (1982) *The Evolving Self: Problem and Process in Human Development*, Cambridge, MA, Harvard University Press. Describes the evolution of developmental stages with particular attention to the elements of growth and loss, the balance achieved at each stage, and transformation to the next stage.

KOHLBERG, L. (1981) *The Philosophy of Moral Development*, New York, Harper and Row. Collection of Kohlberg's writing on moral stages in relation to: the aims of education, the idea of justice, legal and political issues and problems beyond justice.

KOHLBERG, L. (1984) *The Psychology of Moral Development*, New York, Harper and Row. Collection of Kohlberg's early writings and recent research on moral development theory, descriptions of empirical methods and results, and responses to critics.

LOEVINGER, J. (1976) *Ego Development*, San Francisco, CA, Jossey-Bass. Description of the stages of ego development and the empirical basis and research data on the Sentence Completion Test.

LYONS, N. (1983) 'Two perspectives: On self, relationship and morality', *Harvard Educational Review*, 53, 2, pp. 125–45. Proceeding from the work of Gilligan, Lyons identifies two perspectives of autonomy/justice and connection/care and documents women's predominant perspective of connection and care.

NODDINGS, N. (1984) *Caring: A Feminine Approach to Ethics and Moral Education*, Berkeley, CA, University of California Press. Identifies women's approach to moral problems and describes moral education as ethical caring between teacher and student.

MODGIL, S. and MODGIL, C. (Eds) (1986) *Lawrence Kohlberg: Consensus and Controversy*, Lewes, Falmer Press. Current debates on Kohlberg's moral development theory and moral education practice by a wide variety of theorists and researchers representing particular areas of knowledge.

OJA, S. N. (1980) 'Adult development is implicit in staff development,' *The Journal of Staff Development*, 1, 2, pp. 7–56. A condensed review of theories of adult development, including the developmental task and stage theorists with applications of the theories for teacher development.

PERRY, W. (1970) *Forms of Intellectual and Ethical Development in the College Years*, New York, Holt, Rinehart and Winston. In-depth interviews and longitudinal data on Harvard students from their freshman to senior years gives vivid descriptions of the emotional turmoil connected with intellectual growth from positions of dualism and multiplism to relativism and commitment.

REST, J. R. (1986) *Moral Development: Advances in Research and Theory*, New York, Praeger. Reports the theory and research conducted using the Defining Issues Test of moral judgment with one section focusing on deliberate educational interventions designed to promote moral judgment development.

SCHON, D. (1983) *The Reflective Practitioner: How Professionals Think in Action*, New York, Basic Books. Illustrates the process of reflection on practice; practitioners are defined as more effective if they can redefine problems, as well as accept problems as presented, and if they can create an atmosphere of collaborative commitment with others, as well as delegating or acting unilaterally.

SELMAN, R. L. (1980) *The Growth of Interpersonal Understanding*, New York, Academic Press. One more framework within stage development constructs, this theory of interpersonal understanding identifies five levels of social perspective taking based on both the individual's cognitive capability and the social context.

Bibliography

ADELMAN, C. (1985) 'Some problems of ethnographer culture shock' in BURGESS, R. (Ed) *Field Methods in the Study of Education*, Lewes, Falmer Press, pp. 37–50.

ANNING, A. (1986) 'Curriculum in action' in HUSTLER, D., CASSIDY, T. and CUFF, T. (Eds) *Action Research in Classrooms and Schools*, London, Allen and Unwin, pp. 56–66.

ARLIN, P. K. (1975) 'Cognitive development in adulthood: A fifth stage?', *Developmental Psychology*, 13, pp. 297–8.

ARGYRIS, C. and SCHON, D. A. (1978) *Organizational Learning: A Theory of Action Perspectives*, Reading, MA, Addison-Wesley Press.

BALES, R. F. (1951) *Interaction Process Analysis*, Cambridge, MA, Addison-Wesley Press.

BALES, R. F. and STRODTBECK, F. L. (1951) 'Phases in group problem solving', *Journal of Abnormal and Social Psychology*, 46, 4, pp. 485–95.

BALL, S. J. (1984) 'Beachside reconsidered: Reflections on a methodological apprenticeship' in BURGESS, R. (Ed) *The Research Process in Educational Settings: Ten Case Studies*, Lewes, Falmer Press, pp. 69–96.

BASSECHES, M. (1984) *Dialectical Thinking and Adult Development*, Norwood, NJ, Ablex.

BASSEY, M. (1986) 'Does action research require sophisticated research methods' in HUSTLER, D., CASSIDY, T. and CUFF, T. (Eds) *Action Research in Classrooms and Schools*, London, Allen and Unwin, pp. 18–24.

BELENKY, M. F., CLINCHY, B. M., GOLDBERGER, N. and TARULE, J. (1986) *Women's Ways of Knowing: The Development of Self, Voice, and Mind*, New York, Basic Books.

BENNIS, W. G. and SHEPARD, H. A. (1956) 'A theory of group development', *Human Relations*, 9, 4, pp. 415–57.

BERNIER, J. (1976) 'A psychological education interaction for teacher development', unpublished doctoral dissertation, University of Minnesota.

BION, W. R. (1959) *Experiences in Groups*, New York, Basic Books.

BLOMQUIST, R., BORNSTEIN, S., FINK, G., MICHAUD, R., OJA, S. N. and SMULYAN, L. (1983) *Action Research on Change in Schools: The Relationship between Teacher Morale/Job Satisfaction and Organizational Changes in a Junior High*, Durham, New Hampshire, University of New Hampshire, Collaborative Research Projects Office. (ERIC Document Reproduction Service No. ED269873)

BLUMBERG, A. and GREENFIELD, W. (1980) *The Effective Principal: Perspectives on School Leadership*, Boston, MA, Allyn and Bacon.

BOLMAN, L. (1983) personal communication, Cambridge, MA.

BONNER, H. (1959) *Group Dynamics: Principles and Applications*, New York, The Ronald Press Co.

BOOTH, E., and HALL, N. (1986) 'Making sense of literacy' in HUSTLER, D., CASSIDY, T. and CUFF, T. (Eds) *Action Research in Classrooms and Schools*, London, Allen and Unwin, pp. 95–104.

BORG, W. G. (1965) *Educational Research: An Introduction*, New York, David McKay, Co., Inc.

BOWN, O. H. (1987) 'On the care and feeding of cohabitating practitioners and researchers', paper presented at the annual meeting of the American Educational Research Association, New York.

BURGESS, R. (Ed) (1984) *The Research Process in Educational Settings: Ten Case Studies*, Lewes, Falmer Press.

BURGESS, R. (Ed) (1985a) *Field Methods in the Study of Education*, Lewes, Falmer Press.

BURGESS, R. (Ed) (1985b) *Issues in Educational Research: Qualitative Methods*, Lewes, Falmer Press.

BURGESS, R. (Ed) (1985c) *Strategies of Educational Research: Qualitative Methods* Lewes, Falmer Press.

CARR, W. and KEMMIS, S. (1986) *Becoming Critical: Education, Knowledge, and Action Research*, Lewes, Falmer Press.

CARTWRIGHT, D. and ZANDER, A. (1968) *Group Dynamics*, Evanston, IL, Row, Peterson, and Co.

CASSIDY, T. (1986) 'Initiating and encouraging action research in comprehensive schools' in HUSTLER, D., CASSIDY, T. and CUFF, T. (Eds) *Action Research in Classrooms and Schools*, London, Allen and Unwin, pp. 133–42.

CHEIN, I., COOK, S. W. and HARDING, J. (1948) 'The field of action research', *American Psychologist*, 3, 2, pp. 43–50.

CLIFFORD, G. J. (1973) 'A history on the impact of research on teaching' in TRAVERS, R. W. (Ed) *Second Handbook on the Research of Teaching*, New York, Rand McNally, pp. 1–46.

COHEN, M. and FINCH, M. (1987) 'Teacher leadership and collaboration: Key concepts and issues in school change', paper presented at the annual meeting of the American Educational Research Association, Washington, D.C.

COREY, S. (1952) 'Action research and the solution of practical problems', *Educational Leadership*, 9, 8, pp. 478–84.

COREY, S. M. (1953) *Action Research to Improve School Practices*, New York, Teachers College, Columbia University.

CROSBIE, P. (1975) *Interaction in Small Groups*, New York, Macmillan Publishing Co., Inc.

CUMMINGS, C. (1985) 'Qualitative research in the infant classroom: A personal account' in BURGESS, R. (Ed) *Issues in Educational Research: Qualitative Methods*, Lewes, Falmer Press, pp. 216–50.

CUMMINGS, C. and HUSTLER, D. (1986) 'Teachers' professional knowledge' in HUSTLER, D., CASSIDY, T. and CUFF, T. (Eds) *Action Research in Classrooms and Schools*, London, Allen and Unwin, pp. 36–47.

DAY, C. (1985) 'Professional learning and researcher intervention: An action research perspective', *British Educational Research Journal*, 2, 2, pp. 133–51.

DESFORGES, C., COCKBURN, A. and BENNETT, N. (1986) 'Teachers' perspectives on matching: Implications for action research' in HUSTLER, D., CASSIDY, T. and CUFF, T. (Eds) *Action Research in Classrooms and Schools*, London, Allen and Unwin, pp. 67–72.

EBBUTT, D. (1985) 'Educational action research: Some general concerns and specific quibbles' in BURGESS, R. (Ed) *Issues in Educational Research: Qualitative Methods*, Lewes, Falmer Press, pp. 152–74.

EDMONDS, R. (1979) 'Effective schools for the urban poor', *Educational Leadership*, 37, pp. 15–24.

EDMONDS, R. (1982) 'Programs of school improvement: An overview', paper presented at National Institute of Education Conference, The Implications of Research for Practice, Airlie House, Virginia.

ELLIOTT, J. (1977) 'Developing hypotheses about classrooms from teachers' practical constructs: An account of the work of the Ford Teaching Project', *Interchange*, 7, 2, pp. 2–21.

ELLIOTT, J. (1981) *Action Research: A Framework for Self-Evaluation in Schools*, TIQL Working paper no. 1, mimeo., Cambridge, Cambridge Institute of Education.

ELLIOTT, J. (1985) 'Facilitating action research in schools: Some dilemmas' in BURGESS, R. (Ed) *Field Methods in the Study of Education*, Lewes, Falmer Press, pp. 235–62.

ENRIGHT, L. (1981) 'The diary of a classroom' in NIXON, J. (Ed) *A Teacher's Guide to Action Research*, London, Grant McIntyre Ltd., pp. 37–51.

EVANS, C., STUBBS, M., DUCKWORTH, E. and DAVIS, C. (1981) *Teacher Initiated Research: Professional Development for Teachers and a Method for Designing Research Based on Practice*, Cambridge, MA, Technical Education Research Center, Inc.

FERVER, J. C. (1980) 'University collaboration in school inservice', unpublished report, Madison, WI, Extension Programs in Education.

FINCH, J. (1985) 'Social policy and education: Problems and possibilities of using qualitative research' in BURGESS, R. (Ed) *Issues in Educational Research: Qualitative Methods*, Lewes, Falmer Press, pp. 109–128.

FISHER, C. W. and BERLINER, D. C. (1979) 'Critical inquiry in research on classroom teaching and learning', *Journal of Teacher Education*, 30, 6, pp. 42–8.

FLORIO, S. (1983) 'The written literacy forum: An analysis of teacher/researcher collaboration', paper presented at the annual meeting of the American Educational Research Association, Montreal.

FULLER, M. (1984) 'Dimensions of gender in a school: Reinventing the wheel' in BURGESS, R. (Ed) *The Research Process in Educational Settings: Ten Case Studies*, Lewes, Falmer Press, pp. 97–115.

GILLIGAN, C. (1982) *In a Different Voice: Psychological Theory and Women's Development*, Cambridge, MA, Harvard University Press.

GLASSBERG, S. and OJA, S. N. (1981) 'A developmental model for enhancing teachers' personal and professional growth', *Journal of Research and Development in Education*, 14, 2, pp. 59–70.

GOOD, C. V. (1963) *Introduction to Educational Research*, New York, Appleton-Century-Crofts.

GOULD, R. (1978) *Transformations: Growth and Change in Adult Life*, New York, Simon and Schuster.

GRIFFIN, G. A., LIEBERMAN, A., and JACULLO-NOTO, J. (1983) *Interactive Research and Development on Schooling: Executive Summary of the Final Report*, Austin, TX, University of Texas at Austin, Research and Development Center for Teacher Education.

GRIFFITHS, G. (1985) 'Doubts, dilemmas, and diary-keeping: Some reflections on teacher-based research' in BURGESS, R. (Ed) *Issues in Educational Research: Qualitative Methods*, Lewes, Falmer Press, pp. 197–215.

GRIFFORE, R. J. and LEWS, J. (1978) 'Characteristics of teacher's moral judgment', *Educational Research Quarterly*, 3, pp. 20–30.

GRIMMETT, P. (1983) 'Effective clinical supervision conference interventions: A preliminary investigation of participants' conceptual functioning', paper presented at the annual meeting of the American Educational Research Association, Montreal.

GROARKE, J., OVENS, P. and HARGREAVES, M. (1986) 'Towards a more open classroom' in HUSTLER, D., CASSIDY, T. and CUFF, T. (Eds) *Action Research in Classrooms and Schools*, London, Allen and Unwin, pp. 79–86.

GRUNDY, S. and KEMMIS, S. (1982) 'Educational action research in Australia: The state of the art', *The Action Research Reader*, Victoria, Australia, Deakin University, pp. 83–97.

GUBA, E. and CLARK, D. L. (1980) *The Configurational Perspective: A View of Educational Knowledge Production and Utilization*, Washington, D.C., Council for Educational Development and Research.

HAAN, N., STROUD, J. and HOLSTEIN, C. (1973) 'Moral and ego stages in relationship to ego processes: A study of hippies', *Journal of Personality*, 41, pp. 596–612.

HALL, B. L. (1975) 'Participatory research: An approach for change', *Convergence*, 8, 2, pp. 24–31.

HALL, G. E. and LOUCKS-HORSLEY, S. F. (1978) 'Teacher concerns as a basis for facilitating and personalizing staff development', *Teachers College Record*, 80, 1, pp. 36–54.

HALPIN, A. W. and CROFT, D. B. (1963) *The Organizational Climate of Schools*, Chicago, IL, University of Chicago.

HAMMERSLEY, M. (1984) 'The researcher exposed: A natural history' in BURGESS, R. (Ed) *The Research Process in Educational Settings: Ten Case Studies*, Lewes, Falmer Press, pp. 39–67.

HARE, A. P. (1976) *Handbook of Small Group Research*, New York, The Free Press.

HARVEY, O. J. (1970) 'Beliefs and behavior: Some complications for education', *Science Teacher*, 37, pp. 10–14.

HAUSER, S. T. (1976) 'Loevinger's model and measure of ego development: A critical review', *Psychological Bulletin*, 83, pp. 928–55.

HEMBROFF, L. and MYERS, D. (1984) 'Status characteristics: Degrees of task relevance and decision processes', *Social Psychology Quarterly*, 47, 4, pp. 337–46.

HERSEY, P. and BLANCHARD, K. H. (1982) *Management of Organization Behavior*, Englewood Cliffs, NJ, Prentice Hall.

HIGGINS, A. (1983) 'Recent findings in adult moral development', paper presented to the Association for Moral Education, Boston, MA.

HODGKINSON, H. L. (1957) 'Action research: A critique', *Journal of Educational Sociology*, 31, 4, pp. 137–53.

HOLLEY, F. M. (1977) 'The public school R and E unit looks at research, researchers, and school district needs', paper presented at the annual meeting of the American Educational Research Association, New York.

HORD, S. M. (1981) *Working Together: Cooperation or Collaboration*, Austin, Texas, University of Texas at Austin, Research and Development Center for Teacher Education.

HULING, L. (1981) 'The effects on teachers of participation in an interactive research and development project', unpublished doctoral dissertation, Texas Technology University, and presented to the annual meeting of the American Educational Research Association, New York, 1982.

HUNT, D. E. (1970) 'A conceptual level matching model for coordinating learner characteristics with educational approaches', *Interchange*, 1, pp. 68–82.

HUNT, D. E. (1971) *Matching Models in Education: The Coordination of Teaching Methods with Student Characteristics*, Toronto, Ontario Institute for Studies in Education.

HUNT, D. E. (1975) 'The B-P-E paradigm for theory, research, and practice', *Canadian Psychological Review*, 16, pp. 185–97.

HUNT, D. E., GREENWOOD, J., NOY, J. E. and WATSON, N. (1973) *Assessment of Conceptual Level: Paragraph Completion Method (PCM)*, Toronto, Ontario Institute for Studies in Education.

HUNT, D. E., JOYCE, B. R., GREENWOOD, J., NOY, J. E., REID, R. and WEIL, M. (1974) 'Student conceptual level and models of teaching: Theoretical and empirical coordination of the two models', *Interchange*, 5, pp. 19–30.

HUSTLER, D., CASSIDY, T. and CUFF, T. (Eds) (1986) *Action Research in Classrooms and Schools*, London, Allen and Unwin.

JACULLO-NOTO, J. (1984) 'Interactive research and development: Partners in craft', *Teachers College Record*, 86, 1, pp. 208–22.

JAMES, M. and EBBUTT, D. (1981) 'Problems and potentials' in NIXON, J. (Ed) *A Teacher's Guide to Action Research*, London, Grant-McIntyre, pp. 81–95.

JOHNSON, D. F. and OJA, S. N. (1983) 'Review of the literature: Teachers' life-age cycles and stages of cognitive-structural development' in OJA, S. N. and PINE, G. J. (Eds) *Appendices to the Final Report: A Two Year Study of Teacher Stages of Development in Relation to Collaborative Action Research in Schools*, Washington, D.C., National Institute of Education, pp. 261–310. (ERIC Document Reproduction Service No. ED 248227)

JOYCE, B. (1980) 'Learning how to learn', *Theory into Practice*, 19, 1, pp. 15–27.

KEGAN, R. (1982) *The Evolving Self*, Cambridge, MA, Harvard University Press.

KEGAN, R. (1986) 'Kohlberg and the psychology of ego development: A predominantly positive evaluation' in MODGIL, S. and MODGIL, C. (Eds) *Lawrence Kohlberg: Consensus and Controversy*, Lewes. Falmer Press, pp. 163–81.

KELLY, A. (1985) 'Action research: What is it and what can it do?' in BURGESS, R. (Ed) *Issues in Educational Research: Qualitative Methods*, Lewes, Falmer Press, pp. 129–51.

KEMMIS, S. (1980) 'Action research in retrospect and prospect', paper presented to the annual meeting of the Australian Association for Research in Education, Sydney.

KEMMIS, S. (1982) *The Action Research Reader*, Victoria, Deakin University.

KEMMIS, S. and MCTAGGART, R. (1982) *The Action Research Planner*, Victoria, Deakin University.

KING, P. (1987) 'The development of reflective judgment and formal operational thinking in adolescents and young adults', unpublished doctoral dissertation, University of Minnesota.

KITCHENER, K. S. and KING, P. M. (1979) 'Intellectual development beyond adolescence: Reflective judgment, formal operations and verbal reasoning', unpublished manuscript, University of Minnesota.

KOHLBERG, L. (1971) 'Stages of moral development as a basis for moral education' in BECK, C. M., CRITTENDON, B. S. and SULLIVAN, E. V. (Eds) *Moral Education: Interdisciplinary Approaches*, Toronto, University of Toronto Press, pp. 23–92.

KOHLBERG, L. (1976) 'Moral stages and moralization: The cognitive-developmental approach' in LICKONA, T. (Ed) *Moral Development and Behavior*, New York, Holt, Rinehart & Winston, pp. 31–53.

KOHLBERG, L. (1981) *The Philosophy of Moral Development*, New York, Harper and Row.

KOHLBERG, L. (1984) *The Psychology of Moral Development*, New York, Harper and Row.

KOHLBERG, L. and HIGGINS, A. (1984) 'Continuities and discontinuities in childhood and adult development revisited — Again' in KOHLBERG, L. (Ed) *The Psychology of Moral Development*, New York, Harper and Row, pp. 426–97.

KOHLBERG, L. and TURIEL, E. (1971) 'Moral development and moral education' in LESSER, G. (Ed.) *Psychology and Educational Practice*, Glenview, IL, Scott, Foresman & Co., pp. 410–65.

KRATHWOHL, D. R. (1974) 'An analysis of the perceived ineffectiveness of educational research and some recommendations', *Educational Psychologist*, 11, 2, pp. 73–86.

LAWTON, D. (1980) *The Politics of School Curriculum*, London, Routledge & Kegan Paul.

LEARY, M., ROBERTSON, R. and BARNES, B. (1986) 'Self presentations of small group leaders: Effects of role requirements and leadership orientation', *Journal of Personality and Social Psychology*, 51, 4, pp. 742–8.

LEVINSON, D. (1978) *The Seasons of a Man's Life*, New York, Alfred A. Knopf.

LEWIN, K. (1948) *Resolving Social Conflicts*, New York, Harper and Brothers.

LEWIN, K. (1952) 'Group decision and social change' in NEWCOMB, T. M. and HARTLEY, E. L. (Eds), *Readings in Social Psychology*, New York, Holt, pp. 459–73.

LIEBERMAN, A. (1983) 'Interactive research and development on schooling: Case studies of collaborative action inquiry in three contexts', paper presented at the annual meeting of the American Educational Research Association, Montreal.

LIEBERMAN, A. (1986) 'Collaborative research: Working with, not working on', *Educational Leadership*, 43, 5, pp. 28–33.

LIEBERMAN, A. and MILLER, L. (1984) 'School improvement: Themes and variations', *Teachers College Record*, 86, 1, pp. 4–19.

LITTLE, J. W. (1981) 'School success and staff development in urban desegregated schools: A summary of recently completed research', paper presented at the annual meeting of the American Educational Research Association, Los Angeles.

LITTLE, J. W. (1984) 'Seductive images and organizational realities in professional development', *Teachers College Record*, 86, 1, pp. 84–102.

LOEVINGER, J. (1966) 'The meaning and measurement of ego development', *American Psychologist*, 21, pp. 195–206.

LOEVINGER, J. (1969) 'Theories of ego development' in BREGER, L. (Ed) *Clinical-Cognitive Psychology: Models and Integrations,* Englewood Cliffs, NJ, Prentice-Hall.

LOEVINGER, J. (1976) *Ego Development: Conceptions and Theories,* San Francisco, CA, Jossey-Bass.

LOEVINGER, J. (1986) 'On Kohlberg's contributions to ego development' in MODGIL, S. and MODGIL, C. (Eds) *Lawrence Kohlberg: Consensus and Controversy*, Lewes, Falmer Press, pp. 183–93.

LOEVINGER, J. and WESSLER, R. (1970) *Measuring Ego Development, Vol. 1,* San Francisco, CA, Jossey-Bass.

LOEVINGER, J., WESSLER, R. and REDMORE, C. (1970) *Measuring Ego Development, Vol. 2*, San Francisco, CA, Jossey-Bass.

LYONS, N. (1983) 'Two perspectives: On self, relationship and morality', *Harvard Educational Review*, 53, 2, pp. 125–245.

MAC AN GHAILL, M. (1988) 'Sociology and teacher practice: A fruitful alliance' in WOODS, P. and POLLARD, A. (Eds) *Sociology and Teaching*, London, Croom Helm, pp. 209–34.

MCCUTCHEON, G. (1981) 'The impact of the insider' in NIXON, J. *A teacher's Guide to Action Research*, London, Grant Mcintyre Ltd., pp. 186–93.

MCLAUGHLIN, M. W. and MARSH, D. D. (1978) 'Staff development and school change', *Teachers College Record*, 80, 1, pp. 69–84.

MASLACH, C. and JACKSON, S. E. (1980) *Maslach Burnout Inventory: Research Edition Manual*, Palo Alto, CA, Consulting Psychologists Press, Inc.

MERGENDOLLER, J. H. (1981) *Mutual Inquiry: The Role of Collaborative Research on Teaching in School-based Staff Development*, San Francisco, CA, Far West Laboratory for Educational Research and Development.

MILLER, A. (1981) 'Conceptual matching models and interactional research in education', *Review of Educational Research*, 51, pp. 33–84.

MILLER, C., JACKSON, P. and MUELLER, J. (1987) 'Some social psychological effects of group decision rules', *Journal of Personality and Social Psychology*, 52, 2, pp. 325–32.

MISHLER, E. G. (1979) 'Meaning in context: Is there any other kind?', *Harvard Educational Review*, 49, 1, pp. 1–19.

MODGIL, S. and MODGIL, C. (1986) *Lawrence Kohlberg: Consensus and Controversy*, Lewes, Falmer Press.

MOSHER, R. (1974) 'Knowledge from practice: Clinical research and development in research', *The Counseling Psychologist*, 114, 4, pp. 73–81.

NISBET, J. and BROADFOOT, P. (1980) *The Impact of Research on Policy and Practice in Education*, Aberdeen, Aberdeen University Press.

NIXON, J. (1981) *A Teachers' Guide to Action Research*, London, Grant-McIntyre, Ltd.

NODDINGS, N. (1984) *Caring: A Feminine Approach to Ethics and Moral Education*, Berkeley, CA, University of California Press.

NOFFKE, S. E. and ZEICHNER, K. M. (1987) 'Action research and teacher thinking: The first phase of the AR on AR Project at the University of Wisconsin, Madison', paper presented at the annual meeting of the American Educational Research Association, Washington, D.C.

OBERT, S. (1983) 'Developmental patterns of organizational task groups: A preliminary study', *Human Relations*, 36, 1, pp. 37–52.

OJA, S. N. (1978) 'A cognitive-structural approach to adult ego, moral and conceptual development through in-service teacher education' unpublished doctoral dissertation, University of Minnesota.

OJA, S. N. (1979) 'Adapting research findings in psychological education: A case study' in MORRIS, L. (Ed) *Adapting Educational Research: Staff Development Approaches*, Norman, OK, pp. 97–112.

OJA, S. N. (1980a) 'Adult development is implicit in staff development', *Journal of Staff Development*, 1, 2, pp. 7–56.

OJA, S. N. (1980b) 'Models of change: Impact of teacher corps activity on changes in teachers stages of development', paper presented at the National Teacher Corps Research Cluster Meeting, Boston.

OJA, S. N. (1980c) 'The structure of change and stages of adult development' in MORRIS, L. A. (Ed) *A Journal of Research Adaptation*, Vol. II, Norman, OK, University of Oklahoma, pp. 31–5.

OJA, S. N. (1983) 'Life age/cycle characteristics of ARCS teachers' in OJA, S. N. and PINE, G. J., (Eds) *Appendices to the Final Report: A Two Year Study of Teachers' Stages of Development in Relation to Collaborative Action Research in Schools*, Washington, D.C., National Institute of Education, pp. 735–77. (ERIC Document Reproduction Service No. ED 248227)

OJA, S. N. (1984a) 'Developmental stage characteristics of teachers participating in a collaborative action research project', paper presented at the annual meeting of the American Educational Research Association, New Orleans. (ERIC Document Reproduction Service No. ED 246038)

OJA, S. N. (1984b) 'Role issues in practical collaborative research on change in schools', paper presented at the annual meeting of the American Educational Research Association, New Orleans. (ERIC Document Reproduction Service No. ED 247249)

OJA, S. N. (1985) 'Review of the literature: Adult development and teacher education', unpublished manuscript, Durham, NH, University of New Hampshire Collaborative Research Projects Office.

OJA, S. N. (1988a) *Program Assessment Report: A Collaborative Approach to*

Leadership in Supervision, Durham, NH, University of New Hampshire Collaborative Research Projects Office.

OJA, S. N. (1988b) 'Teachers ages and stages of development' in HOLLY, M. L. and MCLOUGHLIN, C. S. (Eds) *Perspectives on Teacher Professional Development*, Lewes, Falmer Press.

OJA, S. N. and HAM, M. C. (1984) 'A cognitive-developmental approach to collaborative action research with teachers', *Teachers College Record*, 86, 1, pp. 171–92.

OJA, S. N. and HAM, M. C. (1987) 'A collaborative approach to leadership in supervision: An OERI project', paper presented at the annual meeting of the American Association of Colleges of Teacher Education, Washington, D.C. (ERIC Document Reproduction Service No. ED277696)

OJA, S. N. and PINE, G. J. (1981) *A Two Year Study of Teacher Stages of Development in Relation to Collaborative Action Research On Schools*, Washington, D.C., National Institute of Education Research Proposal.

OJA, S. N. and PINE, G. J. (1983) *A Two Year Study of Teachers' Stages of Development in Relation to Collaborative Action Research in Schools*, Washington, D.C. National Institute of Education. (ERIC Document Reproduction Service No. ED 248227).

OJA, S. N. and PINE, G. J. (1984) *Executive Summary: Collaborative Action Research: A Two Year Study of Teachers' Stages of Development and School Contexts*, Washington, D.C., National Institute of Education.

OJA, S. N. and PINE, G. J. (1988) 'Collaborative action research: Teachers' stages of development and school contexts', *Peabody Journal of Education*, 64, 1.

OJA, S. N. and SPRINTHALL, N. A. (1978) 'Psychological and moral development for teachers' in SPRINTHALL, N. A. and MOSHER, R. A. (Eds) *Value Development as the Aim of Education*, Schenectady, NY, Character Research Press, pp. 117–34.

PERRY, W. (1970) *Forms of Intellectual and Ethical Development in the College Years*, New York, Holt, Rinehart and Winston.

PERRY, W. (1981) 'Cognitive and ethical growth: The making of meaning' in CHICKERING, A. (Ed) *The Modern American College*, San Francisco, CA, Jossey-Bass, pp. 76–116.

PERVIN, L. A. (1970) *Personality: Theory Assessment and Research,* New York, John Wiley and Sons.

PIAGET, J. (1972) 'Intellectual evolution from adolescence to adulthood', *Human Development*, 15, pp. 1–12.

PINE, G. J. (1979) *University of New Hampshire — Portsmouth Teacher Corps Project Final Report*, Durham, NH, University of New Hampshire.

PINE, G. J. (1981) 'Collaborative action research: The integration of research and service', paper presented at the American Association of College Teachers of Education, Detroit.

PINE, G. J. (1983) 'School context variables and collaborative action research' in OJA, S. N. and PINE, G. J. (Eds) *Appendices to the Final Report: A Two Year Study of Teacher Stages of Development in Relation to Collaborative Action Research in Schools*, Washington, D.C., National Institute of Education, pp. 781–826. (ERIC Document Reproduction Service No. ED 248227)

POLLARD, A. (1985) 'Opportunities and difficulties of a teacher-ethnographer' in BURGESS, R. (Ed) *Field Methods in the Study of Education*, Lewes, Falmer Press, pp. 217–33.

POLLARD, A. (1988) 'Reflective teaching — The sociological contribution' in WOODS, P. and POLLARD, A. (Eds) *Sociology and Teaching*, London, Croom Helm, pp. 54–75.

RAPOPORT, R. N. (1970) 'Three dilemmas in action research', *Human Relations*, 23, 6, pp. 499–513.

REST, J. (1974) *Manual for the Defining Issues Test: An Objective Test of Moral Judgment*, Minneapolis, MN, University of Minnesota Press.

REST, J. (1979) *Development in Judging Moral Issues*, Minneapolis, MN, University of Minnesota Press.

REST, J. (1986) *Moral Development: Advances in Research and Theory*, New York, Praeger.

RICHARDSON, A. and PIPER, W. (1986) 'Leader style, leader consistency, and participant personality effects on learning in small groups', *Human Relations*, 39, 9, pp. 817–36.

RIEGEL, K. (1973) 'Dialectical operations: The final period of cognitive development', *Human Development*, 16, pp. 345–76.

RUTTER, M., MAUGHAN, B., MORTIMORE, P. and OUSTEN, J. (1979) *Fifteen Thousand Hours*, Cambridge, MA, Harvard University Press.

SANFORD, N. (1970) 'Whatever happened to action research?', *Journal of Social Issues*, 26, 4, pp. 3–23.

SARASON, S. B. (1971) *The Culture of School and the Problem of Change*, Boston, MA, Allyn and Bacon, Inc.

SCHAEFER, R. J. (1967) *The School as the Center of Inquiry*, New York, Harper and Row.

SCHEIN, E. (1969) *Process Consultation: Its Role in Organizational Development*, Reading, MA, Addison-Wesley Publishing Co.

SCHON, D. (1983) *The Reflective Practitioner: How Professionals Think in Action*, New York, Basic Books.

SCHUTZ, W. C. (1958) *FIRO: A Three Dimensional Theory of Interpersonal Behavior*, New York, Rinehart.

SCHWAB, R. L. (1983) 'Teacher burnout', *Theory Into Practice*, 22, 1, pp. 21–5.

SELMAN, R. L. (1979) *Assessing Interpersonal Understanding: An Interview and Scoring Manual in Five Parts*, Cambridge, MA, Harvard-Judge Baker Social Reasoning Project.

SELMAN, R. L. (1980) *The Growth of Interpersonal Understanding*, New York, Academic Press.

SHARPLES, D. (1983) 'An overview of school based action research', paper presented at the Action Research in Classrooms and Schools Conference, Manchester Polytechnic.

SHEARD, D. (1981) 'Spreading the message' in NIXON, J. (Ed) *A Teachers' Guide to Action Research*, London, Grant-McIntyre, pp. 175–85.

SHEEHY, G. (1976) *Passages: Predictable Crises of Adulthood*, New York, E. P. Dutton and Company.

SMULYAN, L. (1984) 'The collaborative process in action research: A case study', unpublished dissertation, Harvard University.

SMULYAN, L. (1988) 'The group process of collaborative action research', *Educational Research Quarterly*.

SPRINTHALL, N. and BERNIER, J. (1978) 'Moral and cognitive development of teachers', *New Catholic World*, 1121, pp. 179–84.

SPRINTHALL, N. and THIES-SPRINTHALL, L. (1983) 'The teacher as an adult learner: A cognitive-developmental view' in GRIFFIN, G. (Ed) *Staff Development, 82nd Yearbook of the National Society for the Study of Education*, Chicago, IL, University of Chicago Press, pp. 13–35.

SRIVASTVA, S., OBERT, S., and NEILSON, E. (1977) 'Organizational analysis through group processes: A theoretical perspective for organization development' in COOPER, C. (Ed) *Organizational Development in the UK and USA*, London, Macmillan Press.

STENHOUSE, L. (1975) *An Introduction to Curriculum Research and Development*, London, Heinemann.

STREET, L. (1986) 'Mathematics, teachers, and an action research course' in HUSTLER, D., CASSIDY, T. and CUFF, T. (Eds) *Action Research in Classrooms and Schools*, London, Allen and Unwin, pp. 123–32.

THIBAUT, J. and KELLY, H. H. (1986) *The Social Psychology of Groups*, New York, John Wiley and Sons, Inc.

THIES-SPRINTHALL, L. (1984) 'Promoting developmental growth of supervising teachers: Theory, research progress, and implications', *Journal of Teacher Education*, 35, 3, pp. 53–60.

THREADGOLD, M. W. (1985) 'Bridging the gap between teachers and researchers' in BURGESS, R. (Ed) *Issues in Educational Research: Qualitative Methods*, Lewes, Falmer Press, pp. 251–70.

TIKUNOFF, W. J., WARD, B. A. and GRIFFEN, G. A. (1979) *Interactive Research and Development on Teaching Study: Final Report*, San Francisco, CA, Far West Regional Laboratory for Educational Research and Development.

TRUBOWITZ, S. (1986) 'Stages in the development of school-college collaboration', *Educational Leadership*, 43, 5, pp. 18–21.

TUCKMAN, B. W. (1965) 'Developmental sequence in small groups', *Psychological Bulletin*, 63, 6, pp. 384–9.

TUCKMAN, B. W. and JENSEN, M. C. (1977) 'Stages of small group development revisited', *Group and Organization Studies*, 2, 4, pp. 419–27.

WALLAT, C., GREEN, J. L., CONLIN, S. M. and HARAMIS, M. (1981) 'Issues related to action research in the classroom — The teacher and researcher as a team' in GREEN, J. L. and WALLAT, C. (Eds) *Ethnography and Language in Educational Settings*, Norwood, NJ, Ablex, pp. 87–114.

WARD, B. and TIKUNOFF, W. (1982) 'Collaborative research', paper presented at the National Institute of Education sponsored conference, The Implications of Research on Teaching for Practice.

WHYTE, J. (1986) *Girls into Science and Technology: The Story of a Project*, London, Routledge & Kegan Paul.

WITHERELL, C. (1978) 'A structural-developmental analysis of teachers' conceptions of teaching and human development in relation to patterns of teaching behavior: Five case studies', unpublished doctoral dissertation, University of Minnesota.

ZANDER, A. (1982) *Making Groups Effective*, San Francisco, CA, Jossey-Bass.

Subject Index

Note: ARCS stands for Action Research on Change in Schools.

Name Index